2018 International Plumbing Code® Study Companion

2018 International Plumbing Code®
Study Companion

ISBN: 978-1-60983-795-2

Manager of Development:	Doug Thornburg
Publications Manager:	Mary Lou Luif
Project Editor:	Greg Dickson
Production Technician:	Emily Sargent
Cover Design:	Ricky Razo

COPYRIGHT © 2018
by
INTERNATIONAL CODE COUNCIL, INC.

ALL RIGHTS RESERVED. This publication is a copyrighted work owned by the International Code Council, Inc. ("ICC"). Without advance written permission from the ICC, no part of this book may be reproduced, distributed or transmitted in any form or by any means, including, without limitation, electronic, optical or mechanical means (by way of example, and not limitation, photocopying, or recording by or in an information storage retrieval system). For information on use rights and permissions, please contact: ICC Publications, 4051 Flossmoor Road, Country Club Hills, IL 60478. Phone 1-888-ICC-SAFE (422-7233).

The information contained in this document is believed to be accurate; however, it is being provided for informational purposes only and is intended for use only as a guide. Publication of this document by the ICC should not be construed as the ICC engaging in or rendering engineering, legal or other professional services. Use of the information contained in this workbook should not be considered by the user as a substitute for the advice of a registered professional engineer, attorney or other professional. If such advice is required, it should be sought through the services of a registered professional engineer, licensed attorney or other professional.

Trademarks: "International Code Council," the "International Code Council" logo, "ICC," the "ICC" logo, "International Plumbing Code," "IPC" and other names and trademarks appearing in this book are registered trademarks of the International Code Council, Inc., and/or its licensors (as applicable), and may not be used without permission.

Errata on various ICC publications may be available at www.iccsafe.org/errata.

First Printing: August 2018

PRINTED IN THE USA

TABLE OF CONTENTS

Study Session 1:

   2018 IPC Chapter 1—Scope and Administration 1

   Quiz 21

Study Session 2:

   2018 IPC Sections 301 through 307—General Regulations I 27

   Quiz 42

Study Session 3:

   2018 IPC Sections 308 through 316—General Regulations II 49

   Quiz 63

Study Session 4:

   2018 IPC Sections 401 through 411—Fixtures, Faucets and Fixture Fittings I 69

   Quiz 92

Study Session 5:

   2018 IPC Sections 412 through 426—Fixtures, Faucets and Fixture Fittings II 97

   Quiz 116

Study Session 6:

   2018 IPC Chapter 5—Water Heaters 123

   Quiz 141

Study Session 7:

   2018 IPC Sections 601 through 605—Water Supply and Distribution I 147

   Quiz 165

Study Session 8:

   2018 IPC Sections 606 through 613 —Water Supply and Distribution II 171

   Quiz... 190

Study Session 9:

2018 IPC Sections 701 through 707—Sanitary Drainage I 197

Quiz 211

Study Session 10:

2018 IPC Sections 708 through 716—Sanitary Drainage II 217

Quiz 235

Study Session 11:

2018 IPC Chapter 8—Indirect/Special Waste 241

Quiz 258

Study Session 12:

2018 IPC Sections 901 through 909—Vents I 265

Quiz 282

Study Session 13:

2018 IPC Sections 910 through 920—Vents II 289

Quiz 306

Study Session 14:

2018 IPC Chapter 10—Traps, Interceptor and Separators 313

Quiz 333

Study Session 15:

2018 IPC Chapters 11 through 14—
　　Storm Drainage, Special Piping and Storage Systems, Nonpotable
　　Water Systems and Subsurface Landscape Irrigation Systems 339

Quiz 360

Answer Keys 367

INTRODUCTION

This study companion provides practical learning assignments for independent study of the provisions of the 2018 *International Plumbing Code®* (IPC®). The independent study format affords a method for the student to complete the program in an unregulated time period. Progressing through the workbook, the learner can measure his or her level of knowledge by using the exercises and quizzes provided for each study session.

The workbook is also valuable for instructor-led programs. In jurisdictional training sessions, community college classes, vocational training programs and other structured educational offerings, the study guide and the IPC can be the basis for classroom instruction.

All study sessions begin with a general learning objective specific to the session, the specific code sections or chapter under consideration and a list of questions summarizing the key points of study. Each session addresses selected topics from the IPC and includes code text, a commentary on the code provisions, illustrations representing the provisions under discussion and multiple choice questions that can be used to evaluate the student's knowledge. Before beginning the quizzes, the student should thoroughly review the IPC, focusing on the key points identified at the beginning of each study session.

The workbook is structured so that after every question the student has an opportunity to record his or her response and the corresponding code reference. The correct answers are found in the back of the workbook in the answer key.

Although this study companion is primarily focused on those subjects of specific interest to plumbing inspectors and contractors, it is a valuable resource to any individuals who would like to learn more about the IPC provisions. The information presented may be of importance to many building officials, plans examiners and combination inspectors.

The 2018 *International Plumbing Code Study Companion* has been completely revised and updated from previous editions. Steve Van Note of ICC was responsible for developing the updated content with assistance from ICC staff member Fred Grable, P.E.

The information presented in this publication is believed to be accurate; however, it is provided for informational purposes only and is intended for use only as a guide. As there is a limited discussion of selected code provisions, the code itself should always be referenced for more complete information. In addition, the commentary set forth may not necessarily represent the views of any enforcing agency, as such agencies have the sole authority to render interpretations of the IPC.

Questions or comments concerning this workbook are encouraged. Please direct your comments to ICC at *studycompanion@iccsafe.org*.

About the International Code Council

The International Code Council is a member-focused association. It is dedicated to developing model codes and standards used in the design, build and compliance process to construct safe, sustainable, affordable and resilient structures. Most U.S. communities and many global markets choose the International Codes. ICC Evaluation Service (ICC-ES) is the industry leader in performing technical evaluations for code compliance fostering safe and sustainable design and construction.

Governmental Affairs: 500 New Jersey Avenue, NW, 6th Floor, Washington, DC 20001-2070

Regional Offices: Eastern Regional Office (BIR); Central Regional Office (CH); Western Regional Office (LA)

888-ICC-SAFE (422-7233)

www.iccsafe.org

2018 IPC Chapter 1
Scope and Administration

OBJECTIVE: To develop an understanding of the purpose, scope and administrative provisions of the *International Plumbing Code* (IPC), including the duties and responsibilities of the plumbing code official, the issuance of permits and inspection procedures.

REFERENCE: Chapter 1, 2018 *International Plumbing Code*

KEY POINTS:
- What is the purpose and scope of the 2018 *International Plumbing Code*?
- Which code regulates the installation of fuel gas distribution piping and equipment?
- Which code is referenced for plumbing installations in one- and two-family dwellings and townhouses?
- Under what circumstances are the appendix chapters considered a part of the code?
- When different sections of the code appear to be in conflict, which section applies?
- How are existing systems addressed by the code?
- What authority does the code official have in regulating the maintenance of plumbing systems?
- What regulations apply to historic buildings?
- To what extent are the referenced codes and standards considered part of the code?
- What is the remedy for a conflict between the code and a referenced code or standard?
- Who is responsible for enforcing the code and interpreting its provisions?
- Who determines the applicability of any requirements that are not specifically addressed in the code?
- Under what conditions may a code official enter a building for inspection purposes?
- What types of records are required to be kept by the code official?
- What are the conditions for approvals of alternatives?
- Under what conditions would a code official require tests?

KEY POINTS:
(Cont'd)

- What information is required to be shown on construction documents?
- When are plumbing permits required? What work is exempt from permit requirements?
- What information is required on the permit application?
- Under what circumstances would a permit become invalid?
- Who is responsible for notifying the code official when work is ready for inspection?
- What inspections are required? Is the code official authorized to require additional inspections?
- Under what conditions may the code official allow temporary connection of utilities?
- What actions may be taken by the code official to resolve a violation?
- What conditions would justify the disconnection of utilities?
- What is the purpose of the board of appeals?
- What limitations are placed on the authority of the board of appeals?
- Who may attend hearings before the board of appeals?

Topic: Scope
Reference: IPC 101.2

Category: Scope and Administration
Subject: General Requirements

Code Text: *The provisions of* the International Plumbing Code *shall apply to the erection, installation, alteration, repairs, relocation, replacement, addition to, use or maintenance of plumbing systems within this jurisdiction.* The International Plumbing Code *shall regulate nonflammable medical gas, inhalation anesthetic, vacuum piping, nonmedical oxygen systems and sanitary and condensate vacuum collection systems. Provisions in the appendices shall not apply unless specifically adopted.*

Discussion and Commentary: The *International Plumbing Code* establishes minimum regulations applicable to the design, installation and maintenance of plumbing systems. Although the code focuses primarily on piping, fixtures and equipment to provide a safe and healthy water supply and drain-waste-vent system, it also addresses other piping systems and equipment.

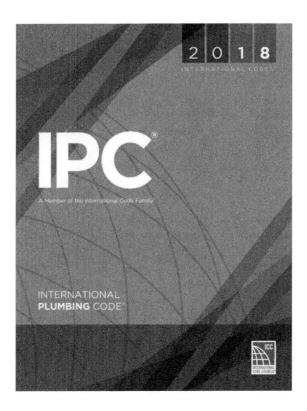

Although an appendix may provide some guidelines or examples of recommended practices, or assist in the determination of alternate materials or methods, it will have no legal status and cannot be enforced until it is specifically recognized in the adopting legislation.

Topic: Scope
Reference: IPC 101.2 and Exception
Category: Scope and Administration
Subject: General Requirements

Code Text: *The installation of fuel gas distribution piping and equipment, fuel gas-fired water heaters and water heater venting systems shall be regulated by the* International Fuel Gas Code. *Detached one- and two-family dwellings and multiple single-family dwellings (townhouses) not more than three stories high with separate means of egress and their accessory structures shall comply with the* International Residential Code.

Discussion and Commentary: The *International Fuel Gas Code®* (IFGC®) regulates fuel gas piping and the installation of gas-fired appliances, including their venting system. *The International Residential Code®* (IRC®) applies to all aspects of construction for detached single-family dwellings, detached duplexes, townhouses and all structures accessory to such buildings. The IRC limits building height to three stories and requires a separate means of egress for each dwelling unit. This comprehensive, stand-alone residential code includes provisions for structural elements, fire and life safety, a healthy living environment, energy conservation, and mechanical, fuel gas, plumbing and electrical systems. The fuel gas portions of the IRC are based on the provisions of the IFGC.

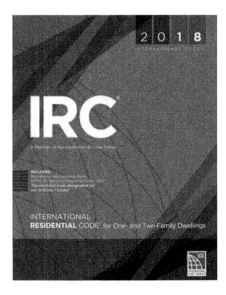 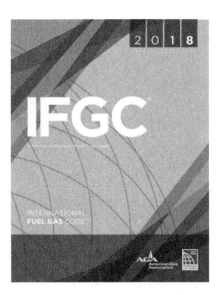

A townhouse is a single-family dwelling unit constructed in a group of three or more units. To fall under the scope of the IRC, each townhouse unit must extend from foundation to roof with a yard or public way on at least two sides.

Topic: Intent	**Category:** Scope and Administration
Reference: IPC 101.3	**Subject:** General Requirements

Code Text: *The purpose of* the International Plumbing Code *is to establish minimum standards to provide a reasonable level of safety, health, property protection and public welfare by regulating and controlling the design, construction, installation, quality of materials, location, operation and maintenance or use of plumbing equipment and systems.*

Discussion and Commentary: The intent of the code is to set forth material, design and installation requirements that establish the minimum acceptable level for public health, safety and welfare in the built environment. The intent becomes important in the administration of the code, particularly in resolving conflicts between requirements, adopting policies and procedures, ruling on alternative materials, methods and equipment, and in making interpretations of the code provisions. These administrative actions require sound judgment on the part of the code official or inspector based on the intent of the code.

Plumbing inspectors make interpretations and judgment calls on a daily basis for installations that meet the intent of the code.

Topic: Existing Installations
Reference: IPC 102.2

Category: Scope and Administration
Subject: Applicability

Code Text: *Plumbing systems lawfully in existence at the time of the adoption of this code shall be permitted to have their use and maintenance continued if the use, maintenance or repair is in accordance with the original design and no hazard to life, health or property is created by such plumbing system.*

Discussion and Commentary: The code is designed to regulate new work and is not intended to be applied retroactively to existing buildings, except where existing plumbing systems create unsafe conditions as specifically addressed in this section and Section 108.

An existing building such as the above, which had its plumbing system designed and installed based on the rules in effect at the time of construction, is not required to be brought up to current code except to remedy hazardous conditions.

Topic: Additions, Alterations or Repairs   **Category:** Scope and Administration
Reference: IPC 102.4   **Subject:** Applicability

Code Text: *Additions, alterations, renovations or repairs to any plumbing system shall conform to that required for a new plumbing system without requiring the existing plumbing system to comply with all the requirements of this code. Additions, alterations or repairs shall not cause an existing system to become unsafe, insanitary or overloaded. Minor additions, alterations, renovations and repairs to existing plumbing systems shall meet the provisions for new construction, unless such work is done in the same manner and arrangement as was in the existing system, is not hazardous and is approved.*

Discussion and Commentary: The intent of this section is to allow the continued use of existing plumbing systems and equipment that may not be designed and constructed as required for new installations. Additions, alterations and repairs are permitted without bringing the existing system into compliance with the code provided the alterations and repairs are safe and sanitary. For minor alterations and repairs, the new work is permitted to conform to the existing system.

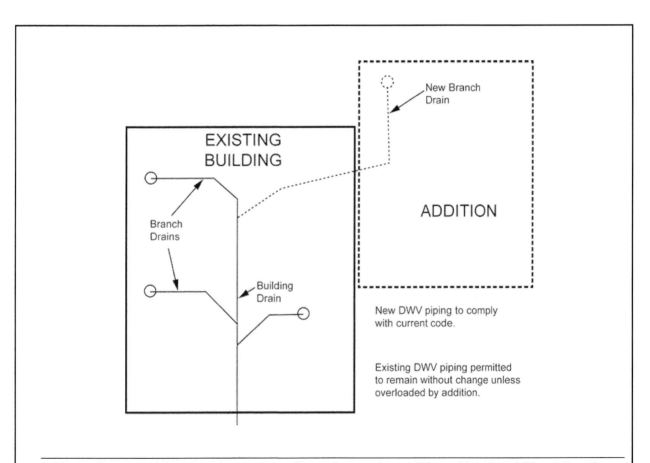

Many elements of the plumbing system will require repair or will be subject to addition, alteration or replacement during the building lifetime. Except for minor repairs or additions, the currently adopted plumbing provisions apply to the new work.

Topic: Historic Buildings	Category: Scope and Administration
Reference: IPC 102.6	Subject: Applicability

Code Text: *The provisions of* the International Plumbing Code *relating to the construction, alteration, repair, enlargement, restoration, relocation or moving of buildings or structures shall not be mandatory for existing buildings or structures identified and classified by the state or local jurisdiction as historic buildings when such buildings or structures are judged by the code official to be safe and in the public interest of health, safety and welfare regarding any proposed construction, alteration, repair, enlargement, restoration, relocation or moving of buildings.*

Discussion and Commentary: This section provides the code official with the widest possible flexibility in enforcing the code when the building in question has historic value. This flexibility, however, is not provided without conditions. The most important criterion for application of this section is that the building must be specifically classified as being of historic significance by the proper authority at the state or local level of government.

The most important issue for consideration regarding historic buildings is whether the proposed plumbing work will alter or destroy the historic elements or features of the building.

Topic: Referenced Codes and Standards **Category:** Scope and Administration
Reference: IPC 102.8 **Subject:** Applicability

Code Text: *The codes and standards referenced in the International Plumbing Code shall be those that are listed in Chapter 15 and such codes and standards shall be considered as part of the requirements of this code to the prescribed extent of each such reference. Where conflicts occur between provisions of this code and the referenced standards, the provisions of this code shall apply. Where the extent of the reference to a referenced code or standard includes subject matter that is within the scope of this code, the provisions of this code, as applicable, shall take precedence over the provisions in the referenced code or standard.*

Discussion and Commentary: The code references many standards promulgated and published by other organizations. A complete list of referenced standards appears in Chapter 14. The wording of this provision referencing Chapter 14 was carefully chosen in order to establish the edition of the standard that is enforceable under the code. The reference to a standard means that only the portions pertaining to the IPC provision regulating a specific subject are in effect, and not the entire standard.

CHAPTER 15
REFERENCED STANDARDS

This chapter lists the standards that are referenced in various sections of this document. The standards are listed herein by the promulgating agency of the standard, the standard identification, the effective date and title, and the section or sections of this document that reference the standard. The application of the referenced standards shall be as specified in Section 102.8.

ANSI
American National Standards Institute
25 West 43rd Street
Fourth Floor
New York, NY 10036

AWS
American Welding Society
550 N.W. LeJeune Road
Miami, FL 33126

ISEA
International Safety Equipment Association
1901 N. Moore Street, Suite 808
Arlington, VA 22209

ASME
American Society of Mechanical Engineers
Three Park Avenue
New York, NY 10016-5990

AWWA
American Water Works Association
6666 West Quincy Avenue
Denver, CO 80235

NFPA
National Fire Protection Association
1 Batterymarch Park
Quincy, MA 02169-7471

ASPE
American Society of Plumbing Engineers
8614 Catalpa Avenue, Suite 1007
Chicago, IL 60656-1116

CISPI
Cast Iron
Soil Pipe Institute
5959 Shallowford Road, Suite 419
Chattanooga, TN 37421

NSF
NSF International
789 Dixboro Road
Ann Arbor, MI 48105

ASSE
American Society of
Sanitary Engineering
901 Canterbury Road
Westlake, OH 44145

CSA
Canadian Standards Association
5060 Spectrum Way.
Mississauga, Ontario, Canada

PDI
Plumbing and Drainage Institute
800 Turnpike Street, Suite 300
North Andover, MA 01845

ASTM
ASTM International
100 Barr Harbor Drive
West Conshohocken, PA 19428-2959

ICC
International Code Council, Inc.
500 New Jersey Ave, NW
6th Floor
Washington, DC 20001

UL
Underwriters Laboratories, Inc.
333 Pfingsten Road
Northbrook, IL 60062-2096

There are a variety of standards promulgated by various organizations listed in Chapter 15, which address piping, fittings, materials, fixtures, equipment and other components. The provisions of the IPC always take precedence over provisions in the referenced codes and standards listed in Chapter 15.

Topic: Creation, Appointment and Deputies **Category:** Administration
Reference: IPC 103 **Subject:** Department of Plumbing Inspection

Code Text: *The department of plumbing inspection is hereby created and the executive official in charge thereof shall be known as the code official. The code official shall be appointed by the chief appointing authority of the jurisdiction. In accordance with the prescribed procedures of this jurisdiction and with the concurrence of the appointing authority, the code official shall have the authority to appoint a deputy code official, other related technical officers, inspectors and other employees. Such employees shall have powers as delegated by the code official.*

Discussion and Commentary: The code official is an appointed officer of the jurisdiction who has administrative responsibilities for the department of plumbing inspection, including the appointment of deputies and inspectors. It is not uncommon for the jurisdiction to use a different position title to identify the code official, such as Building Official or Director of Building Services. Regardless of the jurisdiction title, the code recognizes the individual in charge as the code official.

Inspectors, plan reviewers and other staff are typically given some degree of authority to act on behalf of the code official.

Topic: General Requirements	Category: Administration
Reference: IPC 104.1	Subject: Duties and Powers of the Code Council

Code Text: *The code official is hereby authorized and directed to enforce the provisions of this code. The code official shall have the authority to render interpretations of this code and to adopt policies and procedures in order to clarify the application of its provisions. Such interpretations, policies and procedures shall be in compliance with the intent and purpose of this code. Such policies and procedures shall not have the effect of waiving requirements specifically provided for in this code.*

Discussion and Commentary: The code official must have adequate knowledge to rule on those issues that are not directly addressed or are unclear in the code. Often, determining compliance with the intent and purpose of the code involves some research on the particular design or installation. The administrative authority to adopt policies and procedures is most frequently used to establish administrative rules for the department's efficient and effective operation.

Code official duties
- Enforce the code
- Review construction documents
- Issue permits
- Issue notices and orders
- Conduct inspections
- Maintain records

Code official authority
- Make interpretations
- Adopt policies and procedures
- Approve modifications and alternatives

} Comply with intent and purpose of code

Limitations on authority
- Not authorized to waive code requirements
- Not authorized to require more than the code requires

The IPC gives broad authority to the code official in interpreting the code and adopting rules for its application. With this authority comes great responsibility. The code official must base decisions on the intent and purpose of the code and has no authority to waive code requirements.

Topic: Alternate Materials, Methods and Equipment **Category:** Administration
Reference: IPC 105.2 **Subject:** Approval

Code Text: *The provisions of this code are not intended to prevent the installation of any material or to prohibit any method of construction not specifically prescribed by this code, provided that any such alternative has been approved. An alternative material or method of construction shall be approved where the code official finds that the proposed alternative material, method or equipment complies with the intent of the provisions of this code and is at least the equivalent of that prescribed in this code. Where the alternative material, design or method of construction is not approved, the code official shall respond in writing, stating the reasons why the alternative was not approved.*

Discussion and Commentary: It is virtually impossible for the code to address every scenario in plumbing system installations, particularly in light of continuously evolving technology and the introduction of new materials. The code official has the authority and even the obligation to approve alternative methods and materials that comply with the intent of the code. These provisions encourage innovation in design, construction and materials to meet the performance level intended by the IPC. To ensure satisfactory performance of alternative products, the building official is authorized to require research or testing reports from an approved agency.

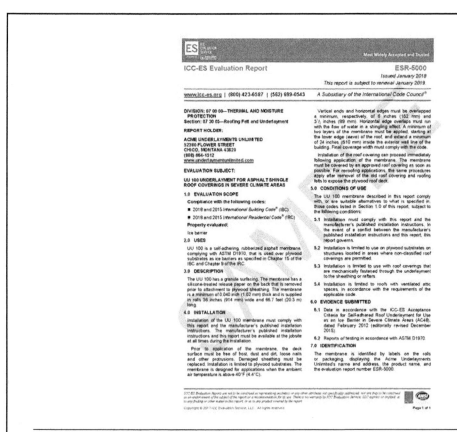

ICC Evaluation Service (ES) reports are developed based upon acceptance criteria for products to verify performance equivalent to that prescribed by the code. These reports are valuable tools in determining equivalency for alternative materials and methods.

Topic: Material and Equipment Reuse
Reference: IPC 105.4.1

Category: Scope and Administration
Subject: Approval

Code Text: *Materials, equipment and devices shall not be reused unless such elements have been reconditioned, tested, placed in good and proper working condition and approved.*

Discussion and Commentary: The code criteria for materials and equipment have changed over the years. Evaluation of testing and materials technology has permitted the development of new criteria, which the old materials may not satisfy. As a result, used materials are required to be evaluated in the same manner as new materials. Used (previously installed) equipment must be equivalent to that required by the code if it is to be utilized in a new installation.

Reconditioned materials and devices are acceptable if approved. By definition in Section 202, "approved" means acceptable to the code official or other authority having jurisdiction.

Study Session 1

Topic: Application for Permit **Category:** Administration
Reference: IPC 106.3 **Subject:** Permits

Code Text: *Each application for a permit, with the required fee, shall be filed with the code official on a form furnished for that purpose and shall contain a general description of the proposed work and its location. The application shall be signed by the owner or the owner's authorized agent. The permit application shall indicate the proposed occupancy of all parts of the building and of that portion of the site or lot, if any, not covered by the building or structure and shall contain such other information required by the code official.*

Discussion and Commentary: This section limits persons who may apply for a permit to the building owner or an authorized agent. An owner's authorized agent could be anyone who is given written permission to act in the owner's interest for the purpose of obtaining a permit, such as an architect, engineer, contractor, tenant or other. Permit forms generally have sufficient space to write a very brief description of the work to be accomplished, which is acceptable for small jobs. For larger projects, the description will be augmented by construction documents.

Plumbing Permit Application

City Department of Plumbing Inspection

Project Address _____

Owner _____

Contractor _____

Project Type: ☐ New ☐ Addition ☐ Alteration ☐ Repair ☐ Demolition

Proposed Occupancy _____

Work Description _____
_____
_____

Applicant _____

Signature of owner or owner's authorized agent

Permit Fee _____ Date _____

Each jurisdiction can develop its own permit application forms and fee schedules to be compatible with its jurisdictional rules, policies and requirements.

Topic: Fee Schedule
Reference: IPC 106.6.2

Category: Administration
Subject: Permits

Code Text: *The fees for all plumbing work shall be as indicated in the following schedule:*
[JURISDICTION TO INSERT APPROPRIATE SCHEDULE]

Discussion and Commentary: A published fee schedule must be established for plans examination, permits and inspections. Ideally, the department should generate revenues that cover operating costs and expenses. The permit fee schedule is an integral part of this process. Many jurisdictions have a book of fees or a fee ordinance that shows the schedule of fees for all jurisdictional services including permit fees.

APPENDIX A
PLUMBING PERMIT FEE SCHEDULE

The provisions contained in this appendix are not mandatory unless specifically referenced in the adopting ordinance.

User note:

About this appendix: *Appendix A provides an example of a permit fee schedule that can be used by a jurisdiction.*

Permit Issuance

1. For issuing each permit _____
2. For issuing each supplemental permit _____

Unit Fee Schedule

1. For each plumbing fixture or trap or set of fixtures on one trap (including water, drainage piping and backflow protection thereof) _____
2. For each building sewer and each trailer park sewer _____
3. Rainwater systems—per drain (inside building) _____
4. For each cesspool (where permitted) _____
5. For each private sewage disposal system _____
6. For each water heater and/or vent _____
7. For each industrial waste pretreatment interceptor including its trap and vent, excepting
8. For installation, alteration or repair of water-piping and/or water-treating equipment, each _____
9. For repair or alteration of drainage or vent piping, each fixture _____
10. For each lawn sprinkler system on any one meter including backflow protection devices therefor _____
11. For atmospheric-type vacuum breakers not included in Item 2:

    1 to 5 _____

    over 5, each _____
12. For each backflow protective device other than atmospheric-type vacuum breakers:

    2 inches (51 mm) and smaller

Plumbing fees are sometimes combined with other fees related to the same project. Sometimes referred to as *project permits*, such permits cover all aspects of a project, such as plumbing, mechanical, electrical and general building construction, with a project permit fee.

Topic: General Requirements
Reference: IPC 107.1
Category: Administration
Subject: Inspections and Testing

Code Text: *The code official is authorized to conduct such inspections as are deemed necessary to determine compliance with the provisions of the International Plumbing Code. Construction or work for which a permit is required shall be subject to inspection by the code official. It shall be the duty of the permit applicant to cause the work to remain visible and able to be accessed for inspection purposes.*

Discussion and Commentary: Inspections are necessary to determine that an installation conforms to all code requirements. Because the majority of a plumbing system is hidden within the building enclosure, periodic inspections are necessary before portions of the system are concealed. All inspections that are necessary to provide such verification must be conducted.

The code official is required to determine that plumbing systems and equipment are installed in accordance with the approved construction documents and the applicable code requirements.

Topic: Testing of Systems
Reference: IPC 107.4.1
Category: Administration
Subject: Inspections and Testing

Code Text: *New plumbing systems and parts of existing systems that have been altered, extended or repaired shall be tested as prescribed herein to disclose leaks and defects, except that testing is not required in the following cases:*

1. *In any case that does not include addition to, replacement, alteration or relocation of any water supply, drainage or vent piping.*
2. *In any case where plumbing equipment is set up temporarily for exhibition purposes.*

Discussion and Commentary: Every plumbing system must be tested before it is placed into service. Testing is necessary to make sure that the system is free from leaks or other defects. Testing is also required, to the extent practicable, for portions of existing systems that have been repaired, altered or extended.

Because plumbing pipes and components are for the most part concealed within the building construction, any leaks could cause substantial damage, expense and inconvenience for the owner or occupants.

Topic: Approval
Reference: IPC 107.5

Category: Administration
Subject: Inspections and Testing

Code Text: *After the prescribed tests and inspections indicate that the work complies in all respects with the* International Plumbing Code, *a notice of approval shall be issued by the code official.*

Discussion and Commentary: After the code official has performed the required inspections and observed the required equipment and system tests (or has received written reports of the results of such tests), he or she must determine if the installation or work is in compliance with all applicable sections of the code. Once the installation passes inspection, the code official must issue a notice of approval.

Department of Plumbing Inspection

INSPECTION APPROVED

☐ Under slab ☐ DWV test
☐ Rough-in ☐ Final
☐ Water piping test ☐ Other

Description _____

Comments _____
_____
_____
_____
_____

Date _____

Inspector _____

Department of Plumbing Inspection

CORRECTION NOTICE

Address _____

Description _____

The following work is not in compliance with the Code and requires correction:
_____
_____
_____
_____

Work shall not be covered until inspected and approved by this department. When corrections are completed, call the department of plumbing inspection for re-inspection.

Date _____

Inspector _____

The notice of approval is sometimes referred to as a *green tag* because traditionally it has been coded green to signify the contractor may proceed. Because many approval tags could still contain minor corrective instructions, some jurisdictions have moved away from the color scheme for tags. In accordance with Section 107.2.3, the code official notifies the permit holder of any portions of the work that do not comply with the code. This may be in the form of a correction notice that is posted at the job site.

Topic: Stop Work Orders **Category:** Administration
Reference: IPC 108.5 **Subject:** Violations

Code Text: *Upon notice from the code official, work on any plumbing system that is being done contrary to the provisions of this code or in a dangerous or unsafe manner shall immediately cease. Such notice shall be in writing and shall be given to the owner of the property, or to the owner's agent, or to the person performing the work. The notice shall state the conditions under which work is authorized to resume. Where an emergency exists, the code official shall not be required to give a written notice prior to stopping the work. Any person who shall continue any work in or about the structure after having been served with a stop work order, except such work as that person is directed to perform to remove a violation or unsafe condition, shall be liable to a fine of not less than [AMOUNT] dollars or more than [AMOUNT] dollars.*

Discussion and Commentary: A stop work order can result in both an inconvenience and a monetary loss to the contractor or owner; therefore, the code official must be prudent in exercising this authority. However, a stop work order has the potential to prevent a violation from becoming worse and more difficult or expensive to correct. A stop work order may be issued when work is proceeding without a permit or to prevent work that is in violation of the code from being covered.

Department of Plumbing Inspection

STOP WORK

Address _____
Description _____

Notice

This work has been inspected and the following does not comply with the code:

_____
_____
_____
_____
_____
_____

Work shall not resume until authorization to proceed is granted. Please call the Department of Plumbing Inspection before any additional work is done.

_____   _____
Inspector   Date

Do Not Remove This Notice

As an example, a stop work order may be justified if a plumbing contractor cuts a structural member while installing a plumbing system and fails to make corrections to restore the structural integrity of the weakened member or system.

Topic: Application for Appeal
Reference: IPC 109.1
Category: Administration
Subject: Means of Appeal

Code Text: *Any person shall have the right to appeal a decision of the code official to the board of appeals. An application for appeal shall be based on a claim that the true intent of this code or the rules legally adopted thereunder have been incorrectly interpreted, the provisions of this code do not fully apply, or an equally good or better form of construction is proposed. The application shall be filed on a form obtained from the code official within 20 days after the notice was served.*

Discussion and Commentary: This section allows any person to appeal a decision of the code official. In practice, this section has been interpreted to permit appeals only by those aggrieved parties with a material or definitive interest in the decision of the code official. An aggrieved party may not appeal a code requirement per se. The intent of the appeal process is not to waive or set aside the code requirement; rather, it is intended to provide a means of reviewing a code official's decision on an interpretation or application of the code, or to review the equivalency of an installation to the code requirements.

Department of Plumbing Inspections

PLUMBING BOARD OF APPEALS

Appeal for interpretation of the Plumbing Code

Project address _____

Type of construction _____

Building use _____

Owner's name _____ Phone _____

Owner's address _____

In accordance with the provisions of the City Plumbing Regulations Section 109.1, I hereby appeal to the Plumbing Board of Appeals the determination made by the Code Official relative to the interpretation of Section_____, which provides that _____, in order that I might perform the plumbing work for the above project as proposed and shown on the attachments.

Application for Appeal is based on a claim that:
- ☐ the true intent of the plumbing code has been incorrectly interpreted
- ☐ the provisions of the plumbing code do not fully apply
- ☐ the appellant proposes an equally good or better form of construction

_____   _____
Signature of owner or appellant   Date

The jurisdiction must create an atmosphere of trust in which the contractors feel comfortable appealing those decisions of code officials that they truly believe are contrary to the intent of the code.

Quiz

Study Session 1
IPC Chapter 1

1. The *International Residential Code* (IRC) is applicable to plumbing work in townhouses not more than _____ in height with a separate means of egress.

    a. 35 feet 　　　　　　　b. 45 feet

    c. three stories　　　　　d. four stories

    Reference _____

2. The provisions of the appendices do not apply unless _____.

    a. referenced in the code

    b. applicable to specific conditions

    c. specifically adopted

    d. relevant to fire or life safety

    Reference _____

3. In order to safeguard life, health and property, the IPC regulates all of the following within the built environment, except _____.

    a. design　　　　　　　　b. maintenance

    c. use　　　　　　　　　　d. cost

    Reference _____

4. Where different sections of the code specify different requirements, the _____ requirement shall apply.

   a. general   b. most restrictive
   c. least restrictive d. specific

   Reference _____

5. Existing plumbing systems must be brought into compliance with the IPC if the system is _____.

   a. repaired   b. added on to
   c. a hazard to property d. nonconforming

   Reference _____

6. Where code provisions are in conflict with the referenced standard, the _____ provisions shall apply.

   a. code   b. referenced standard
   c. most restrictive d. more specific

   Reference _____

7. Where the code official finds that a proposed alternative material does not comply with the intent of the code provisions, the code official shall _____.

   a. request additional information from the manufacturer
   b. state the reason for disapproval in writing to the applicant
   c. contact a third-party agency to authorize additional testing
   d. place limitations on the use of the alternative material

   Reference _____

8. For materials not specifically covered by the code, supporting data necessary to verify compliance with the code must include _____.

   a. a referenced standard
   b. research reports
   c. testing and listing
   d. the manufacturer's instructions

   Reference _____

9. Tests performed by _____ may be required by the code official where there is insufficient evidence of code compliance.

    a. the owner   b. the contractor

    c. an approved agency   d. a design professional

    Reference _____

10. Required department records shall be retained _____.

    a. permanently

    b. as required by the code official

    c. for as long as the building is in existence

    d. as required for public records

    Reference _____

11. The code official shall be appointed by the _____.

    a. chief appointing authority

    b. building official

    c. director of the plumbing inspection department

    d. jurisdiction attorney

    Reference _____

12. The prescribed portions of standards referenced in the IPC and listed in Chapter 15 are considered _____.

    a. requirements   b. guidelines

    c. alternatives   d. modifications

    Reference _____

13. The code official shall require construction documents and specifications to be prepared by a registered design professional when _____.

    a. the proposed construction does not comply with the code
    b. the building exceeds two stories in height
    c. required by state law
    d. special conditions exist

    Reference _____

14. Which of the following information is not specifically required on a permit application?

    a. location   b. type of construction
    c. the proposed occupancy   d. description of the work

    Reference _____

15. Who is responsible for inspection scheduling?

    a. the permit holder   b. the code official
    c. the contractor   d. the owner

    Reference _____

16. A permit is not required for _____.

    a. replacement of a water heater
    b. rearrangement of valves or pipes
    c. replacement of a concealed vent pipe
    d. repairing of leaks in pipes, valves or fixtures

    Reference _____

17. Permits expire if work is not commenced within _____ days of issuance.

    a. 30   b. 60

    c. 120   d. 180

Reference _____

18. An application for an appeal of the code official's decision must be filed within _____ days after receipt of the notice.

    a. 10   b. 20

    c. 30   d. 60

Reference _____

19. The code official is authorized to suspend or revoke a permit _____.

    a. when work proceeds without approved construction documents

    b. when work does not commence within 120 days of issuance

    c. for failure to call for required inspections

    d. that was issued based on inaccurate information

Reference _____

20. Where tests are required as evidence of compliance with the code, the test reports shall be retained for _____.

    a. 180 days after completion of the project

    b. the period required for retention of public records

    c. 90 days after completion of the project

    d. 120 days after occupancy of the building

Reference _____

21. When a plumbing permit is issued, the construction documents shall be stamped _____.

    a. APPROVED FOR CONSTRUCTION

    b. APPROVED

    c. ACCEPTED AS REVIEWED

    d. REVIEWED FOR CODE COMPLIANCE

Reference _____

22. Generally, one set of approved construction documents shall be retained by the code official for at least _____ days following completion of the work.

    a. 180 b. 120
    c. 90   d. 60

    Reference _____

23. The board of appeals is not authorized to rule on an appeal based on a claim that _____.

    a. the provisions of the code do not fully apply
    b. a code requirement should be waived
    c. the rules have been incorrectly interpreted
    d. a better form of construction is proposed

    Reference _____

24. Construction documents for buildings more than _____ stories in height shall indicate the materials and methods for maintaining the required fire-resistance rating.

    a. 2 b. 3
    c. 4 d. 6

    Reference _____

25. The code official may allow temporary connection to the utility source _____.

    a. pending the outcome of an appeal
    b. for a period not exceeding 60 days
    c. for construction purposes
    d. for testing plumbing systems

    Reference _____

2018 IPC Sections 301 through 307
General Regulations I

OBJECTIVE: To develop an understanding of those general provisions regarding plumbing systems that are not specifically addressed in other chapters of the code. To develop an understanding of the provisions that apply to materials in all plumbing applications.

REFERENCE: Sections 301 through 307, 2018 *International Plumbing Code*

KEY POINTS:
- What fixtures and components are required to be connected to the drainage system?
- What fixtures are permitted to discharge to an approved nonpotable water system?
- What items are required to be connected to the water supply?
- Where are plumbing systems and fixtures prohibited? What are the conditions for allowing exceptions?
- What materials are prohibited from being introduced into a sewer system?
- What are the identification requirements for plumbing materials?
- Under what circumstances do standards apply to the installation of materials? Manufacturer's instructions?
- When is third-party certification required?
- What methods are required to prevent the entry of rodents?
- What requirements apply to pipes penetrating foundation walls?
- When is protection against freezing required?
- When are shield plates required?
- What are the excavation and bedding requirements for underground piping systems?
- What materials are approved for backfill and how are the materials placed?
- What measures are implemented to protect pipe from damage in underground installations?
- What limitations are placed on cutting, notching or boring of framing members?
- What documentation and approvals are required for alterations to trusses?

KEY POINTS:
(Cont'd)
- How is the location of pipe trenches regulated to prevent damage to existing footings or foundation walls?
- Which code regulates piping material exposed within plenums?

Topic: System Installation	**Category:** General Regulations
Reference: IPC 301.2, 307.2	**Subject:** General Provisions

Code Text: *Plumbing shall be installed with due regard to preservation of the strength of structural members and prevention of damage to walls and other surfaces through fixture usage. A framing member shall not be cut, notched or bored in excess of limitations specified in the International Building Code.*

Discussion and Commentary: Building structural systems are either engineered or constructed according to the conventional construction provisions of the *International Building Code*® (IBC®). In either case, excessive cutting, notching, boring or otherwise altering the original structural components could negatively impact the performance of the structural system. Installers and code officials alike should inspect fixtures and piping to verify that the installation and use of these components do not have adverse effects on the structure or finished surfaces.

Code Violation

The *International Building Code* (IBC) and the *International Residential Code* (IRC) limit the amount of notching and boring of wood framing members to preserve the integrity of the framing system.

Topic: Prohibited Locations
Reference: IPC 301.6
Category: General Regulations
Subject: General Provisions

Code Text: *Plumbing systems shall not be located in an elevator shaft or in an elevator equipment room.*

> ***Exception:*** *Floor drains, sumps and sump pumps shall be permitted at the base of the shaft provided they are indirectly connected to the plumbing system and comply with Section 1003.4.*

Discussion and Commentary: An elevator pit at the base of an elevator shaft typically has a means for preventing the accumulation of water that may enter the pit. The code permits the installation of floor drains, sumps and sump pumps for this purpose if both of two conditions are satisfied. First, the drain or pump must be indirectly connected to the drainage system through an air gap or air break. The intent of this requirement is to prevent sewer gas from entering the shaft. Secondly, an oil separator in accordance with Section 1003.4 is required to prevent hydraulic oil or other contaminants from entering the building drainage system.

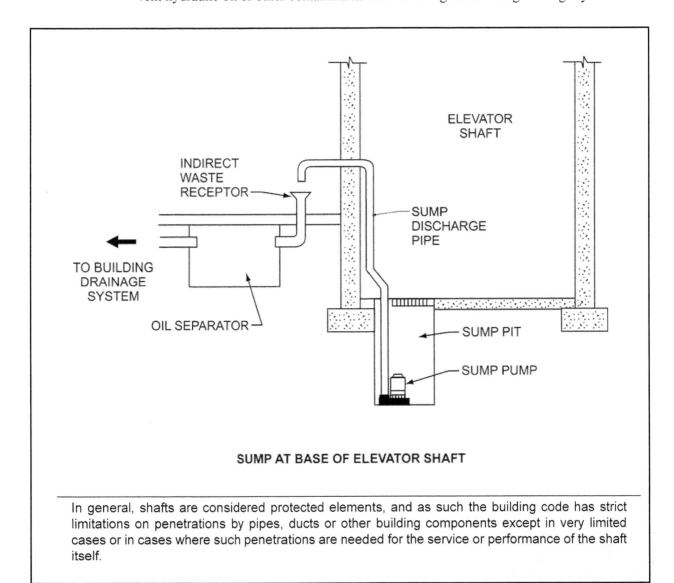

SUMP AT BASE OF ELEVATOR SHAFT

In general, shafts are considered protected elements, and as such the building code has strict limitations on penetrations by pipes, ducts or other building components except in very limited cases or in cases where such penetrations are needed for the service or performance of the shaft itself.

Topic: Identification
Reference: IPC 303.1

Category: General Regulations
Subject: Materials

Code Text: *Each length of pipe and each pipe fitting, trap, fixture, material and device utilized in a plumbing system shall bear the identification of the manufacturer and any markings required by the applicable referenced standards.*

Discussion and Commentary: In addition to bearing the identification of the manufacturer, all pipe, fittings, fixtures and plumbing components are required to meet the marking requirements of the applicable referenced standard. This will help ensure that the marks of the third-party certification agencies are applied to listed products and will assist the inspector in verifying compliance with the referenced standards and the code.

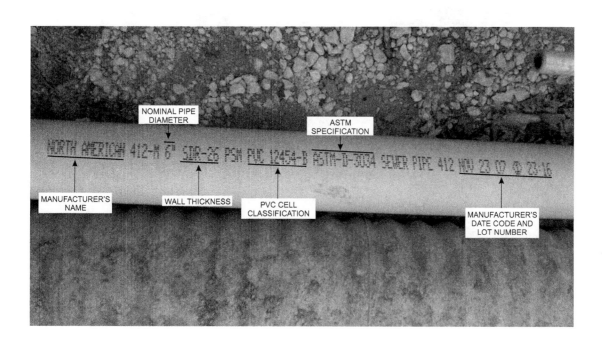

Section 303.4 requires all plumbing products and materials to be listed by a third-party certification agency as complying with the referenced standards. Because certification is mandated for all products, the inspector is able to verify compliance without reviewing third-party test reports.

Topic: Plastic Pipe, Fittings and Components **Category:** General Regulations
Reference: IPC 303.3 **Subject:** Materials

Code Text: *All plastic pipe, fittings and components shall be third-party certified as conforming to NSF 14.*

Discussion and Commentary: All plastic piping, fittings and plastic pipe-related components, including solvent cements, primers, tapes, lubricants and seals used in plumbing systems, are required to be tested and certified as conforming to NSF 14. This includes all water service, water distribution, drainage piping and fittings, and plastic piping system components, including but not limited to pipes, fittings, valves, joining materials, gaskets and appurtenances. This section does not apply to components that only include plastic parts such as brass valves with a plastic stem, or to fixture fittings such as fixture stop valves. Plastic piping systems, fittings and related components intended for use in the potable water supply system must comply with NSF 61 in addition to NSF 14.

NSF International Standards are developed under the American National Standards Institute (ANSI) consensus process. This process allows participation by all interested or affected segments of the industry, and presents a balanced representation for committee decisions.

| Topic: Third-Party Certification | Category: General Regulations |
| Reference: IPC 303.4 | Subject: Materials |

Code Text: *All plumbing products and materials required by the code to be in compliance with a referenced standard shall be listed by a third-party certification agency as complying with the referenced standards. Products and materials shall be identified in accordance with Section 303.1.*

Discussion and Commentary: The code requires that all plumbing products and materials must be certified (often referred to as "listed") as complying with the applicable referenced standards. By definition, certification indicates that the function and performance characteristics of a product or material have been determined by testing and ongoing surveillance by an approved third-party certification agency. One such agency is ICC Evaluation Service (ICC-ES), which evaluates and certifies plumbing products as well as other construction materials. Certification is verified through identification in accordance with the requirements of the third-party certification agency.

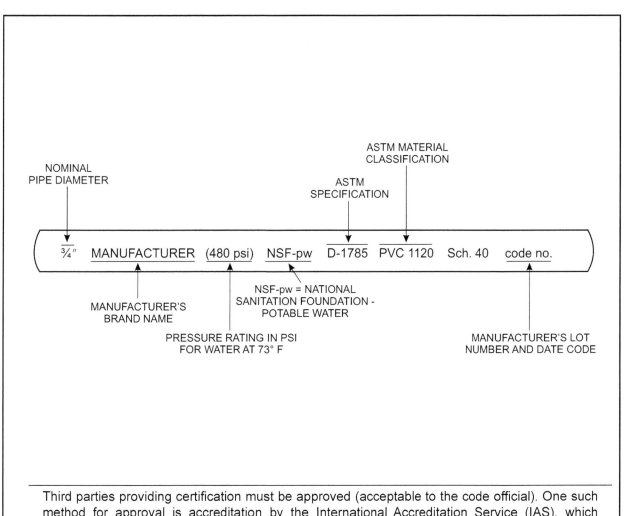

Third parties providing certification must be approved (acceptable to the code official). One such method for approval is accreditation by the International Accreditation Service (IAS), which accredits product certification agencies under ISO/IEC Guide 65, *General Requirements for Bodies Operating Product Certification Systems.*

| Topic: Pipes through Foundation Walls | Category: General Regulations |
| Reference: IPC 305.3 | Subject: Protection of Pipes and Components |

Code Text: *Any pipe that passes through a foundation wall shall be provided with a relieving arch, or a pipe sleeve pipe shall be built into the foundation wall. The sleeve shall be two pipe sizes greater than the pipe passing through the wall.*

Discussion and Commentary: Piping installed through a foundation wall must be structurally protected from any transferred loading from the structure. This protection may be provided through the use of a relieving arch or a pipe sleeve. When a sleeve is used, it should be sized such that it is two pipe sizes larger than the penetrating pipe. For example, a 4-inch penetrating pipe would require a 6-inch sleeve. This space will allow for any differential movement of the pipe. By providing structural protection to the piping system, the piping will not be subjected to undue stresses that could cause it to rupture and leak.

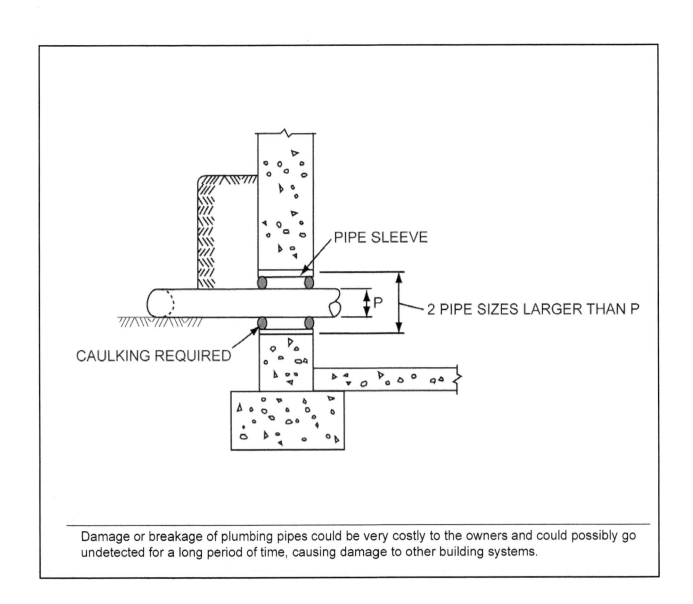

Damage or breakage of plumbing pipes could be very costly to the owners and could possibly go undetected for a long period of time, causing damage to other building systems.

Topic: Freezing
Reference: IPC 305.4
Category: General Regulations
Subject: Protection of Pipes and Components

Code Text: *Water, soil and waste pipes shall not be installed outside of a building, in attics or crawl spaces, concealed in outside walls, or in any other place subjected to freezing temperature unless adequate provision is made to protect such pipes from freezing by insulation or heat or both. Exterior water supply system piping shall be installed not less than 6 inches (152 mm) below the frost line and not less than 12 inches (305 mm) below grade.*

Discussion and Commentary: When a water or drain pipe is installed in an exterior wall or unheated space, such as a crawl space or attic, freeze protection can be achieved through thermal insulation. No amount of insulation alone (without a heat source) can prevent freezing; insulation can only delay freezing by slowing the rate of heat loss. Hose bibbs and wall hydrants located on the exterior wall must be protected when installed in areas subject to freezing temperature. This can be accomplished by installing devices, such as freezeproof hose bibbs, that locate the valve seat within the heated space and allow residual water within the hydrant to drain after the valve is closed.

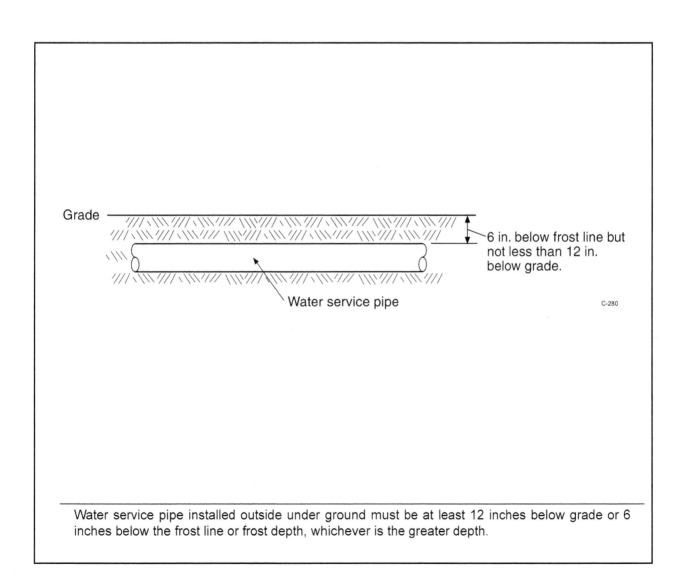

Water service pipe installed outside under ground must be at least 12 inches below grade or 6 inches below the frost line or frost depth, whichever is the greater depth.

Topic: Waterproofing
Reference: IPC 305.5

Category: General Regulations
Subject: Protection of Pipes and Components

Code Text: *Joints at the roof and around vent pipes shall be made water tight by the use of lead, copper, galvanized steel, aluminum, plastic or other approved flashings or flashing material. Exterior wall openings shall be made water tight.*

Discussion and Commentary: Where a pipe penetrates a roof, the pipe must be provided with flashing to prevent the entry of moisture. If improperly flashed, moisture from precipitation can enter the structure and damage the surrounding structure and finishes. Because the vertical surface of exterior walls readily shed moisture and penetrations are not subjected to the same severity of exposure as a roof, the space around pipes that penetrate exterior walls does not require flashing. Openings in exterior walls can be sealed with an approved sealant to prevent moisture penetration and air infiltration into the structure.

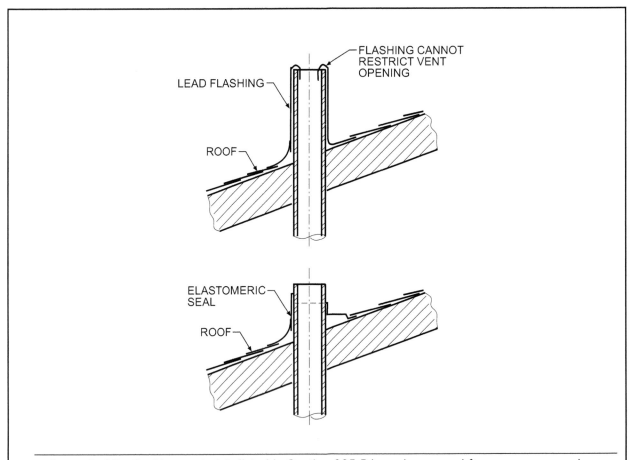

Several of the flashing materials listed in Section 305.5 have been used for many years and are recognized as effective moisture penetration protection. This section also provides for the use of new and innovative materials that are not specifically listed when approved by the code official.

Topic: Protection against Physical Damage
Reference: IPC 305.6

Category: General Regulations
Subject: Protection of Pipes and Components

Code Text: *In concealed locations where piping, other than cast-iron or galvanized steel, is installed through holes or notches in studs, joists, rafters or similar members less than $1^{1}/_{4}$ inches (32 mm) from the nearest edge of the member, the pipe shall be protected by steel shield plates. Such shield plates shall have a thickness of not less than 0.0575 inch (1.463 mm) (No. 16 gage). Such plates shall cover the area of the pipe where the member is notched or bored, and shall extend a minimum of 2 inches (51 mm) above sole plates and below top plates.*

Discussion and Commentary: Plumbing piping is often installed through bored holes in studs and joists. When piping material such as copper or plastic is less than $1^{1}/_{4}$ inches from the face of the framing members it is subject to nail or screw penetration during the application of gypsum board or other finish materials. In such cases, the code requires the installation of steel shield plates on the face of the framing to protect the piping.

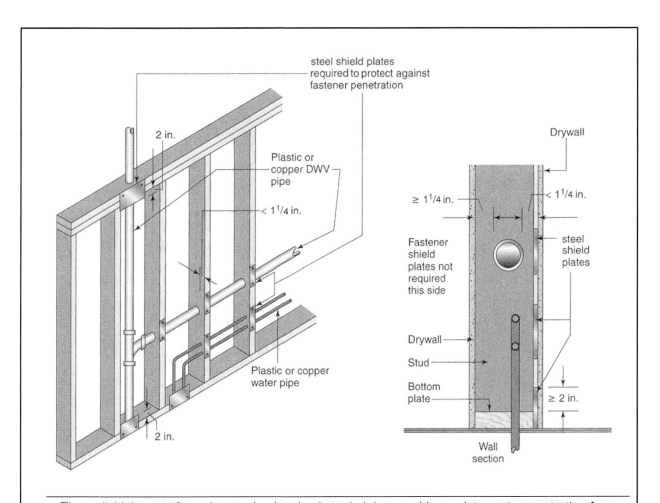

The wall thickness of cast iron and galvanized steel piping provides resistance to penetration from nails or screws that is equivalent to the steel shield plates. Therefore, additional protection is not required for these piping materials.

Topic: Protection of Components
Reference: IPC 305.7

Category: General Regulations
Subject: Protection of Pipes and Components

Code Text: *Components of a plumbing system installed along alleyways, driveways, parking garages or other locations exposed to damage shall be recessed into the wall or otherwise protected in an approved manner.*

Discussion and Commentary: To maintain exposed portions of plumbing systems in a safe and sanitary condition, the code requires protection from vehicle impact damage when components are installed in garages or adjacent to driveways, alleys or parking areas. When piping or other components are recessed behind the face of the wall, they are considered protected. Otherwise, an approved barrier is required to prevent damage to the system.

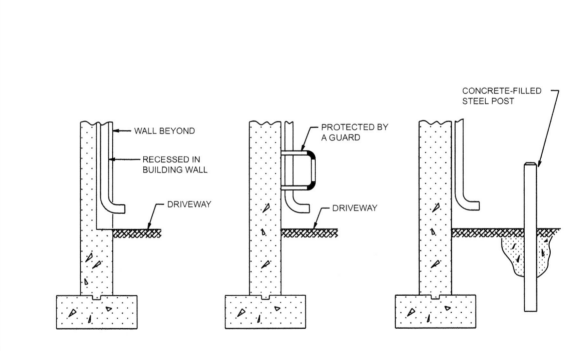

NOTE: OTHER METHODS OF PROTECTION OF PLUMBING COMPONENTS ARE POSSIBLE, SUBJECT TO APPROVAL BY THE CODE OFFICIAL.

The most common method of protection from vehicle impact is a steel pipe bollard filled with concrete. Other than recessing the pipe into the wall, any method of protection must be approved by the code official.

Topic: Trenching and Bedding
Reference: IPC 306.2
Category: General Regulations
Subject: Trenching, Excavation and Backfill

Code Text: *Where trenches are excavated such that the bottom of the trench forms the bed for the pipe, solid and continuous load-bearing support shall be provided between joints. Bell holes, hub holes and coupling holes shall be provided at points where the pipe is joined. Such pipe shall not be supported on blocks to grade. Where trenches are excavated below the installation level of the pipe such that the bottom of the trench does not form the bed for the pipe, the trench shall be backfilled to the installation level of the bottom of the pipe with sand or fine gravel placed in layers not greater than 6 inches (152 mm) in depth and such backfill shall be compacted after each placement.*

Discussion and Commentary: To maintain proper alignment, integrity and connections of underground piping systems, the code requires continuous support at the bottom of the excavation. Preparation of the trench bed must also accommodate the additional thickness of bells, hubs or hubless couplings at the joint locations to maintain the continuous support of the pipe. For some materials, the manufacturer may require specific bedding material, such as sand or fine gravel, support of the sides of the pipe with the same material, or other installation criteria that exceed the code provisions. In such cases, the more restrictive requirements prevail.

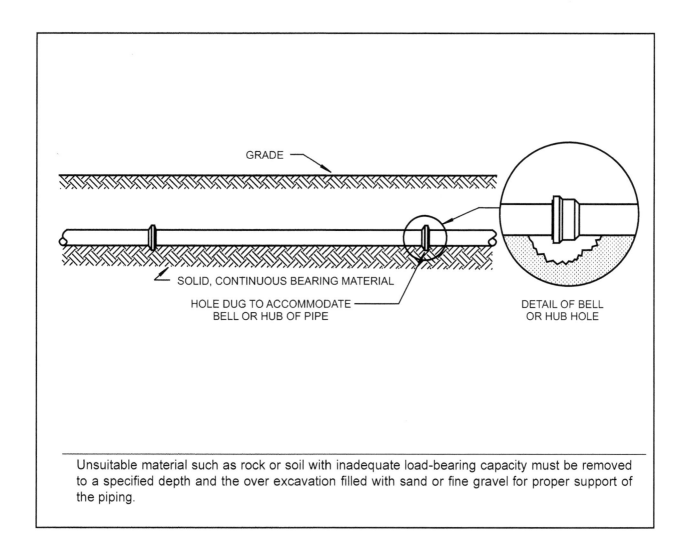

Unsuitable material such as rock or soil with inadequate load-bearing capacity must be removed to a specified depth and the over excavation filled with sand or fine gravel for proper support of the piping.

Topic: Backfilling
Reference: IPC 306.3

Category: General Regulations
Subject: Trenching, Excavation and Backfill

Code Text: *Backfill shall be free from discarded construction material and debris. Loose earth free from rocks, broken concrete and frozen chunks shall be placed in the trench in 6-inch (152 mm) layers and tamped in place until the crown of the pipe is covered by 12 inches (305 mm) of tamped earth. The backfill under and beside the pipe shall be compacted for pipe support. Backfill shall be brought up evenly on both sides of the pipe so that the pipe remains aligned.*

Discussion and Commentary: In addition to proper continuous support under the pipe, care must be taken in backfilling around and above the pipe with suitable materials to prevent damage, distortion or misalignment of the underground piping system. Fine gravel, sand or suitable loose soil must be placed evenly in 6-inch lifts and compacted to provide at least 12 inches of cover over the pipe and to provide protection from any loads placed on the soil above that point.

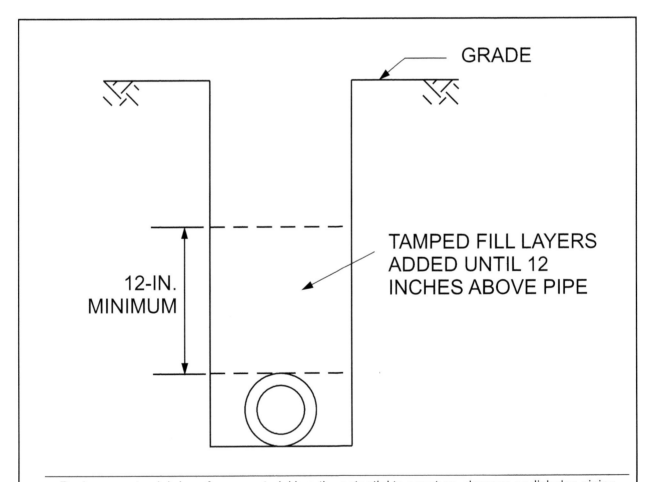

Rock, concrete, debris or frozen material has the potential to puncture, damage or dislodge piping during backfill operations, and the code prohibits the use of such materials. Use of these materials may also cause differential settling at a later date causing damage to the piping system or the structure.

Topic: Protection of Footings	Category: General Regulations
Reference: IPC 307.5	Subject: Structural Safety

Code Text: *Trenching installed parallel to footings and walls shall not extend into the bearing plane of a footing or wall. The upper boundary of the bearing plane is a line that extends downward, at an angle of 45 degrees (0.79 rad) from horizontal, from the outside bottom edge of the footing or wall.*

Discussion and Commentary: A footing requires a minimum load-bearing area to distribute the weight of the building. This load-bearing distribution plane extends downward at approximately a 45-degree angle from the base of the footing. Water and sewer piping must not be installed below this load-bearing plane, nor can excavation for the installation of pipe extend below the plane, so as not to affect the load capacity of the footing, or cause the excavation to collapse.

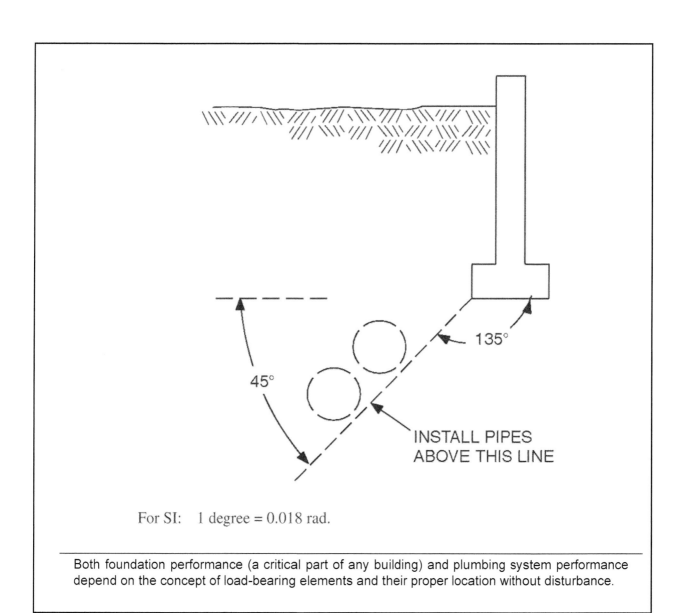

For SI: 1 degree = 0.018 rad.

Both foundation performance (a critical part of any building) and plumbing system performance depend on the concept of load-bearing elements and their proper location without disturbance.

Quiz

Study Session 2
IPC Sections 301 through 307

1. A _____ is permitted to discharge to an approved nonpotable water system.

    a. bidet
    b. clothes washer
    c. floor drain
    d. sink

    Reference _____

2. When there is a conflict between the requirements of the code and the manufacturer's installation instructions, the _____ requirements apply.

    a. code
    b. more specific
    c. more restrictive
    d. manufacturer's

    Reference _____

3. A sump pump is permitted at the base of an elevator shaft when the discharge is _____.

    a. monitored by an alarm system
    b. protected by a backflow device
    c. directly connected to a storm drain
    d. indirectly connected to the plumbing system

    Reference _____

4. Materials required by the code to comply with a referenced standard must be listed by a(n) _____ agency.

    a. evaluation service   b. third-party testing

    c. third-party certification   d. accreditation service

    Reference _____

5. The approved methods for preventing rodents from entering a structure do not include _____.

    a. caulking   b. strainer plates

    c. building traps   d. meter box design

    Reference _____

6. The minimum burial depth of exterior water service piping is _____ inches below grade.

    a. 6   b. 12

    c. 24   d. 30

    Reference _____

7. Where the frost line is established at 30 inches, water service pipe shall be installed a minimum of _____ inches below grade.

    a. 30   b. 32

    c. 36   d. 42

    Reference _____

8. The code does not permit the use of _____ to support and maintain the grade of drainage piping in a trench.

    a. gravel   b. sand

    c. clay soil   d. blocks

    Reference _____

9. Shield plates required to protect piping installed through notches or bored holes in framing members shall extend a minimum of _____ inch/es above sole plates and below top plates.

    a. 1
    b. 2
    c. 3
    d. 4

    Reference _____

10. For water piping adjacent and parallel to a wall footing, and installed at a depth of 12 inches below the bottom of the footing, the trench shall be located not less than _____ inches horizontally from the footing.

    a. 24
    b. 12
    c. 6
    d. 18

    Reference _____

11. The _____ regulates piping materials that are exposed in plenums.

    a. *International Fire Code*® (IFC®)
    b. *International Fuel Gas Code*® (IFGC®)
    c. *International Mechanical Code*® (IMC®)
    d. *International Plumbing Code*® (IPC®)

    Reference _____

12. Where concealed copper piping passes through holes bored in wood studs, shield plates are not required if the bored holes are at least _____ from the nearest edge of the studs.

    a. 5/8 inch
    b. 1 inch
    c. 1 1/4 inches
    d. 1 1/2 inches

    Reference _____

13. A pipe sleeve in a masonry foundation wall shall be at least _____ greater than the pipe passing through the wall.

    a. 2 inches
    b. 1 inch
    c. 2 pipe sizes
    d. 1 pipe size

    Reference _____

14. Where poor soil conditions exist at the bottom of the trench, the pipe bed shall be over excavated a minimum of _____ below the installation depth of the pipe.
    a. 4 inches
    b. 6 inches
    c. one pipe diameter
    d. two pipe diameters

    Reference _____

15. The initial backfill over pipe installed in a trench shall be in maximum _____ layers of loose earth.
    a. 4-inch
    b. 6-inch
    c. 8-inch
    d. 12-inch

    Reference _____

16. Compaction is required for the first _____ inches of backfill above a pipe installed in a trench.
    a. 6
    b. 12
    c. 16
    d. 20

    Reference _____

17. Alterations to trusses require written approval of _____.
    a. a registered design professional
    b. the manufacturer
    c. the general contractor
    d. the building official

    Reference _____

18. _____ piping shall not be placed in direct contact with concrete walls or floors.
    a. Ductile iron
    b. Cast iron
    c. Galvanized steel
    d. Copper

    Reference _____

19. Sheathing or wrapping for corrosion protection of pipes shall be not less than _____ - inch thick.
    a. 0.008
    b. 0.030
    c. 0.035
    d. 0.025

    Reference _____

20. When concealed piping requires protection against physical damage, the steel shield plates shall be not less than _____ - inch thick.
    a. 0.0620
    b. 0.0575
    c. 0.0520
    d. 0.0475

    Reference _____

21. When excavating a trench for underground piping installation, rock shall be removed to a depth at least _____ below the bottom of the pipe.
    a. 3 inches
    b. 6 inches
    c. one pipe diameter
    d. two pipe diameters

    Reference _____

22. The minimum burial depth for a building sewer is _____ .
    a. 18 inches
    b. 12 inches
    c. 24 inches
    d. as determined by the local jurisdiction

    Reference _____

23. Where the bedding for piping installed in a trench consists of backfill, _____ is an approved material.
    a. loose soil free from rocks or frozen material
    b. sandy clay
    c. fine gravel
    d. organic silty clay

    Reference _____

24. Piping installed by tunneling shall be protected from _____.
    a. uneven loading   b. expansion
    c. contraction   d. excavation

    Reference _____

25. Vent pipes through the roof require _____.
    a. protection from freezing   b. caulking
    c. a termination cap   d. flashing

    Reference _____

Study Session

2018 IPC Sections 308 through 316
General Regulations II

OBJECTIVE: To develop an understanding of those general provisions regarding plumbing systems that are not specifically addressed in other chapters of the code. To develop an understanding of the provisions that apply to materials in all plumbing applications

REFERENCE: Sections 308 through 316, 2018 *International Plumbing Code*

KEY POINTS:
- What piping is required to be supported? What seismic requirements apply?
- What types of materials are permitted to be used for hangers, anchors and supports?
- How is the interval of support for both horizontal and vertical piping determined?
- When is sway bracing required?
- When are piping restraints required, and what methods are acceptable?
- What requirements apply to hot and cold water piping installed in bundles?
- What regulations apply to plumbing systems and equipment installed in flood hazard areas?
- What plumbing systems are required to be located above the designated flood elevation?
- What plumbing systems are permitted to be located below the designated flood elevation?
- What light, ventilation and interior finish requirements apply to washrooms and toilet rooms?
- What plumbing facilities are required for construction workers?
- When is testing required for piping systems? What are the methods for testing?
- What criteria apply to the maximum increments in test gauges?
- When is pressure air testing not permitted?
- What test requirements apply to shower liners?
- What components of a plumbing system require annual inspection and testing?

KEY POINTS:
(Cont'd)
- What requirements apply to the collection and disposal of condensate wastes?
- When are auxiliary systems required for the disposal of condensate wastes?
- When are traps required for condensate piping systems?
- When are pipe penetrations required to be sealed? What materials are approved for sealing around the pipes?
- How are pipe penetrations of fire-resistance-rated assemblies regulated?
- What specific design, submittal, documentation and inspection requirements apply to alternative engineered designs?

Topic: Sway Bracing
Reference: IPC 308.6

Category: General Regulations
Subject: Piping Support

Code Text: *Where horizontal pipes 4 inches (102 mm) and larger convey drainage or waste, and where a pipe fitting in that piping changes the flow direction greater than 45 degrees (0.79 rad), rigid bracing or other rigid support arrangements shall be installed to resist movement of the upstream pipe in the direction of pipe flow. A change of flow direction into a vertical pipe shall not require the upstream pipe to be braced.*

Discussion and Commentary: For larger pipes, hangers alone may not be sufficient to resist the forces created by water movement within horizontal piping at a change in direction. To maintain alignment and prevent damage to the piping system adjacent to the elbow fitting, rigid sway bracing is required when the horizontal change in direction exceeds 45 degrees and the piping is 4 inches or greater in diameter.

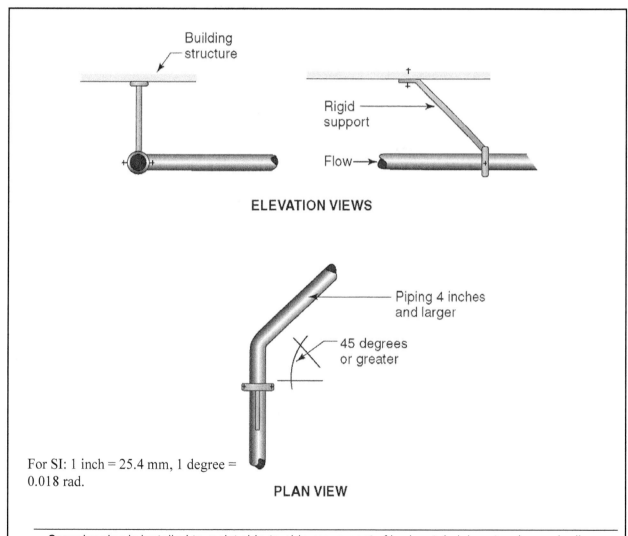

For SI: 1 inch = 25.4 mm, 1 degree = 0.018 rad.

Sway bracing is installed to resist side-to-side movement of horizontal piping at a change in direction. A change in horizontal direction of 45 degrees or less is not considered significant enough to cause pipe movement.

Study Session 3

Topic: Anchorage
Reference: IPC 308.7

Category: General Regulations
Subject: Piping Support

Code Text: *Anchorage shall be provided to restrain drainage piping from axial movement. For pipe sizes greater than 4 inches (102 mm), restraints shall be provided for drain pipes at all changes in direction and at all changes in diameter greater than two pipe sizes. Braces, blocks, rodding and other suitable methods as specified by the coupling manufacturer shall be utilized.*

Discussion and Commentary: This section requires a method of resisting axial movement of piping systems in order to prevent joint separation, regardless of the type of fittings or connections used. In particular, mechanical couplings using an elastomeric seal (typically hubless piping systems) have a limited ability to resist axial movement (pulling apart); therefore, pipe restraints must be provided to prevent joint separation. Section 308.7.1 requires axial restraints for pipe sizes greater than 4 inches at each change in direction and at each location with a change greater than two pipe sizes. Such joints also have a limited ability to resist shear forces. The hanger and support system must, therefore, prevent the couplings and connections from being subjected to shear forces that can damage the joint.

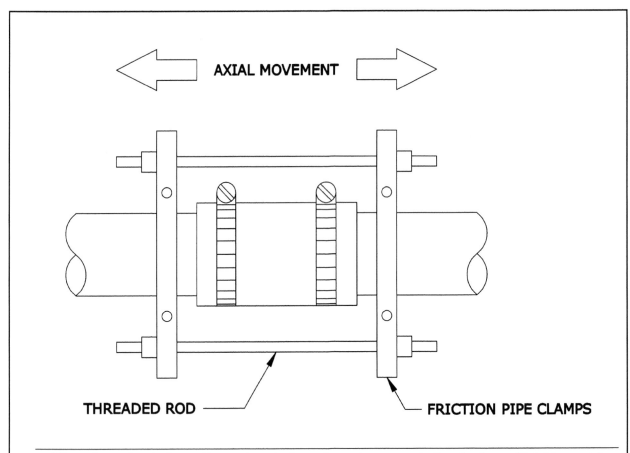

Although mechanical couplings using elastomeric seals are most often the type of joint to experience damage that is due to axial movement, this restraint requirement applies to changes in direction for all types of piping that exceed 4 inches in diameter.

Topic: Parallel Water Distribution Systems **Category:** General Regulations
Reference: IPC 308.9 **Subject:** Piping Support

Code Text: *Piping bundles for manifold systems shall be supported in accordance with Table 308.5. Support at changes in direction shall be in accordance with the manufacturer's instructions. Where hot water piping is bundled with cold or hot water piping, each hot water pipe shall be insulated.*

Discussion and Commentary: Typically, manifold systems distribute individual water supply lines to each fixture using PEX or some other semirigid plastic piping or tubing. The individual lines may be bundled together, and such bundles are treated as a single unit for determining hanger spacing. Installation also must comply with the manufacturer's installation instructions, which include the required supports at changes in direction to maintain a smooth transition without damaging, deforming or reducing the cross-sectional area of the piping.

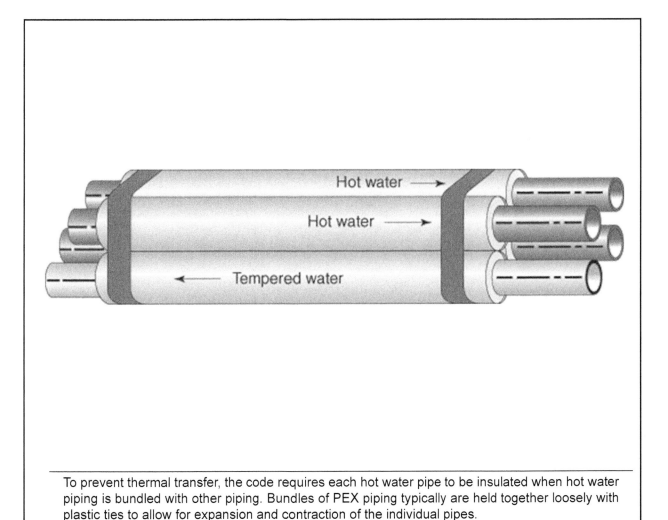

To prevent thermal transfer, the code requires each hot water pipe to be insulated when hot water piping is bundled with other piping. Bundles of PEX piping typically are held together loosely with plastic ties to allow for expansion and contraction of the individual pipes.

Topic: Test Gauges
Reference: IPC 312.1.1
Category: General Regulations
Subject: Tests and Inspections

Code Text: *Gauges used for testing shall be as follows:*

1. *Tests requiring a pressure of 10 pounds per square inch (psi) (69 kPa) or less shall utilize a testing gauge having increments of 0.10 psi (0.69 kPa) or less.*
2. *Tests requiring a pressure of greater than 10 psi (69 kPa) but less than or equal to 100 psi (689 kPa) shall utilize a testing gauge having increments of 1 psi (6.9 kPa) or less.*
3. *Tests requiring a pressure of greater than 100 psi (689 kPa) shall utilize a testing gauge having increments of 2 psi (14 kPa) or less*

Discussion and Commentary: A test gauge must be chosen to accurately measure the air pressure and clearly indicate any drop in pressure so as to detect a leak in the piping system. For example, a test gauge with increments of 1 or 2 psi will not provide the necessary accuracy when testing a piping system with only 5 psi of air pressure. In such a case, a small drop in pressure would not be noticeable on the gauge.

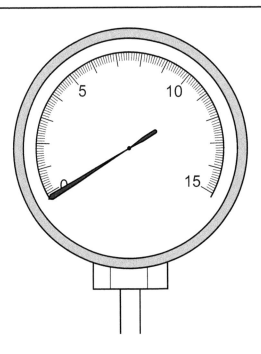

PRESSURE GAUGE WITH
0.10 PSI INCREMENTS FOR
TESTING AT 10 PSI OR LESS

The permit holder is responsible for performing the tests and giving reasonable advance notice to the code official that the system is ready for inspection and observation of the testing.

Topic: Drainage and Vent Water Test
Reference: IPC 312.2
Category: General Regulations
Subject: Tests and Inspections

Code Text: *A water test shall be applied to the drainage system either in its entirety or in sections. In testing successive sections, at least the upper 10 feet (3048 mm) of the next preceding section shall be tested so that no joint or pipe in the building, except the uppermost 10 feet (3048 mm) of the system, shall have been submitted to a test of less than a 10-foot (3048 mm) head of water. This pressure shall be held for not less than 15 minutes. The system shall then be tight at all points.*

Discussion and Commentary: All drain, waste and vent (DWV) piping must be tested in an appropriate manner to verify that there are no leaks in the system. For a water test (the most common method of testing the DWV system) all portions of the system are filled with water, including 10 feet of water-filled vertical pipe above all piping being tested. The uppermost 10 feet of the system that includes the highest vent through the roof only needs to be filled with water and does not require 10 feet of head pressure.

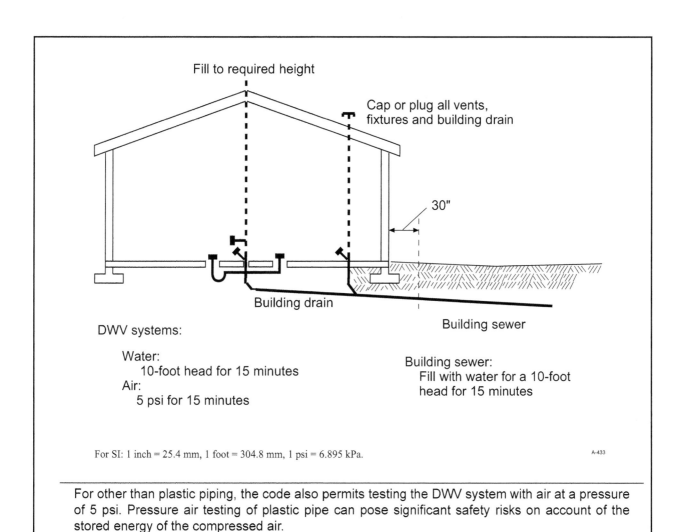

For SI: 1 inch = 25.4 mm, 1 foot = 304.8 mm, 1 psi = 6.895 kPa.

For other than plastic piping, the code also permits testing the DWV system with air at a pressure of 5 psi. Pressure air testing of plastic pipe can pose significant safety risks on account of the stored energy of the compressed air.

Study Session 3

Topic: Water Supply System Test
Reference: IPC 312.5

Category: General Regulations
Subject: Tests and Inspections

Code Text: *Upon completion of a section of or the entire water supply system, the system, or portion completed shall be tested and proved tight under a water pressure not less than the working pressure of the system; or, for piping systems other than plastic, by an air test of not less than 50 psi (344 kPa). This pressure shall be held for not less than 15 minutes. The water utilized for tests shall be obtained from a potable source of supply. The required tests shall be performed in accordance with this section and Section 107.*

Discussion and Commentary: Water piping typically is tested by capping the outlets and connecting to the domestic potable water supply. In cases where the water supply is not yet available or to test isolated portions of the system, the code also permits testing of copper water piping with air at a pressure of 50 psi.

Testing with air is not permitted on plastic piping systems because of the hazards of a sudden release of energy, which could cause a separated piece of piping or a fitting to become a projectile causing serious injury.

Topic: Shower Liner Test	**Category:** General Regulations
Reference: IPC 312.9	**Subject:** Tests and Inspections

Code Text: *Where shower floors and receptors are made water-tight by the application of materials required by Section 417.5.2, the completed liner installation shall be tested. The pipe from the shower drain shall be plugged water tight for the test. The floor and receptor area shall be filled with potable water to a depth of not less than 2 inches (51 mm) measured at the threshold. The water shall be retained for a test period of not less than 15 minutes, and there shall not be evidence of leakage.*

Discussion and Commentary: For other than prefabricated receptors, shower floors, typically tile, require a water-tight liner of approved materials. Because shower floor leaks can go undetected for long periods of time and cause considerable damage, the code requires this liner to be tested by plugging the shower drain pipe and filling the area above the liner with water 2 inches deep. The test is monitored for 15 minutes to verify there is no evidence of a leak.

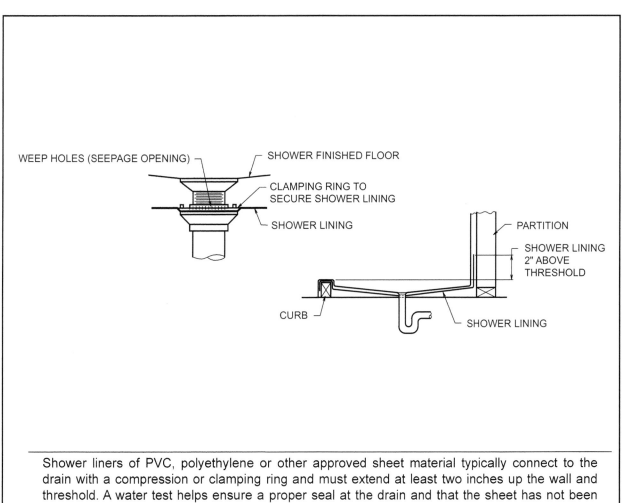

Shower liners of PVC, polyethylene or other approved sheet material typically connect to the drain with a compression or clamping ring and must extend at least two inches up the wall and threshold. A water test helps ensure a proper seal at the drain and that the sheet has not been damaged during installation.

Topic: Fuel-Burning Appliances
Reference: IPC 314.1

Category: General Regulations
Subject: Condensate Disposal

Code Text: *Liquid combustion by-products of condensing appliances shall be collected and discharged to an approved plumbing fixture or disposal area in accordance with the manufacturer's installation instructions. Condensate piping shall be of approved corrosion-resistant material and shall not be smaller than the drain connection on the appliance. Such piping shall maintain a minimum horizontal slope in the direction of discharge of not less than one-eighth unit vertical in 12 units horizontal (1-percent slope).*

Discussion and Commentary: High-efficiency appliances, such as Category IV furnaces, have low-temperature flue gases that also produce condensate in the vent. The condensate collection is integral with the appliance and must drain to an approved location, typically a floor drain or other indirect waste receptor.

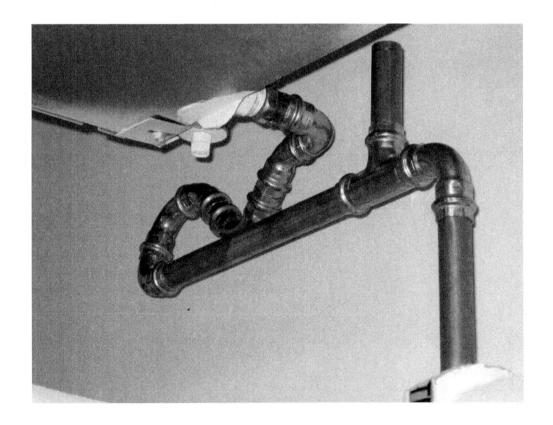

Condensate piping is part of the mechanical system and is covered as part of the appliance installation provisions of the IMC as well as by the general regulations of the IPC. Inclusion in the IPC recognizes that appliance drain systems use products approved for plumbing systems and may be installed by plumbers.

Topic: Evaporators and Cooling Coils
Reference: IPC 314.2
Category: General Regulations
Subject: Condensate Disposal

Code Text: *Condensate drain systems shall be provided for equipment and appliances containing evaporators or cooling coils. Condensate drain systems shall be designed, constructed and installed in accordance with Sections 314.2.1 through 314.2.4. Condensate from all cooling coils and evaporators shall be conveyed from the drain pan outlet to an approved place of disposal. Such piping shall maintain a minimum horizontal slope in the direction of discharge of not less than one-eighth unit vertical in 12 units horizontal (1-percent slope). Condensate shall not discharge into a street, alley or other areas so as to cause a nuisance.*

Discussion and Commentary: Cooling coils and evaporators installed in forced air furnaces as part of the air conditioning system generate condensate that is collected within the appliance in an integral pan. Refrigeration and dehumidification equipment also produce condensate extracted from the air. A drainage system is necessary to dispose of condensate at an approved location.

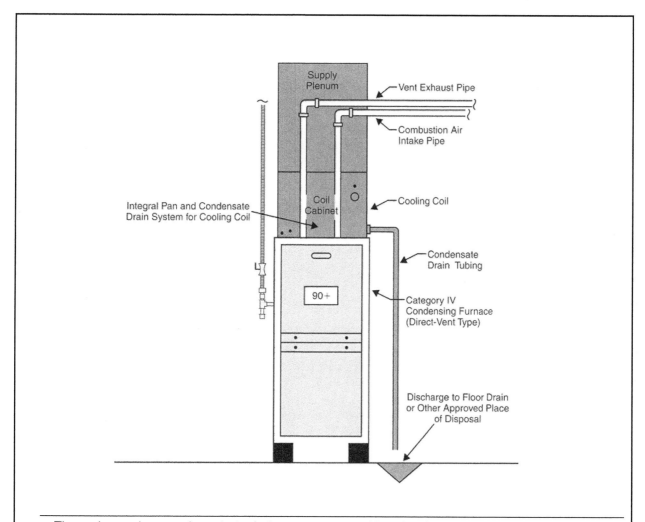

The code requires condensate to drain to an approved location for disposal. In some cases, this may be a floor drain or other receptor connecting to the building drainage system. Another common point of disposal is outside the building at grade, provided the location does not create a nuisance.

Topic: Auxiliary Drain Systems
Reference: IPC 314.2.3
Category: General Regulations
Subject: Condensate Disposal

Code Text: *Where damage to any building components could occur as a result of overflow from the equipment primary condensate removal system, an auxiliary protection method shall be provided for each cooling coil or fuel-fired appliance that produces condensate. An auxiliary drain pan with a separate drain shall be provided under the coils on which condensation will occur. The auxiliary pan drain shall discharge to a conspicuous point of disposal to alert occupants in the event of a stoppage of the primary drain.*

Discussion and Commentary: For condensing appliances installed in basements, on slab-on-ground floors or rooftops, a stoppage and overflow of the primary condensate collection system is not a big concern, as the overflow does not cause damage, is often readily observed and the stoppage may be remedied in short order. On the other hand, for appliances installed in attics or other spaces above finished areas, leakage may cause significant damage to finishes and the structure, and the code requires an auxiliary backup system to prevent such damage. One option is to install an auxiliary pan below the appliance with a separate drain system. The code prescribes the size and materials of the pan and stipulates that it drain to a conspicuous location so as to alert occupants of a stoppage.

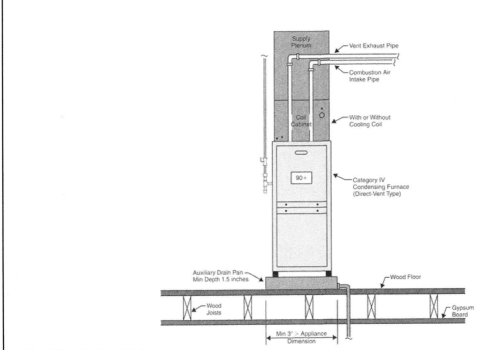

For SI: 1 inch = 25.4 mm

In addition to an auxiliary drain pan with a separate drain, there are three options for providing a backup for the condensate drainage system. The first involves a separate overflow drain line that may be installed at the integral drain pan with discharge to a conspicuous location. The other two options involve a water level detection device that shuts off the equipment before an overflow occurs.

Topic: Water-Level Monitoring Devices
Reference: IPC 314.2.3.1
Category: General Regulations
Subject: Condensate Disposal

Code Text: *On down-flow units and all other coils that do not have a secondary drain or provisions to install a secondary or auxiliary drain pan, a water-level monitoring device shall be installed inside the primary drain pan. This device shall shut off the equipment served in the event that the primary drain becomes restricted. Devices installed in the drain line shall not be permitted.*

Discussion and Commentary: Some appliance installations cannot accommodate the installation of an overflow drain or an auxiliary drain pan. In such cases, the code requires a water-level monitoring device located in the primary drain pan that shuts down the appliance before an overflow can occur.

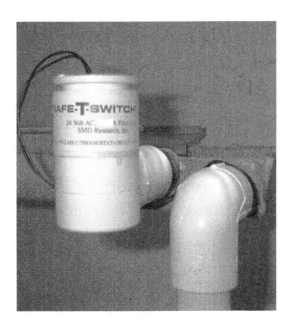

A water-level monitoring device is an alternative to providing an auxiliary or secondary drain system and is only required in locations where an overflow would cause damage to building components.

Topic: Sealing of Annular Spaces
Reference: IPC 315.1
Category: General Regulations
Subject: Penetrations

Code Text: *The annular space between the outside of a pipe and the inside of a pipe sleeve or between the outside of a pipe and an opening in a building envelope wall, floor, or ceiling assembly penetrated by a pipe shall be sealed in an approved manner with caulking material, foam sealant or closed with a gasketing system. The caulking material, foam sealant or gasketing system shall be designed for the conditions at the penetration location and shall be compatible with the pipe, sleeve and building materials in contact with the sealing materials. Annular spaces created by pipes penetrating fire-resistance-rated assemblies or membranes of such assemblies shall be sealed or closed in accordance with Section 714 of the* International Building Code.

Discussion and Commentary: Sealing of all pipe penetrations of the building envelope serve two purposes—to prevent water intrusion into the structure and to protect against air leakage and conserve energy in accordance with the *International Energy Conservation Code* (IECC). The entire annular space does not need to be filled with sealant for the full thickness of the wall or floor. Approved sealant applied to the end of the pipe sleeve or at the exterior building surface around the pipe penetration is adequate to prevent water intrusion and air infiltration. Care must be taken to choose a caulking, foam sealant or gasketing material that is compatible with the piping and surrounding materials and that is designed for the specific application and conditions. For example, the type of sealant should be chosen based on its intended use for the particular materials, weather exposure and temperature range.

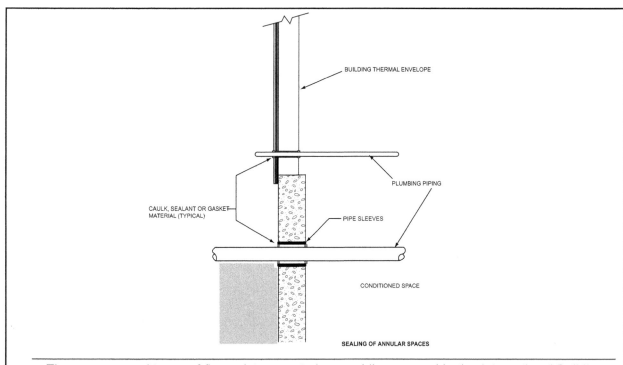

SEALING OF ANNULAR SPACES

There are several types of fire-resistance-rated assemblies covered in the *International Building Code* (IBC), including fire walls, fire barriers, fire partitions and horizontal assemblies. Any penetration of these fire-resistance-rated assemblies with plumbing piping or components must be protected to maintain the fire-resistance rating of the assembly.

Study Session 3
IPC Sections 308 through 316

1. When installed horizontally, $1^{1}/_{4}$-inch polypropylene pipe and tubing shall be supported at maximum intervals of _____.

    a. 32 inches b. 48 inches

    c. 8 feet d. 10 feet

    Reference _____

2. A horizontal 4-inch PVC drainage pipe suspended from the ceiling requires _____ at a 90 degree turn.

    a. axial restraints b. sway bracing

    c. coupling restraints d. thrust blocks

    Reference _____

3. One-half-inch CPVC water pipe installed horizontally shall be supported at maximum intervals of _____ feet.

    a. 6 b. 5

    c. 4 d. 3

    Reference _____

4. Support hangers for 10-foot lengths of cast-iron soil pipe suspended from a ceiling shall be spaced not more than _____ feet.

    a. 2.5   b. 5
    c. 7.5   d. 10

    Reference _____

5. PVC pipe installed vertically requires a guide installed midway between required supports for pipe sizes _____ inch(es) and smaller.

    a. 1   b. 3
    c. 2   d. 1¼

    Reference _____

6. Which of the following is not specifically allowed for sealing around a pipe that passes through an exterior wall?

    a. flashing   b. caulk
    c. foam sealant   d. gasketing system

    Reference _____

7. When located in a flood hazard area, the top of a potable water well casing without a sealed cover shall extend not less than _____ inches above the design flood elevation.

    a. 6   b. 12
    c. 18   d. 24

    Reference _____

8. When performing an air test on cast iron drain, waste and vent (DWV) piping at a pressure of 5 psi, the test gauge shall be marked at maximum _____ psi increments.

    a. 0.10   b. 0.20
    c. 0.50   d. 1.0

    Reference _____

9. A water test on a building drain requires at least a _____ head of water.

   a. 5-foot b. 10-foot
   c. 12-foot d. 15-foot

   Reference _____

10. The _____ is responsible for performing tests on plumbing piping systems.

    a. code official b. owner
    c. person doing the work d. permit holder

    Reference _____

11. The water supply system test must hold a water pressure not less than _____.

    a. 5 psi b. 50 psi
    c. 10-foot head pressure d. the working pressure of the system

    Reference _____

12. Condensate piping must maintain a minimum slope of not less than _____ percent.

    a. 1 b. 2
    c. $1/4$ d. $1/2$

    Reference _____

13. When required on downflow HVAC units to prevent damage from condensate, a water level monitoring device must be installed _____.

    a. at the equipment drain pan outlet
    b. inside the auxiliary drain pan
    c. in the auxiliary drain line
    d. inside the primary drain pan

    Reference _____

Study Session 3

14. For piping bundles in manifold water distribution systems, hot water piping _____.
    a. requires expansion joint fittings
    b. must be individually insulated
    c. must be thermally isolated from cold water piping
    d. is not permitted in bundles containing cold water piping

    Reference _____

15. On construction sites, _____ are required for workers.
    a. water dispensers   b. emergency showers
    c. emergency eye washes d. toilet facilities

    Reference _____

16. Water or air pressure tests on piping systems must be held for not less than _____ minutes.
    a. 15   b. 30
    c. 10   d. 20

    Reference _____

17. Where water supply systems other than plastic are tested with air, the test pressure shall be not less than _____ psi.
    a. 10   b. 20
    c. 30   d. 50

    Reference _____

18. Horizontal 6-inch PVC drainage piping installed above ground requires _____ at a 45-degree change in direction.
    a. support   b. sway bracing
    c. restraint   d. expansion fittings

    Reference _____

19. One inch cross-linked polyethylene (PEX) piping installed horizontally requires hangers at intervals not greater than _____ inches.

    a. 48   b. 36

    c. 32   d. 24

Reference _____

20. The building sewer requires testing under not less than a _____ -foot head of water.

    a. 10   b. 12

    c. 15   d. 8

Reference _____

21. For other than prefabricated shower bases, a water test at least _____ inch(es) deep at the threshold is required for shower liners.

    a. 4   b. 3

    c. 2   d. 1

Reference _____

22. The drain line size for condensate from evaporators and cooling coils shall be not less than _____ -inch internal diameter.

    a. $1/2$ b. $5/8$

    c. $3/4$ d. $3/8$

Reference _____

23. For a condensate drain line serving multiple units with a total equipment capacity of 80 tons of refrigeration, the pipe shall be not less than _____ -inch pipe diameter.

    a. 1   b. $1 1/4$

    c. $1 1/2$ d. 2

Reference _____

24. An auxiliary drain pan shall be at least _____ inches larger than the unit it serves.

    a. 6   b. 4

    c. 3   d. 2

Reference _____

25. Condensate drains separate from the primary drain line shall discharge to_____.

    a. the sanitary drain   b. a floor drain

    c. grade outside the building   d. a conspicuous location

Reference _____

Study Session

4

2018 IPC Sections 401 through 411
Fixtures, Faucets and Fixture Fittings I

OBJECTIVE: To develop an understanding of how the code describes the number and types of plumbing fixtures needed for building occupants and fixture protection requirements.

REFERENCE: Sections 401 through 411, 2018 *International Plumbing Code*

KEY POINTS:
- How is the minimum number of plumbing fixtures in a building determined?
- How is the occupancy classification of a building or space determined?
- When are urinals permitted to be substituted for water closets? What is the ratio?
- How do fixtures in family or assisted use toilet rooms affect the fixture count in a building?
- When are separate facilities required for men and women?
- When are family or assisted use toilet rooms permitted as satisfying the requirement for separate facilities?
- When are public toilet facilities required? How is the route to the facilities regulated?
- What are the requirements for the locations of toilet facilities?
- What is the maximum travel distance to toilet facilities based on the occupancy of a building? To drinking fountains?
- What requirements apply to toilet room locks and signage?
- Proper installation of the water supply lines is required to prevent what from occurring?
- Closet screws and bolts are required to be of what materials?
- What general requirements for water lines, access and installation apply to all fixtures?
- What are the clearance requirements for fixtures in toilet rooms and bathrooms?
- When are toilet compartments required? Urinal partitions? What dimensions apply?
- What connection and anchoring requirements apply to floor outlet water closets? Wall hung water closets?

KEY POINTS:
(Cont'd)
- What requirements apply to the water and waste connections for automatic clothes washers?
- What features are required for bathtub outlets?
- How is the minimum number of wheel chair accessible drinking fountains determined? The minimum number for standing persons?
- When can water dispensers be substituted for drinking fountains?
- Drinking fountains are prohibited in what locations?

Topic: Minimum Plumbing Fixtures
Reference: IPC 403.1
Category: Fixtures, Faucets and Fixture Fittings
Subject: Minimum Plumbing Facilities

Code Text: *Plumbing fixtures shall be provided in the minimum number shown in Table 403.1, based on the actual use of the building or space. Uses not shown in Table 403.1 shall be considered individually by the code official. The number of occupants shall be determined by the* International Building Code.

Discussion and Commentary: Table 403.1 establishes the minimum number of plumbing fixtures required for each building. The occupant load used for calculating the number of fixtures required may be the same occupant load used for determining means of egress in the *International Building Code* (IBC). Fixture count is based on the actual use of the space matching the description in the table. Although the general use categories will typically align with those in the IBC, the IPC no longer uses specific occupancy group designations from the IBC.

TABLE 403.1
MINIMUM NUMBER OF REQUIRED PLUMBING FIXTURES[a]
(See Sections 403.1.1 and 403.2)

NO.	CLASSIFICATION	DESCRIPTION	WATER CLOSETS (URINALS: SEE SECTION 424.2)		LAVATORIES		BATHTUBS/ SHOWERS	DRINKING FOUNTAIN (SEE SECTION 410)	OTHER
			MALE	FEMALE	MALE	FEMALE			
1	Assembly	Theaters and other buildings for the performing arts and motion pictures[d]	1 per 125	1 per 65	1 per 200		—	1 per 500	1 service sink
		Nightclubs, bars, taverns, dance halls and buildings for similar purposes[d]	1 per 40	1 per 40	1 per 75		—	1 per 500	1 service sink
		Restaurants, banquet halls and food courts[d]	1 per 75	1 per 75	1 per 200		—	1 per 500	1 service sink

(continued)

The occupant load used for determining the means of egress requirements in the IBC does not necessarily reflect the day-to-day use of a building but does address the potential capacity for fire and life safety purposes. The ratios for fixtures in Table 403.1 intend to provide reasonable accommodation for occupants under typical use conditions, but a determination of occupancy and fixture count often requires some judgment on the part of the code official.

Topic: Separate Facilities
Reference: IPC 403.2

Category: Fixtures, Faucets and Fixture Fittings
Subject: Minimum Plumbing Facilities

Code Text: *Where plumbing fixtures are required, separate facilities shall be provided for each sex. See exceptions for 1) dwelling units and sleeping units, 2) structures or tenant spaces with a maximum occupant load of 15, 3) mercantile occupancies with a maximum occupant load of 100 and 4) business occupancies with a maximum occupant load of 25.*

Discussion and Commentary: With some exceptions, separate facilities are required for men and women. The rule does not apply to dwelling and sleeping units, where occupant loads are typically quite small and the occupants are often families. Similarly, for small business occupancies with an occupant load of 25 or fewer, and other buildings or tenant spaces with occupant loads not exceeding 15, a single occupant toilet room is deemed adequate to serve both men and women. For fire and life safety reasons, mercantile occupancies often have greater occupant loads based on capacity of the building than actually occur on a day-to-day basis. For this reason and the fact that customers are typically in a store for a short duration, separate facilities are not required until the occupant load exceeds 100.

Where multiple toilet facilities serve each sex, the required lavatories must be distributed proportionately to the required water closets installed in each location.

Topic: Family or Assisted-Use Facilities
Reference: IPC 403.2.1
Category: Fixtures, Faucets and Fixture Fittings
Subject: Minimum Plumbing Facilities

Code Text: *Where a building or tenant space requires a separate toilet facility for each sex and each toilet facility is required to have only one water closet, two family/assisted-use toilet facilities shall be permitted to serve as the required separate facilities. Family or assisted-use toilet facilities shall not be required to be identified for exclusive use by either sex as required by Section 403.4.*

Discussion and Commentary: Except for spaces with very low occupant loads, the code typically requires separate facilities for men and women, with each facility identified by the applicable sign. As an alternative, if the occupant load is relatively low—for example a business occupancy with an occupant load of 50—and only one water closet is required in each of the two restrooms, the code allows two separate family- or assisted-use facilities to satisfy the separate facilities requirement. In this case, men and women can use either of the restrooms. This improves efficiency in the workplace and increases availability of restroom facilities without the need to provide multi-user toilet facilities. This provision may be particularly useful for some smaller business, storage and factory occupancies where the employees are predominantly one gender. Although gender-specific signs are not required, IPC Section 403.1.2 does require signs for single-user, family and assisted-use toilet rooms to indicate that the facilities may be used by either sex.

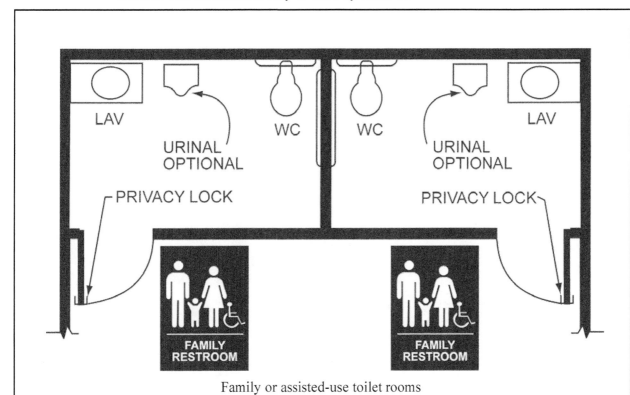

Family or assisted-use toilet rooms

The accessibility provisions of the *International Building Code* limit the fixtures in family or assisted-use facilities to one toilet and one lavatory. A single urinal is optional. In addition, provisions must be available to secure the door from the inside for privacy.

Topic: Employee and Public Toilet Facilities **Category:** Fixtures, Faucets and Fixture Fittings
Reference: IPC 403.3 **Subject:** Minimum Plumbing Facilities

Code Text: *For structures and tenant spaces intended for public utilization, customers, patrons and visitors shall be provided with public toilet facilities. Employees associated with structures and tenant spaces shall be provided with toilet facilities. The number of plumbing fixtures located within the required toilet facilities shall be provided in accordance with Section 403 for all users. Employee toilet facilities shall be either separate or combined employee and public toilet facilities.*

Discussion and Commentary: Restaurants, other assembly occupancies, business and mercantile occupancies, and similar buildings intended for public use must have public toilet facilities that are available to customers, patrons and visitors at all times the building is occupied. Employee toilet facilities are required for all occupancies and may be the same facilities as those used by the public, provided access does not pass through kitchen or storage areas.

An accessible route, a continuous, unobstructed path that complies with Chapter 11 of the *International Building Code* (IBC), is required for access to public toilet facilities.

Topic: Public Toilet Facilities
Reference: IPC 403.3, Exception
Category: Fixtures, Faucets and Fixture Fittings
Subject: Minimum Plumbing Facilities

Code Text: *Public toilet facilities shall not be required in:*

1. *Parking garages operated without parking attendants.*
2. *Structures and tenant spaces intended for quick transactions, including takeout, pickup and dropoff, having a public access area less than or equal to 300 square feet (28 m²).*

Discussion and Commentary: The code provides two exceptions to the requirement for public restrooms. Both are contingent on the limited time the public spends in certain spaces and the limited number of people in the spaces at any given time. Most parking garages meet those criteria and generally serve nearby occupancies that have public facilities. Likewise, limited-size quick-service businesses and tenant spaces are not required to provide public toilet facilities for customers. Examples include shoe repair shops, dry cleaners and take-out food locations, but many other quick-transaction businesses would qualify.

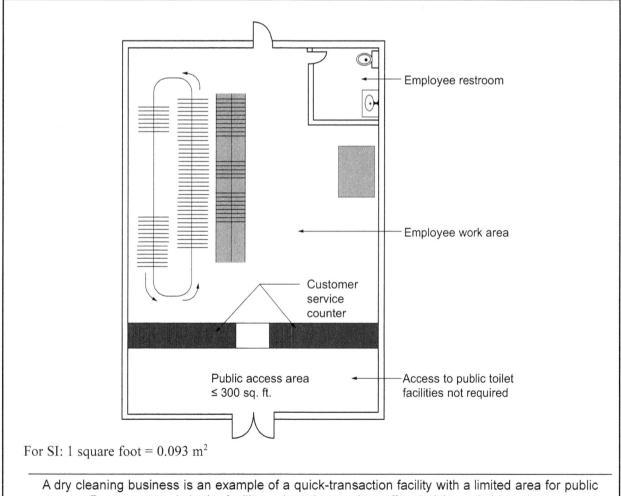

For SI: 1 square foot = 0.093 m²

A dry cleaning business is an example of a quick-transaction facility with a limited area for public access. Patrons are only in the facility a short time to drop off and pick up clothing, the occupant load in the public area is very low, and the code does not anticipate a need for access to public restroom facilities.

Topic: Location of Toilet Facilities
Reference: IPC 403.3.3

Category: Fixtures, Faucets and Fixture Fittings
Subject: Minimum Plumbing Facilities

Code Text: *In occupancies other than covered and open mall buildings, the required public and employee toilet facilities shall be located not more than one story above or below the space required to be provided with toilet facilities, and the path of travel to such facilities shall not exceed a distance of 500 feet (152 m).* See exception for factory and industrial occupancies.

Discussion and Commentary: For all building occupants in other than covered and open malls, including employees, customers, patrons and visitors, the code clearly provides two conditions that must be met: The required toilet facilities must be located within a travel distance of 500 feet, and the occupant must not be required to travel beyond the next adjacent story above or below the space being considered.

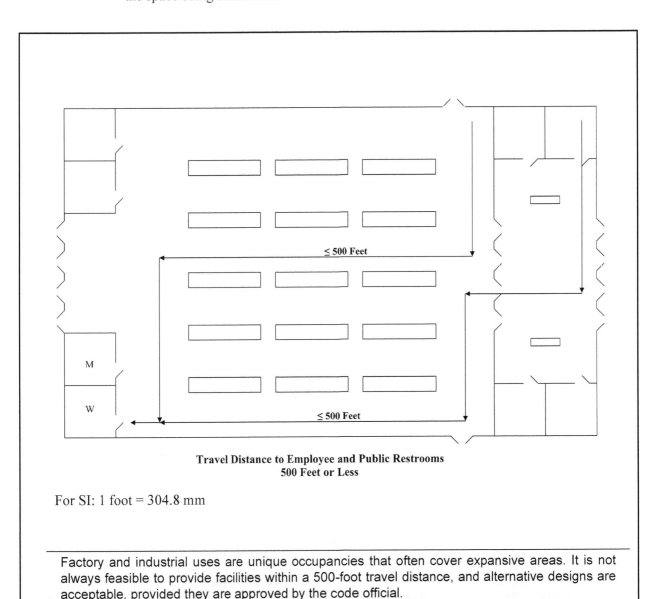

**Travel Distance to Employee and Public Restrooms
500 Feet or Less**

For SI: 1 foot = 304.8 mm

Factory and industrial uses are unique occupancies that often cover expansive areas. It is not always feasible to provide facilities within a 500-foot travel distance, and alternative designs are acceptable, provided they are approved by the code official.

Topic: Location of Toilet Facilities
Reference: IPC 403.3.4

Category: Fixtures, Faucets and Fixture Fittings
Subject: Minimum Plumbing Facilities

Code Text: *In covered and open mall buildings, the required public and employee toilet facilities shall be located not more than one story above or below the space required to be provided with toilet facilities, and the path of travel to such facilities shall not exceed a distance of 300 feet (91 m). In mall buildings, the required facilities shall be based on total square footage within a covered mall building or within the perimeter line of an open mall building, and facilities shall be installed in each individual store or in a central toilet area located in accordance with this section. The maximum distance of travel to central toilet facilities in mall buildings shall be measured from the main entrance of any store or tenant space. In mall buildings, where employees' toilet facilities are not provided in the individual store, the maximum distance of travel shall be measured from the employees' work area of the store or tenant space.*

Discussion and Commentary: In malls, the path of travel to required toilet facilities must not exceed a distance of 300 feet and is measured from the main entrance of any store or tenant space. However, if the tenant space does not have employee facilities, the distance is measured from the employee work area. When compared to buildings other than malls, the shorter travel distance addresses the fact that covered malls are frequently very congested, and occupants are unfamiliar with their surroundings. The minimum number of required plumbing facilities is based on total square footage of the mall, including tenant spaces, and must be installed in each individual store or in a central toilet area.

Covered and open mall buildings are defined in the *International Building Code* (IBC). Anchor buildings are not considered part of a covered or open mall.

Study Session 4

Topic: Drinking Fountain Location
Reference: IPC 403.5
Category: Fixtures, Faucets and Fixture Fittings
Subject: Minimum Plumbing Facilities

Code Text: *Drinking fountains shall not be required to be located in individual tenant spaces provided that public drinking fountains are located within a distance of travel of 500 feet (152 m) of the most remote location in the tenant space and not more than one story above or below the tenant space. Where the tenant space is in a covered or open mall, such distance shall not exceed 300 feet (91 m). Drinking fountains shall be located on an accessible route.*

Discussion and Commentary: The maximum travel distance to required drinking fountains matches the travel distance provisions for toilet facilities: 500 feet for buildings other than malls and 300 feet for covered or open mall buildings.

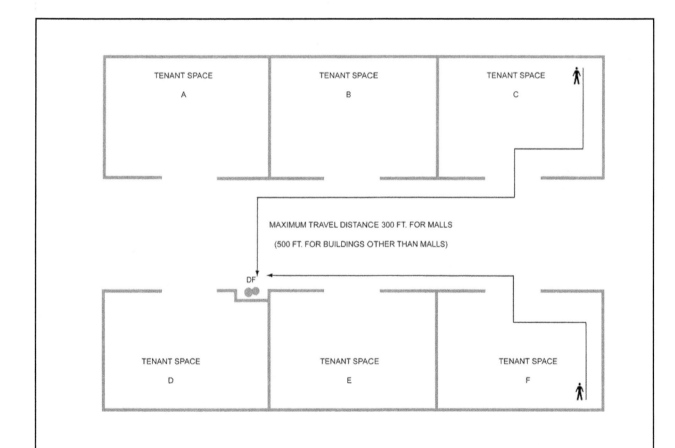

The *International Building Code* (IBC) requires that all drinking fountains that are provided, including those that are not required, must meet the provisions for accessibility for persons with physical disabilities. When drinking fountains are provided, an equal number must be designed for wheel chair users and standing persons. For required drinking fountains, the IPC reprints the applicable IBC provisions in Section 410.

Topic: Water Supply Protection
Reference: IPC 405.1
Category: Fixtures, and Faucets and Fixture Fittings
Subject: Installation of Fixtures

Code Text: *The supply lines and fittings for every plumbing fixture shall be installed so as to prevent backflow.*

Discussion and Commentary: This section identifies minimal installation requirements for water supply protection. Backflow prevention is perhaps the most important aspect of a plumbing system. All plumbing fixtures, plumbing appliances and water distribution system openings, outlets and connections are potentially capable of contaminating the potable water supply. Backflow can occur as a result of backpressure or backsiphonage, both of which are defined terms in the IPC.

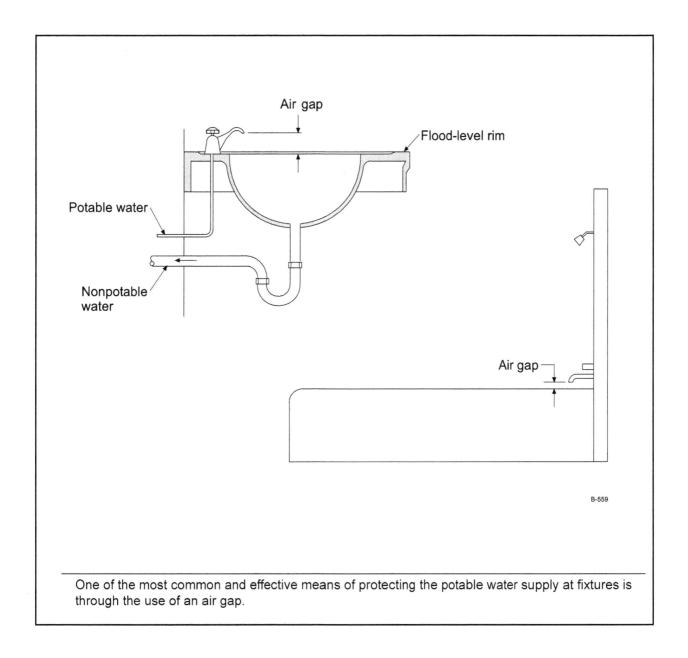

One of the most common and effective means of protecting the potable water supply at fixtures is through the use of an air gap.

Study Session 4

Topic: Fixture Clearances
Reference: IPC 405.3.1
Category: Fixtures, Faucets and Fixture Fittings
Subject: Installation of Fixtures

Code Text: *A water closet, urinal, lavatory or bidet shall not be set closer than 15 inches (381 mm) from its center to any side wall, partition, vanity or other obstruction. Where partitions or other obstructions do not separate adjacent fixtures, fixtures shall not be set closer than 30 inches (762 mm) center to center between adjacent fixtures. There shall be not less than a 21-inch (533 mm) clearance in front of a water closet, urinal, lavatory or bidet to any wall, fixture or door. Water closet compartments shall be not less than 30 inches (762 mm) in width and not less than 60 inches (1524 mm) in depth for floor-mounted water closets and not less than 30 inches (762 mm) in width and 56 inches (1422 mm) in depth for wall-hung water closets.* See the exception for accessible children's water closets.

Discussion and Commentary: This section establishes minimum clearances for mounting of plumbing fixtures. Adequate clearances are critical for proper and comfortable usability and cleaning.

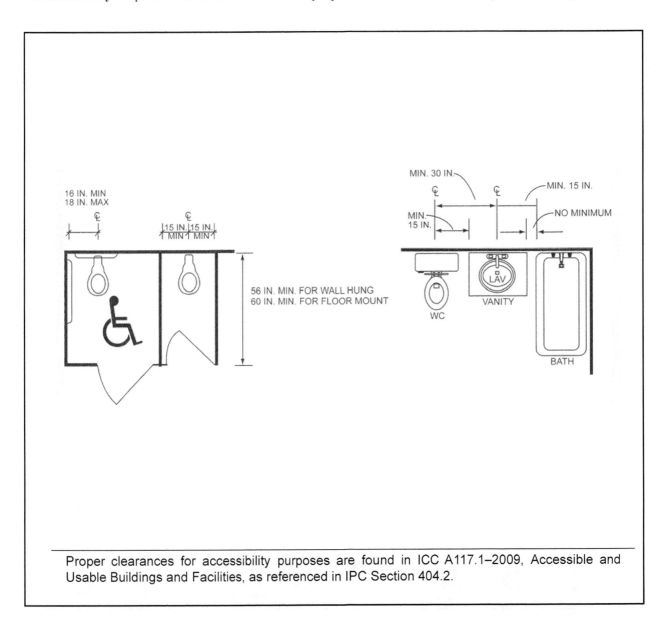

Proper clearances for accessibility purposes are found in ICC A117.1–2009, Accessible and Usable Buildings and Facilities, as referenced in IPC Section 404.2.

Topic: Location of Fixtures and Piping
Reference: IPC 405.3.3

Category: Fixtures, Faucets and Fixture Fittings
Subject: Installation of Fixtures

Code Text: *Piping, fixtures or equipment shall not be located in such a manner as to interfere with the normal operation of windows, doors or other means of egress openings.*

Discussion and Commentary: The code prohibits fixtures and piping located in washrooms or toilet rooms to interfere with the operation of building components such as windows and doors or to adversely affect means of egress openings. Obstructions to the required means of egress system could result in serious injury to the occupants by restricting egress in an emergency condition.

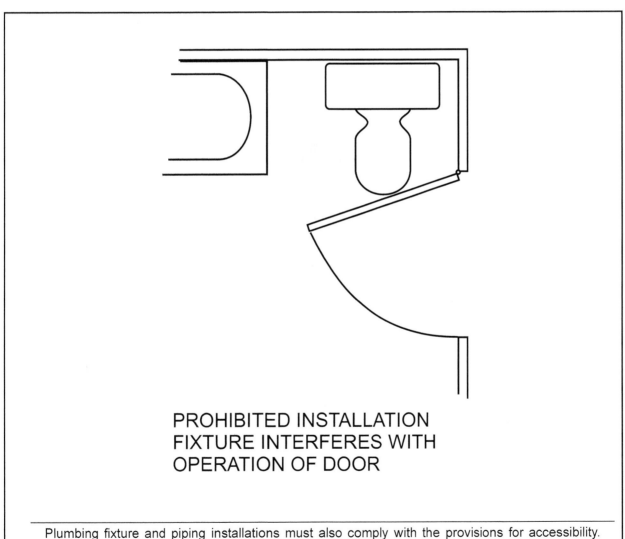

PROHIBITED INSTALLATION
FIXTURE INTERFERES WITH
OPERATION OF DOOR

Plumbing fixture and piping installations must also comply with the provisions for accessibility. The scoping provisions for accessibility are typically found in the IBC, and the technical provisions are located in ICC A117.1 - 2009 as referenced in IPC Section 404.2.

Topic: Water Closet Compartment
Reference: IPC 405.3.4
Category: Fixtures, Faucets and Fixture Fittings
Subject: Installation of Fixtures

Code Text: *Each water closet utilized by the public or employees shall occupy a separate compartment with walls or partitions and a door enclosing the fixtures to ensure privacy.* See the exceptions for 1) single occupant toilet room with lockable door, 2) one water closet in day care facilities, and 3) Group I-3 housing areas.

Discussion and Commentary: Partitioned compartments provide necessary privacy for individuals using bathroom facilities. Also, a single-occupant toilet room with a lockable door is deemed to provide the required privacy as stated in the first exception. The second exception, allowing an unenclosed water closet in a child-care facility, recognizes the need for people to be able to assist children

All areas of a toilet room, including toilet partitions, must be designed such that the toilet room complies with the accessibility requirements.

Topic: Urinal Partitions
Reference: IPC 403.3.5
Category: Fixtures, Faucets and Fixture Fittings
Subject: Installation of Fixtures

Code Text: *Each urinal utilized by the public or employees shall occupy a separate area with walls or partitions to provide privacy. The horizontal dimension between walls or partitions at each urinal shall be not less than 30 inches (762 mm). The walls or partitions shall begin at a height not greater than 12 inches (305 mm) from and extend not less than 60 inches (1524 mm) above the finished floor surface. The walls or partitions shall extend from the wall surface at each side of the urinal not less than 18 inches (457 mm) or to a point not less than 6 inches (152 mm) beyond the outermost front lip of the urinal measured from the finished back wall surface, whichever is greater.* See the exceptions for single occupant toilet room with lockable door and one urinal in day care facilities.

Discussion and Commentary: Privacy concerns for toilet facilities are not limited to water closets. Urinals need to have privacy partitions installed as well.

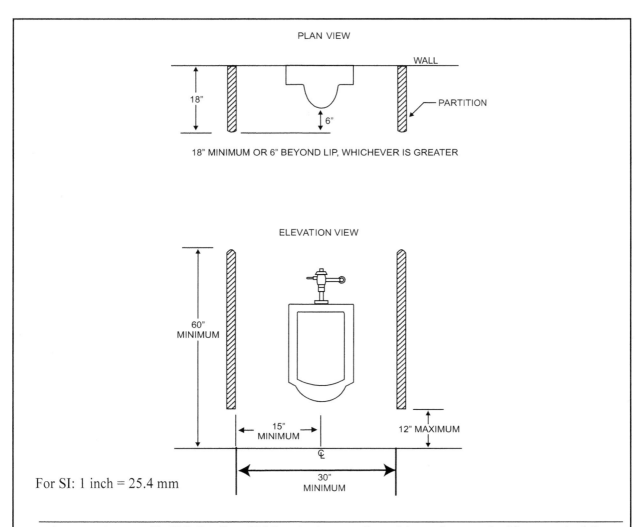

In accordance with IPC Section 424.2, urinals are allowed to replace up to 50 percent of the required number of water closets in all occupancies except in assembly and educational occupancies, where they can replace up to 67 percent of the required number of water closets.

Topic: Floor and Wall Drainage Connections **Category:** Fixtures, Faucets and Fixture Fittings
Reference: IPC 405.4 **Subject:** Installation of Fixtures

Code Text: *Connections between the drain and floor outlet plumbing fixtures shall be made with a floor flange or a waste connector and sealing gasket. The waste connector and sealing gasket joint shall comply with the joint tightness test of ASME A112.4.3 and shall be installed in accordance with the manufacturer's instructions. The flange shall be attached to the drain and anchored to the structure. Connections between the drain and wall-hung water closets shall be made with an approved extension nipple or horn adaptor. The water closet shall be bolted to the hanger with corrosion-resistant bolts or screws. Joints shall be sealed with an approved elastomeric gasket, flange-to-fixture connection complying with ASME A112.4.3 or an approved setting compound.*

Discussion and Commentary: The code permits two connection methods for the installation of floor-mounted water closets—a flanged outlet connection, or a waste connector and sealing gasket. Traditionally, water closets designed for the North American market required a floor flange. A waste connector and sealing gasket design is used almost exclusively in Europe and other locations worldwide. This alternative connection consists of a waste tube connector on the water closet that is inserted into an elastomeric gasket. The waste tube and gasket are then inserted into the drain pipe opening at the floor line, and the gasket provides the seal between the water closet's waste tube and the drain pipe. The water closet fixture is then anchored directly to the floor using mounting brackets or fasteners.

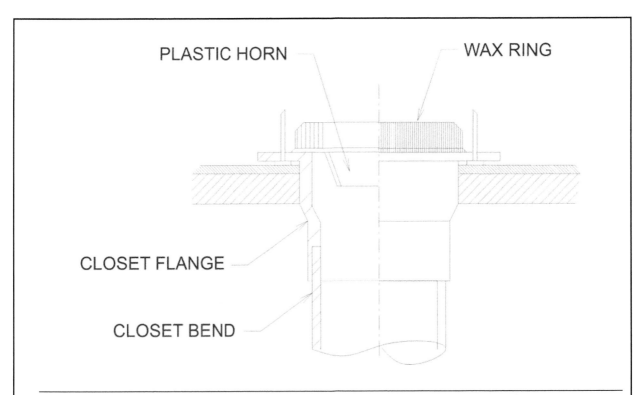

Flanges must be secured to the floor with corrosion-resistant screws or bolts. Brass screws or bolts are required for securing the water closet to the flange.

Topic: Water-Tight Joints	Category: Fixtures, Faucets and Fixture Fittings
Reference: IPC 405.6	Subject: Installation of Fixtures

Code Text: *Joints formed where fixtures come in contact with walls or floors shall be sealed.*

Discussion and Commentary: This section addresses the surface connection of the fixture to the floor or wall. The point of contact does not form a joint with any piping material; however, it is still an important area to seal so as to prevent a concealed fouling surface. The contact joint typically is sealed with a flexible material such as silicon caulking. The exact material selected to seal the joint should be capable of withstanding any anticipated movement of the fixture during its normal use.

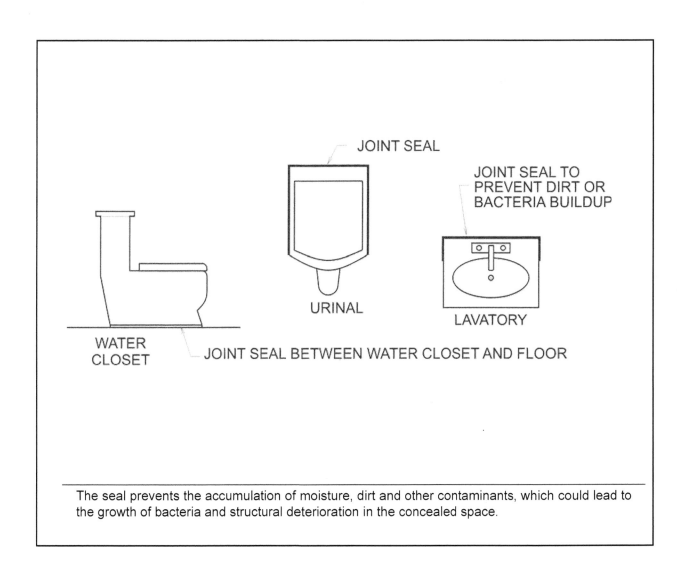

The seal prevents the accumulation of moisture, dirt and other contaminants, which could lead to the growth of bacteria and structural deterioration in the concealed space.

Topic: Waste Connection
Reference: IPC 406.2
Category: Fixtures, Faucets and Fixture Fittings
Subject: Automatic Clothes Washers

Code Text: *The waste from an automatic clothes washer shall discharge through an air break into a standpipe in accordance with Section 802.3.2 or into a laundry sink. The trap and fixture drain for an automatic clothes washer standpipe shall be not less than 2 inches (51 mm) in diameter. The fixture drain for the standpipe serving an automatic clothes washer shall connect to a 3-inch (76 mm) or larger diameter fixture branch or stack. Automatic clothes washers that discharge by gravity shall be permitted to drain to a waste receptor or an approved trench drain.*

Discussion and Commentary: A clothes washer must discharge to the drainage system through an air break. A direct connection could allow waste to back up into the appliance in the event of a blockage in the drain pipe. A clothes washer is usually discharged to an individually trapped standpipe. It is not uncommon, however, to find clothes washer installations where the appliance discharges to a laundry sink or by gravity to a floor drain or trench drain. The actual connection of the discharge pipe needs to be reviewed to verify that the required air break has been maintained.

The discharge tube from the clothes washer is inserted into the top of the standpipe, which satisfies the air break criteria because the discharge is below the flood level rim of the receptor (standpipe) and above the trap seal. Unlike an air gap, an air break does not require clearance above the flood rim of the receptor.

Topic: Bathtub Waste Outlets
Reference: IPC 407.2
Category: Fixtures, Faucets and Fixture Fittings
Subject: Bathtubs

Code Text: *Bathtubs shall be equipped with a waste outlet and an overflow outlet. The outlets shall be connected to waste tubing or piping not less than $1^1/_2$ inches (38 mm) in diameter. The waste outlet shall be equipped with a water-tight stopper.*

Discussion and Commentary: A bathtub is required to have an overflow waste outlet to protect against accidental flooding of the bathroom by an unattended filling operation or to remove displaced water when a bather enters a full tub.

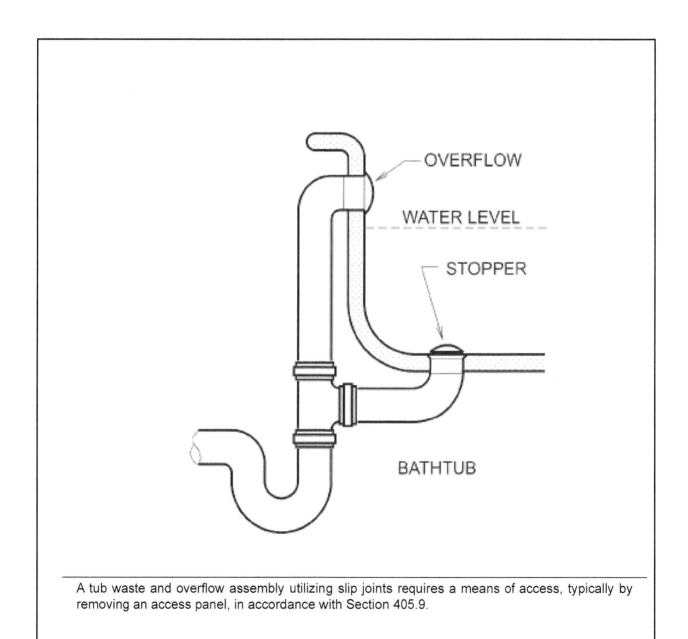

A tub waste and overflow assembly utilizing slip joints requires a means of access, typically by removing an access panel, in accordance with Section 405.9.

Study Session 4

Topic: Bidet Water Temperature
Reference: IPC 408.3

Category: Fixtures, Faucets and Fixture Fittings
Subject: Bidets

Code Text: *The discharge water temperature from a bidet fitting shall be limited to a maximum temperature of 110°F (43°C) by a water temperature limiting device conforming to ASSE 1070/ASME A112.1070/CSA B125.70 or CSA B125.3.*

Discussion and Commentary: ASSE 1070/ASME A112.1070/CSA B125.70, Performance Requirements for Water-temperature Limiting Devices, regulates devices intended for this type of application. The device is a thermostatic mixing valve with a maximum temperature limit adjustment. CSA B125.3, Plumbing Fittings, is another approved standard that covers water-temperature limiting devices in addition to certain other fittings including valves, stops and connectors.

BIDET PLUMBING FIXTURE

TEMPERATURE — LIMITED TO A MAXIMUM OF 110°F

CONTROLLED BY — ASSE 1070-04, PERFORMANCE REQUIREMENTS FOR WATER-TEMPERATURE LIMITING DEVICES

BIDET WATER TEMPERATURE

An air gap or backflow preventer is required for protection of the water supply connected to a bidet.

Topic: Residential Dishwasher Waste
Reference: IPC 409.4

Category: Fixtures, Faucets and Fixture Fittings
Subject: Dishwashing Machines

Code Text: *The waste connection of a residential dishwasher shall connect directly to a wye branch fitting on the tailpiece of the kitchen sink, directly to the dishwasher connection of a food waste disposer, or through an air break to a standpipe. The waste line of a residential dishwasher shall rise and be securely fastened to the underside of the sink rim or counter top.*

Discussion and Commentary: The code gives several options for the discharge of residential dishwashing machines to the building drainage system, all of which provide protection against contamination of the contents and surfaces inside the dishwasher. To satisfy the requirements, dishwashing machines may discharge indirectly through an air break to a standpipe waste receptor. The more common option in residential applications is to connect the discharge line directly to the tailpiece or food waste disposer, with protection provided by the loop in the waste line.

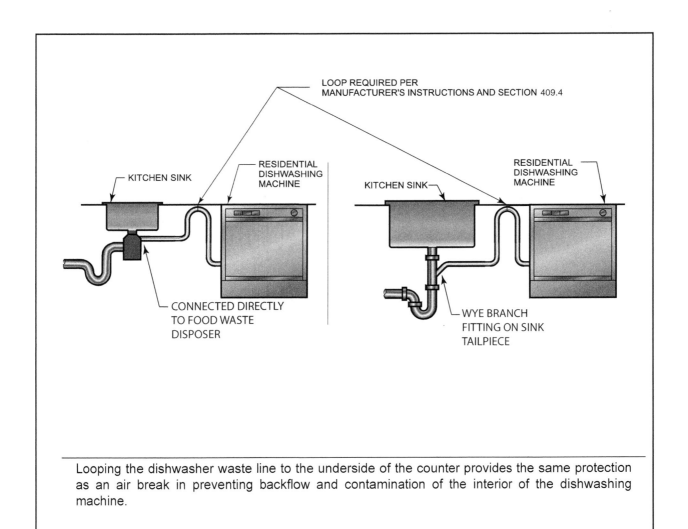

Looping the dishwasher waste line to the underside of the counter provides the same protection as an air break in preventing backflow and contamination of the interior of the dishwashing machine.

Study Session 4

Topic: High and Low Drinking Fountains
Reference: IPC 410.3
Category: Fixtures, Faucets and Fixture Fittings
Subject: Drinking Fountains

Code Text: *Where drinking fountains are required, not fewer than two drinking fountains shall be provided. One drinking fountain shall comply with the requirements for people who use a wheelchair and one drinking fountain shall comply with the requirements for standing persons.* See the exception for a single drinking fountain with two separate spouts that complies with the design criteria both for persons in wheelchairs and standing persons.

Discussion and Commentary: For most occupancies, drinking fountains must be provided for building occupants and others visiting the building. When drinking fountains are required, Section 410.3, which is extracted from the *International Building Code* (IBC), prescribes a minimum of two drinking fountains—one accessible to standing persons and one accessible to wheelchair users. This requirement overrides IPC Table 403.1, which may require only one drinking fountain but does not satisfy these accessibility requirements. Additional provisions in the IBC require any drinking fountains that are provided, whether or not they are required, to be accessible and to be evenly divided for wheelchair users and standing persons. Water fountains are not required in restaurants if water is served free of charge and are not required in occupancies with an occupant load that does not exceed 15.

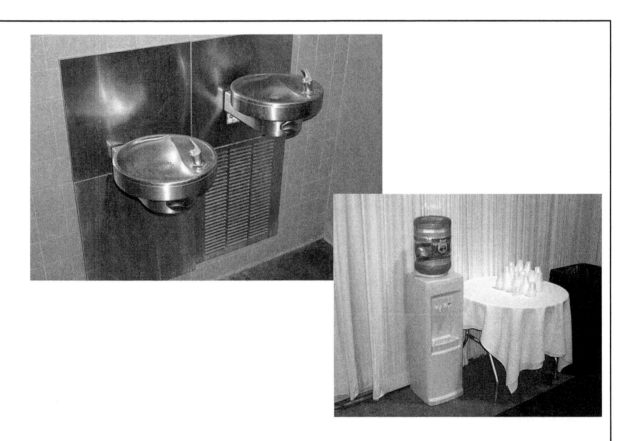

Water dispensers can be considered part of the required number of drinking fountains but cannot account for more than 50 percent of the total number of required fixtures. To prevent contamination of drinking water, drinking fountains, water coolers and water dispensers cannot be located in public restrooms.

Topic: Approval	Category: Fixtures, Faucets and Fixture Fittings
Reference: IPC 411.1	Subject: Emergency Showers and Eyewash Stations

Code Text: *Emergency showers and eyewash stations shall conform to ISEA Z358.1.*

Discussion and Commentary: Emergency showers and eyewash stations are provided in areas where an individual may come in contact with substances that are immediately harmful to the body. These emergency devices provide an instantaneous deluge of water to help neutralize any adverse reactions. Emergency showers and eyewash stations are located where people are exposed to chemicals, acids, nuclear products and fire. The water supply requirements for an emergency eyewash station are dependent on the manufacturer's requirements for the specific equipment installed. Waste connections are not required.

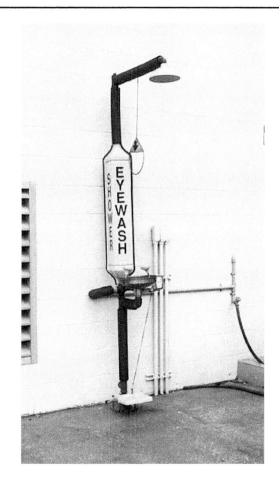

The code does not require the installation of emergency eyewash stations and showers. This section has been provided to address them if installed. Usually, governmental agencies regulating worker and building occupant safety establish where and when these fixtures are required to be installed.

Study Session 4
IPC Sections 401 through 411

1. A business occupancy is permitted to have a maximum occupant load of _____ without requiring installation of a drinking fountain.

    a. 10
    b. 15
    c. 25
    d. 99

    Reference _____

2. A building classified as a business occupancy, with a total occupant load of 320, is required to have a minimum of _____ lavatories in the women's restroom.

    a. 2
    b. 3
    c. 4
    d. 5

    Reference _____

3. An indoor sports arena with a total occupant load of 5,440 requires at least _____ water closets in the women's restrooms.

    a. 103
    b. 68
    c. 58
    d. 46

    Reference _____

4. The same indoor sports arena with an occupant load of 5,440 requires at least _____ lavatories in the women's restrooms.

    a. 14
    b. 27
    c. 19
    d. 37

    Reference _____

5. For an employee toilet room, the required lavatory shall be _____ the required water closet.

   a. not more than 30 inches from

   b. separated by a partition from

   c. not less than 60 inches away from

   d. in the same room as

   Reference _____

6. The fixture drain of an automatic clothes washer shall connect to a minimum _____ -inch branch drain.

   a. 1 1/2   b. 2

   c. 2 1/2   d. 3

   Reference _____

7. The waste line of an automatic clothes washer shall discharge through a(n) _____.

   a. backflow preventer   b. vacuum breaker

   c. air gap   d. air break

   Reference _____

8. Concealed slip joint connections require an access panel not less than _____ inches in the smallest dimension.

   a. 20   b. 18

   c. 12   d. 10

   Reference _____

9. A water closet must be set no closer than _____ inches to a lavatory when measured center to center of the fixtures.

   a. 30   b. 15

   c. 21   d. 28

   Reference _____

Study Session 4

10. An automatic clothes washer requires a minimum _____ -inch fixture drain.

    a. 1½   b. 2
    c. 2½   d. 3

    Reference _____

11. A residential care facility with an occupant load of 300 is required to have at least three drinking fountains. Bottled water dispensers can be substituted for _____ of the required drinking fountains.

    a. none   b. one
    c. two   d. three

    Reference _____

12. A required urinal partition shall extend not less than _____ inches from the wall surface.

    a. 22   b. 12
    c. 16   d. 18

    Reference _____

13. A bottled water dispenser is prohibited from being located in a _____.

    a. kitchen   b. restaurant
    c. public restroom   d. storage area

    Reference _____

14. Privacy partitions for urinals are not required in a(n) _____ toilet room.

    a. employee   b. Group I-3
    c. family/assisted use   d. mercantile

    Reference _____

15. A _____ shall be used to support a wall-mounted water closet.

    a. concealed metal carrier
    b. flush mount hanger
    c. wall flange
    d. horn adaptor

    Reference _____

16. The waste tube of the drain outlet for a bathtub shall be not less than _____ inches in diameter.

    a. 1¼
    b. 1½
    c. 2
    d. 2½

    Reference _____

17. For installation in an employee restroom, a urinal requires not less than a _____ -inch clearance from the centerline of the fixture to a wall or partition.

    a. 30
    b. 21
    c. 15
    d. 12

    Reference _____

18. If approved, the travel distance to an employee toilet room may exceed 500 feet in a _____.

    a. stadium
    b. covered mall
    c. warehouse
    d. factory

    Reference _____

19. Water supply lines and fittings for every plumbing fixture shall be installed so as to prevent _____.

    a. condensation
    b. backflow
    c. vibration
    d. expansion

    Reference _____

20. Separate toilet facilities for each sex shall not be required in mercantile occupancies with a maximum occupant load of _____ or fewer.

    a. 100
    b. 60
    c. 40
    d. 80

    Reference _____

21. The path of travel to required toilet facilities for an employee in a warehouse shall not exceed _____ feet.

    a. 200
    b. 250
    c. 300
    d. 500

    Reference _____

22. The path of travel to required toilet facilities for an employee in a covered mall shall not exceed _____ feet.

    a. 200
    b. 250
    c. 300
    d. 500

    Reference _____

23. There shall be at least _____ inches of clearance in front of the water closet to any wall, fixture or door.

    a. 12
    b. 18
    c. 21
    d. 24

    Reference _____

24. Bidets shall be equipped with a device conforming to ASSE 1070 or CSA B125.3 to limit the discharge water from fittings to a maximum temperature of _____ degrees Fahrenheit.

    a. 105
    b. 110
    c. 120
    d. 130

    Reference _____

25. Waste connections are not required for _____.

    a. laundry trays
    b. emergency eyewash station
    c. automatic clothes washers
    d. floor drains

    Reference _____

2018 IPC Sections 412 through 426
Fixtures, Faucets and Fixture Fittings II

OBJECTIVE: To develop an understanding of requirements for dimensions, access and other provisions related to floor drains, food waste disposers, lavatories, showers, urinals and water closets.

REFERENCE: Sections 412 through 426, 2018 *International Plumbing Code*

KEY POINTS:
- Where are floor drains required? What is the minimum size?
- What requirements apply to domestic and commercial food waste disposers?
- What is required to prevent the discharge of large particles from a food waste disposer into the drainage system?
- What requirements apply to lavatories?
- What are the water supply requirements for public hand-washing facilities?
- What requirements apply to water supply risers serving showers? Waste outlets?
- What is the minimum size of a shower compartment? Access size?
- What requirements apply to shower floors? Shower walls?
- What types of shower liners are approved? What are the installation requirements?
- What types of water closets and seats are required for public and employee use?
- What are the acceptable fittings for water closet connections?
- What are the access requirements for the pump of whirlpool bathtubs?
- What requirements apply to footbaths, pedicure baths and head shampoo sinks?
- What are the valve and water temperature criteria for showers? Bathtubs? Personal hygiene devices?
- What requirements apply to flushing devices for water closets and urinals?

Topic: Hand Showers	**Category:** Fixtures, Faucets and Fixture Fittings
Reference: IPC 412.2	**Subject:** Faucets and Fixture Fittings

Code Text: *Hand-held showers shall conform to ASME A112.18.1/CSA B125.1. Hand-held showers shall provide backflow protection in accordance with ASME A112.18.1/CSA B125.1 or shall be protected against backflow by a device complying with ASME A112.18.3.*

Discussion and Commentary: Similar to a hose and spray assembly, it is possible for a handheld shower to be submerged in the bathtub or shower compartment base, constituting a cross connection. The handheld shower, which is illustrated below, must have adequate protection against backflow. These types of showers are commonly installed in accessible shower enclosures. Their use, however, has increased in popularity within dwelling unit showers. The referenced standards specify the requirements for backflow protection of the handheld shower.

A combination tub filler with a handheld shower creates a potential scalding hazard if the handheld unit can be wall mounted and used as a conventional shower. The requirements of Section 412.3 for individual combination valves to limit the water temperature would apply in such cases.

Topic: Individual Shower Valves
Reference: IPC 412.3

Category: Fixtures, Faucets and Fixture Fittings
Subject: Faucets and Fixture Fittings

Code Text: *Individual shower and tub-shower combination valves shall be balanced pressure, thermostatic or combination balanced-pressure/thermostatic valves that conform to the requirements of ASSE 1016/ASME A112.1016/CSA B125.16 or ASME A112.18.1/CSA B125.1 and shall be installed at the point of use. Shower and tub-shower combination valves required by this section shall be equipped with a means to limit the maximum setting of the valve to 120°F (49°C), which shall be field adjusted in accordance with the manufacturer's instructions. In-line thermostatic valves shall not be utilized for compliance with this section.*

Discussion and Commentary: Every shower must have a control valve that is capable of protecting an individual from being scalded. These devices are also required to protect against thermal shock. Thermal shock is a change in discharge temperature great enough to produce a potentially hazardous reaction. ASSE 1016 requires control valves to protect against rapid temperature fluctuations by automatically maintaining the discharge temperature. The three types of valves available are a balanced pressure-mixing shower valve, a thermostatic-mixing shower valve and a combination mixing valve.

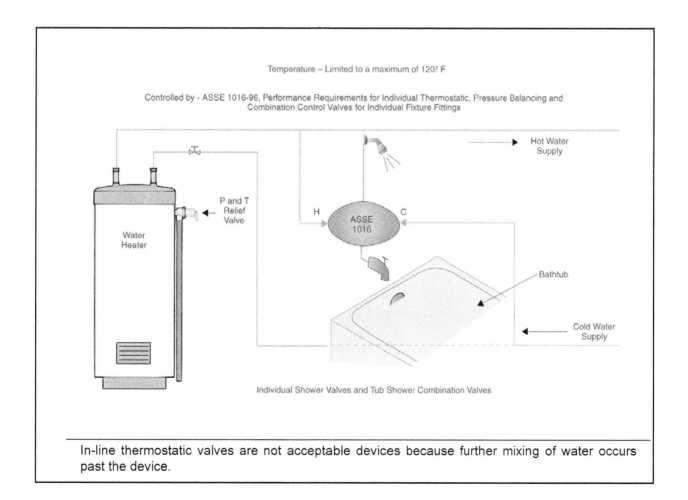

Individual Shower Valves and Tub Shower Combination Valves

In-line thermostatic valves are not acceptable devices because further mixing of water occurs past the device.

Study Session 5

Topic: Multiple (Gang) Showers
Reference: IPC 412.4

Category: Fixtures, Faucets and Fixture Fittings
Subject: Faucets and Fixture Fittings

Code Text: *Multiple (gang) showers supplied with a single-tempered water supply pipe shall have the water supply for such showers controlled by an approved automatic temperature control mixing valve that conforms to ASSE 1069 or CSA B125.3, or each shower head shall be individually controlled by a balanced-pressure, thermostatic or combination balanced-pressure/thermostatic valve that conforms to ASSE 1016/ASME A112.1016/CSA B125.16 or ASME A112.18.1/CSA B125.1 and is installed at the point of use. Such valves shall be equipped with a means to limit the maximum setting of the valve to 120°F (49°C), which shall be field adjusted in accordance with the manufacturers' instructions.*

Discussion and Commentary: The referenced standards address automatic temperature control mixing valves for gang showers.

Many Canadian Standards Association (CSA) standards are referenced in the IPC as acceptable standards in lieu of ASSE or other standards.

Topic: Bathtub and Whirlpool Valves
Reference: IPC 412.5
Category: Fixtures, Faucets and Fixture Fittings
Subject: Faucets and Fixture Fittings

Code Text: *The hot water supplied to bathtubs and whirlpool bathtubs shall be limited to a maximum temperature of 120°F (49°C) by a water temperature limiting device that conforms to ASSE 1070 or CSA B125.3, except where such protection is otherwise provided by a combination tub/shower valve in accordance with Section 412.3.*

Discussion and Commentary: The ASSE 1070 standard is for a water temperature limiting device that is intended for this type of application. The device is a thermostatic mixing valve with a maximum temperature limit adjustment.

The ASSE 1070 standard provides for devices to be installed with the fixture fitting, or they can be integral to the plumbing fixture fitting supplying the water.

Topic: Floor Drains
Reference: IPC 413.2
Category: Fixtures, Faucets and Fixture Fittings
Subject: Floor and Trench Drains

Code Text: *Floor drains shall have removable strainers. The floor drain shall be constructed so that the drain is capable of being cleaned. Access shall be provided to the drain inlet. Ready access shall be provided to floor drains.* See the exception for access to floor drains serving refrigerated display cases.

Discussion and Commentary: The actual floor drain body may or may not have an integral trap. All floor drain installations are required to be trapped. The strainer may be flush with the floor surface or may have a dome grate. The free area of the strainer or grate must not be less than the transverse area of connecting pipe. Most manufacturers provide this information in the product literature. All floor drains must be installed or constructed such that they can be properly cleaned, ensuring that the drain will continue to function properly

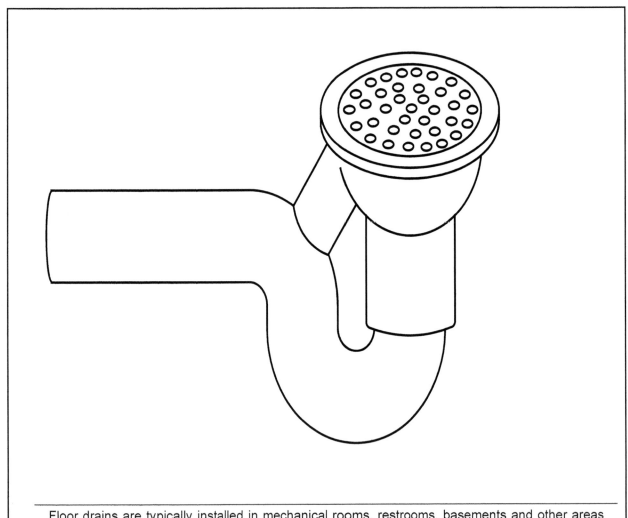

Floor drains are typically installed in mechanical rooms, restrooms, basements and other areas for cleaning or to receive condensate or overflow. However, the IPC only requires floor drains in public laundries and central washing facilities of multi-family dwellings.

Topic: Size of Floor Drains
Reference: IPC 413.3
Category: Fixtures, Faucets and Fixture Fittings
Subject: Floor and Trench Drains

Code Text: *Floor drains shall have a drain outlet not less than 2 inches (51 mm) in diameter.*

Discussion and Commentary: This section emphasizes the requirements of Table 709.1, which provides the minimum size of the drain outlet for the particular dfu value of the floor drain fixture. Section 413.4 requires a minimum floor drain size of 3 inches (76 mm) in public coin-operated laundries and in central washing facilities of multiple-family dwellings.

Floor drains are often used as a receptor for condensate discharge from HVAC equipment.

Study Session 5

Topic: Public Laundries and Washing Facilities **Category:** Fixtures, Faucets and Fixture Fittings
Reference: IPC 413.4 **Subject:** Floor and Trench Drains

Code Text: *In public coin-operated laundries and in the central washing facilities of multiple-family dwellings, the rooms containing automatic clothes washers shall be provided with floor drains located to readily drain the entire floor area. Such drains shall have a minimum outlet of not less than 3 inches (76 mm) in diameter.*

Discussion and Commentary: Floor drains are required in public coin-operated laundries and in central washing facilities of multiple-family dwellings that contain laundry machines. They protect against damage from accidental spills, fixture overflows and leakage. This plumbing fixture is considered an emergency floor drain, which has a drainage fixture unit value of zero. Such fixtures do not add to the load used to compute drainage pipe sizing because their sole purpose is to serve only in the event of an emergency.

Under normal circumstances, an emergency floor drain does not receive any waste and, therefore, is required to be provided with a means to protect the trap seal from loss by evaporation.

Topic: Flushometer Valves and Tanks **Category:** Fixtures, Faucets and Fixture Fittings
Reference: IPC 415.2 **Subject:** Flushing Devices

Code Text: *Flushometer valves and tanks shall comply with ASSE 1037/ASME A112.1037/CSA B125.37 or CSA B125.3. Vacuum breakers on flushometer valves shall conform to the performance requirements of ASSE 1001 or CSA B64.1.1. Access shall be provided to vacuum breakers. Flushometer valves shall be of the water-conservation type and shall not be utilized where the water pressure is lower than the minimum required for normal operation. When operated, the valve shall automatically complete the cycle of operation, opening fully and closing positively under the water supply pressure. Each flushometer valve shall be provided with a means for regulating the flow through the valve. The trap seal to the fixture shall be automatically refilled after each valve flushing cycle.*

Discussion and Commentary: There are a variety of styles of flushometer valves and tanks, all of which must be equipped with a vacuum breaker to prevent backflow. The flushometer valve operation is either a diaphragm type or a piston type. The majority of flushometer valves are diaphragm type, on account of its reliability. The working components of a flushometer valve are either exposed or concealed. When concealed, the valve must be accessible through an access opening, cover or plate.

Flushometers are either manually or automatically operated. Common manual valves are activated by a hand lever, push button or foot valve. Automatic valves are activated electrically by infrared sensors or other devices that sense the presence of an individual using the fixture

Topic: Water Supply Required
Reference: IPC 416.4
Category: Fixtures, Faucets and Fixture Fittings
Subject: Flood Waste Disposer Units

Code Text: *Food waste disposers shall be provided with a supply of cold water. The water supply shall be protected against backflow by an air gap or backflow preventer in accordance with Section 608.*

Discussion and Commentary: A supply of cold water is necessary to act as the transport vehicle during the disposer operation. The water flushes the grinding chamber and carries the waste into the drain. If a waste disposer is used without running water, a drain blockage will result. Note that the water supply serving all waste disposers must be protected from backflow by an air gap or backflow preventer in accordance with Section 608.

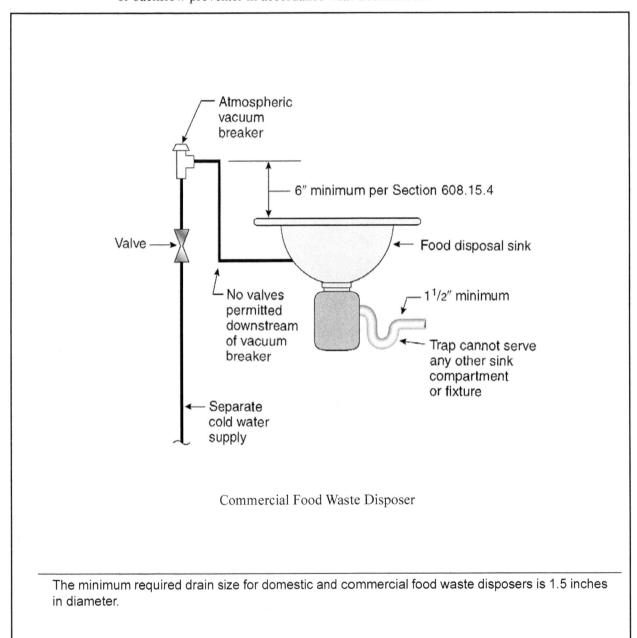

Commercial Food Waste Disposer

The minimum required drain size for domestic and commercial food waste disposers is 1.5 inches in diameter.

Topic: Tempered Water
Reference: IPC 419.5
Category: Fixtures, Faucets and Fixture Fittings
Subject: Lavatories

Code Text: *Tempered water shall be delivered from lavatories and group wash fixtures located in public toilet facilities provided for customers, patrons and visitors. Tempered water shall be delivered through an approved water-temperature limiting device that conforms to ASSE 1070/ASME A112.1070/CSA B125.70 or CSA B125.3.*

Discussion and Commentary: The ASSE 1070/ASME A112.1070/CSA B125.70 and CSA B125.3 standards are for water temperature limiting devices intended for this type of application at public hand-washing facilities to prevent scalding. The device is a thermostatic mixing valve with a maximum temperature limit.

By definition, tempered water has a temperature range between 85°F (29°C) and 110°F (43°C).

Study Session 5

Topic: Water Supply Riser
Reference: IPC 421.2
Category: Fixtures, Faucets and Fixture Fittings
Subject: Showers

Code Text: *Water supply risers from the shower valve to the shower head outlet, whether exposed or concealed, shall be attached to the structure. The attachment to the structure shall be made by the use of support devices designed for use with the specific piping material or by fittings anchored with screws.*

Discussion and Commentary: Proper attachment of the shower supply riser prevents damage from the stress of replacing or adjusting the shower head. This attachment is typically achieved by using a drop-eared elbow (wing-ell) at the top of the riser. This fitting is attached to solid blocking in the wall. The code requires attachment using screws because nails are subject to withdrawal and loosening. A drop-eared elbow securely fastened to blocking receives the threads of the shower arm and provides a stable base to prevent damage to the piping, fittings and wall finish material. Otherwise, damage often occurs. The use of pipe strapping or other means of support that does not adequately attach the pipe to the structure and allows movement or rotation of the riser piping does not meet the intent of the code.

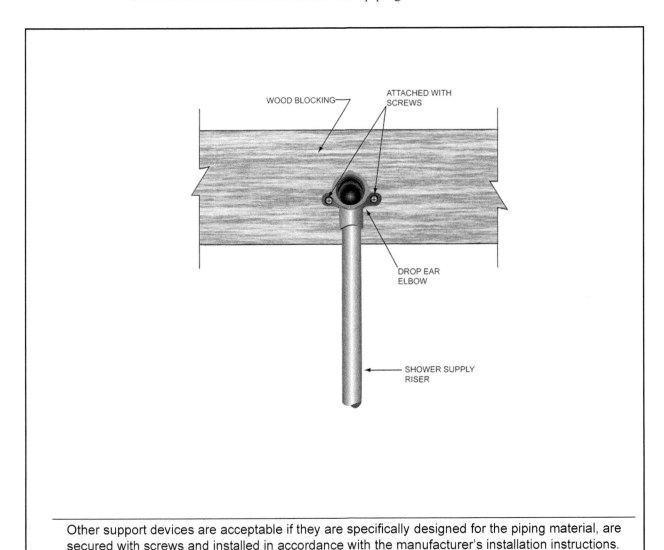

Other support devices are acceptable if they are specifically designed for the piping material, are secured with screws and installed in accordance with the manufacturer's installation instructions.

Topic: Shower Waste Outlet	Category: Fixtures, Faucets and Fixture Fittings
Reference: IPC 421.3	Subject: Showers

Code Text: *Waste outlets serving showers shall be not less than 1½ inches (38 mm) in diameter and, for other than waste outlets in bathtubs, shall have removable strainers not less than 3 inches (76 mm) in diameter with strainer openings not less than 0.25 inch (6.4 mm) in least dimension. Where each shower space is not provided with an individual waste outlet, the waste outlet shall be located and the floor pitched so that waste from one shower does not flow over the floor area serving another shower. Waste outlets shall be fastened to the waste pipe in an approved manner.*

Discussion and Commentary: In gang or multiple showers, the shower room floor must slope toward the shower drains in such a manner as to prevent waste water from flowing from one shower area through another shower area. It would be undesirable and unhygienic for a bather to stand in another person's waste water.

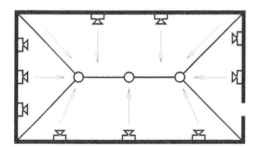

SLOPE OF SHOWER ROOM FLOOR TO PREVENT WATER FROM DRAINING TO ANOTHER SHOWER LOCATION

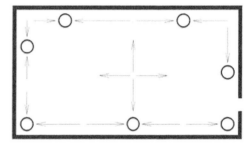

SHOWER WITH PERIMETER DRAINS

The shower drain requirements are written in performance language such that shower drains can be of different designs as long as they accomplish the code's intent.

Topic: Shower Compartments
Reference: IPC 421.4
Category: Fixtures, Faucets and Fixture Fittings
Subject: Showers

Code Text: *All shower compartments shall be not less than 900 square inches (0.58 m²) in interior cross-sectional area. Shower compartments shall not be less than 30 inches (762 mm) in least dimension as measured from the finished interior dimension of the compartment, exclusive of fixture valves, showerheads, soap dishes, and safety grab bars or rails. Except as required in Section 404, the minimum required area and dimension shall be measured from the finished interior dimension at a height equal to the top of the threshold and at a point tangent to its centerline and shall be continued to a height not less than 70 inches (1778 mm) above the shower drain outlet.* See exception for a 1,300 square inch area with a minimum dimension of 25 inches.

Discussion and Commentary: A minimum of 900 square inches of cross-sectional area is required for an average-sized adult to clean the lower body extremities by bending over. A smaller-sized shower would not provide adequate space for the user to bend over while showering. The 30-inch minimum dimension is based on this movement of the body.

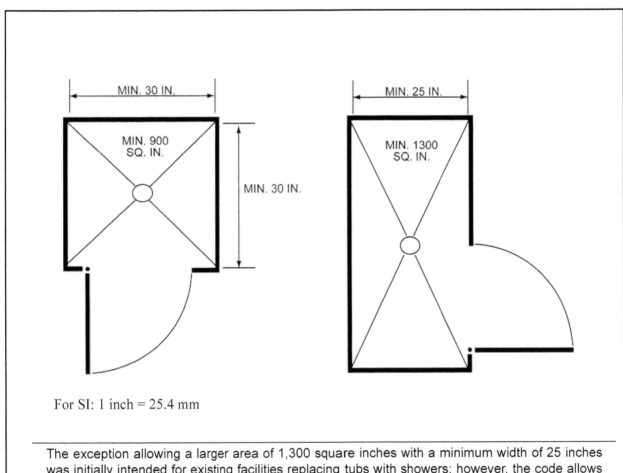

For SI: 1 inch = 25.4 mm

The exception allowing a larger area of 1,300 square inches with a minimum width of 25 inches was initially intended for existing facilities replacing tubs with showers; however, the code allows this for new buildings as well.

Topic: Access
Reference: IPC 421.4.2

Category: Fixtures, Faucets and Fixture Fittings
Subject: Showers

Code Text: *The shower compartment access and egress opening shall have a clear and unobstructed finished width of not less than 22 inches (559 mm). Shower compartments required to be designed in conformance to accessibility provisions shall comply with Section 404.1.*

Discussion and Commentary: For ease of access and to safely egress from the shower, the code sets the minimum clear opening dimension and stipulates that the door must swing out. This not only facilitates access to the user in a medical emergency but is more convenient for maneuvering in the shower while opening and closing the door.

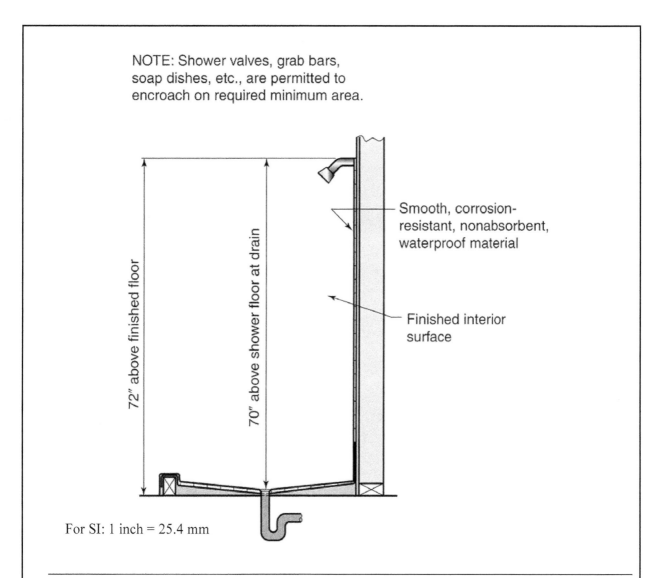

For SI: 1 inch = 25.4 mm

The finished floor and wall surfaces for showers must be of smooth, noncorrosive and nonabsorbent waterproof materials for sanitary purposes and cleaning. The waterproof surface must extend to a minimum of 70 inches above the shower drain and 72 inches above the room floor level.

Topic: Approval
Reference: IPC 424.1
Category: Fixtures, Faucets and Fixture Fittings
Subject: Urinals

Code Text: *Urinals shall conform to ASME A112.19.2/CSA B45.1, ASME A112.19.19 or CSA B45.5/IAPMO Z124. Urinals shall conform to the water consumption requirements of Section 604.4. Water-supplied urinals shall conform to the hydraulic performance requirements of ASME A112.19.2/CSA B45.1 or CSA B45.5/IAPMO Z124.*

Discussion and Commentary: There are four types of water-supplied urinals: stall, blowout, siphon-jet and washdown. A stall urinal is floor mounted, with other urinals being predominantly wall hung. Both blowout and siphon-jet urinals flush completely by siphonic action. The contents of the bowl are completely evacuated during the flushing cycle, and the trap is refilled. A washout urinal does not typically have an integral trap. Some manufacturers, however, design washout urinals with an integral trap. Neither stall nor washout urinals flush with siphon action. The flush cycle is accomplished by a combination of water exchange and dilution.

By definition, a plumbing fixture does not necessarily require connection to a water supply, and waterless urinals complying with the applicable standards are approved. Due to growing interest in water conservation, waterless urinals are gaining wider acceptance.

Topic: Substitution for Water Closets
Reference: IPC 424.2

Category: Fixtures, Faucets and Fixture Settings
Subject: Urinals

Code Text: *In each bathroom or toilet room, urinals shall not be substituted for more than 67 percent of the required water closets in assembly and educational occupancies. Urinals shall not be substituted for more than 50 percent of the required water closets in all other occupancies.*

Discussion and Commentary: Because a urinal is similar to a water closet in its function, it may be substituted for not more than 67 percent of the required water closets in assembly and educational facilities and 50 percent in other occupancies.

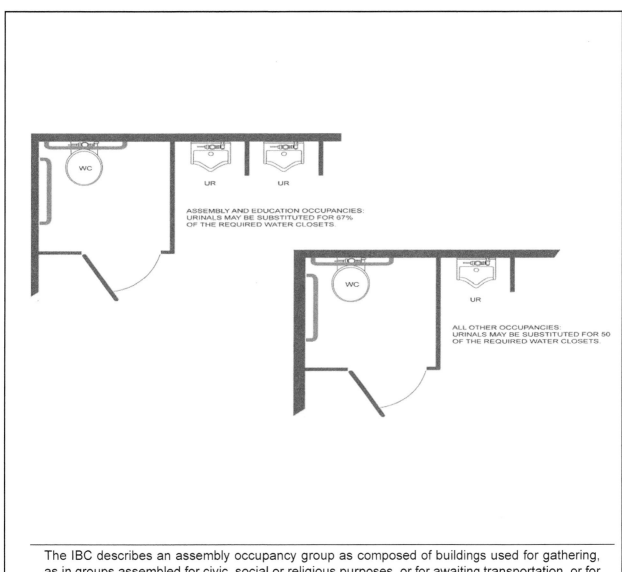

The IBC describes an assembly occupancy group as composed of buildings used for gathering, as in groups assembled for civic, social or religious purposes, or for awaiting transportation, or for recreation, food or drink consumption. Schools and day-care facilities are common examples of educational occupancies.

Topic: Public or Employee Toilet Facilities **Category:** Fixture, Faucets and Fixture Fittings
Reference: IPC 425.2 **Subject:** Water Closets

Code Text: *Water closet bowls for public or employee toilet facilities shall be of the elongated type.*

Discussion and Commentary: An elongated water closet bowl is required for public or employee use because it gives the user an extended area in which to eliminate human waste. The concept is to reduce the possibility of the user missing the bowl and soiling the water closet seat and surroundings. The elongated water closet bowl also has a larger water surface area, which helps keep the inside surface of the bowl clean.

An elongated water closet bowl is 2 inches longer than a regular bowl. The bowl extension is toward the front of the fixture. Elongated bowls are not required for various nonpublic or nonemployee uses, including hotel guestrooms and private facilities.

Topic: Access to Pump
Reference: IPC 426.5
Category: Fixtures, Faucets and Fixture Fittings
Subject: Whirlpool Bathtubs

Code Text: *Access shall be provided to circulation pumps in accordance with the fixture or pump manufacturer's installation instructions. Where the manufacturer's instructions do not specify the location and minimum size of field-fabricated access openings, an opening not less than 12 inches by 12 inches (305 mm by 305 mm) shall be installed to provide access to the circulation pump. Where pumps are located more than 2 feet (609 mm) from the access opening, an opening not less than 18 inches by 18 inches (457 mm by 457 mm) shall be installed. A door or panel shall be permitted to close the opening. In all cases, the access opening shall be unobstructed and of the size necessary to permit the removal and replacement of the circulation pump.*

Discussion and Commentary: A whirlpool circulation pump requires access for maintenance and replacement purposes. The dimension of the access must be either as specified by the manufacturer or as required by the code. Typically, access is gained by removal of an access panel that is constructed on site or is provided by the manufacturer as part of the whirlpool unit. Because the pump is not required to have "ready access" a removable panel is acceptable.

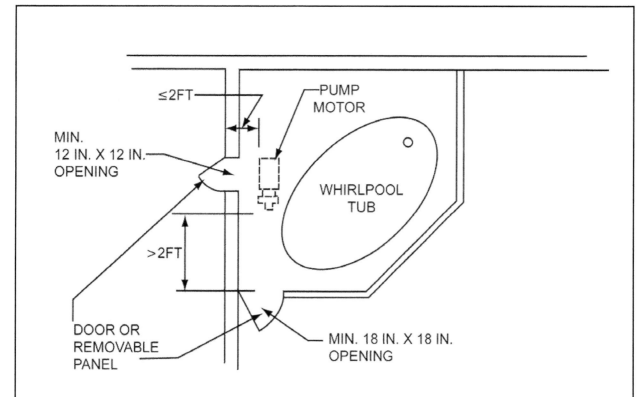

For SI: 1 inch = 25.4 mm, 1 foot = 304.8 mm

A whirlpool bathtub is a plumbing appliance consisting of a bathtub fixture that is equipped and fitted with a circulating piping system designed to accept, circulate and discharge bathtub water upon each use.

Quiz

Study Session 5
IPC Sections 412 through 426

1. Water closets installed in public and employee restrooms do not require _____ seats.
   a. nonabsorbent
   b. elongated
   c. open front
   d. integral

   Reference _____

2. In each toilet room of an institutional occupancy, urinals may be substituted for no more than _____ percent of the required number of water closets.
   a. 50
   b. 33
   c. 67
   d. 75

   Reference _____

3. A temperature-activated, flow reduction device is an approved method for limiting water temperature to _____ °F or less at a faucet outlet.
   a. 110
   b. 115
   c. 120
   d. 105

   Reference _____

4. Water delivered from public hand-washing lavatories shall have a temperature range between _____.
   a. 80°F and 105°F
   b. 85°F and 110°F
   c. 90°F and 115°F
   d. 95°F and 120°F

   Reference _____

5. Unless a shower compartment is designed for accessibility, the minimum clear width of the door opening is _____ inches.

   a. 22
   b. 25
   c. 27
   d. 30

   Reference _____

6. For a shower compartment with an area of 1,300 square inches, the minimum interior dimension is _____ inches.

   a. 22
   b. 25
   c. 27
   d. 30

   Reference _____

7. Unless the manufacturer states otherwise, the minimum size of the access opening to a whirlpool circulation pump located within 24 inches of the opening is _____.

   a. 8 inches x 12 inches
   b. 12 inches x 12 inches
   c. 12 inches x 18 inches
   d. 18 inches x 18 inches

   Reference _____

8. Which of the following is approved for the control of temperature from an individual shower valve?

   a. in-line thermostatic valve
   b. temperature-actuated mixing valve
   c. water-temperature limiting device
   d. combination balanced pressure/thermostatic valve

   Reference _____

9. The maximum allowable setting for water temperature supplied by an individual shower valve is _____.

   a. 100°F
   b. 110°F
   c. 120°F
   d. 140°F

   Reference _____

10. The water supply to a garbage can washer shall be protected against backflow by a backflow preventer or a(n) _____.

    a. air break
    b. check valve
    c. air gap
    d. flushometer valve

    Reference _____

11. In toilet facilities of an educational occupancy, urinals can be substituted for not more than _____ percent of the required water closets.

    a. 33
    b. 50
    c. 67
    d. 75

    Reference _____

12. Generally, the drain outlet for floor drains shall be a minimum of _____ inches in diameter.

    a. $1\frac{1}{2}$
    b. 2
    c. $1\frac{1}{4}$
    d. 3

    Reference _____

13. Floor drains in public coin-operated laundries shall have an outlet of not less than _____ inches in diameter.

    a. 4
    b. 3
    c. 2
    d. $1\frac{1}{2}$

    Reference _____

14. Commercial food waste disposers shall be connected to a drain of not less than _____ inches in diameter.

    a. 2
    b. $1\frac{1}{4}$
    c. 3
    d. $1\frac{1}{2}$

    Reference _____

15. A shower liner must turn up on all sides at least _____ inches above the threshold level.

    a. 2   b. 3
    c. 1.5   d. 2.5

    Reference _____

16. Flushometer valves shall be of the _____ type.

    a. water-pressure   b. diaphragm
    c. water-conservation   d. antisiphon

    Reference _____

17. The opening of the overflow pipe in a flush tank shall be located above the _____ of the water closet or above a secondary overflow in the flush tank.

    a. trap seal   b. flood level rim
    c. fill valve   d. backflow preventer

    Reference _____

18. The only approved method for controlling the delivery temperature at an emergency shower is by a _____.

    a. temperature actuated mixing valve complying with ASSE 1071
    b. temperature-actuated, flow-reduction device conforming to ASSE 1062
    c. water-temperature limiting device conforming to ASSE 1070
    d. balanced-pressure/thermostatic valve conforming to ASSE 1016

    Reference _____

19. A _____ shall not serve more than one fixture.

    a. transfer valve   b. flushing device
    c. temperature limiting device d. vacuum breaker

    Reference _____

20. The fill valve backflow preventer in a flush tank shall be located at least _____ inch(es) above the full opening of the overflow pipe.

   a. ½   b. 1
   c. 1½   d. 2

   Reference _____

21. Head shampoo sink faucets require _____.

   a. temperature control to limit the hot water to 110°F or less
   b. temperature-actuated, flow-reduction devices
   c integral check valves
   d. combination balanced-pressure/thermostatic valves

   Reference _____

22. Lavatories shall have waste outlets not less than _____ inch(es) in diameter.

   a. 1½   b. 1¼
   c. 1   d. 2

   Reference _____

23. Removable strainers at waste outlets of showers shall be not less than _____ inches in diameter.

   a. 3   b. 2
   c. 5   d. 4

   Reference _____

24. Where a whirlpool circulation pump is located more than 24 inches from the access opening, the minimum opening dimensions are _____.

   a. 18 inches x 24 inches   b. 12 inches x 12 inches
   c. 12 inches x 18 inches   d. 18 inches x 18 inches

   Reference _____

25. A water temperature limiting device shall be provided to limit the water supplied to a whirlpool bathtub to a maximum of _____.

    a. 110°F   b. 115°F

    c. 120°F   d. 125°F

Reference _____

Study Session 6

2018 IPC Chapter 5
Water Heaters

OBJECTIVE: To develop an understanding of the requirements for safe installation of water heaters. To develop an understanding of provisions of the code that apply to water heaters used for space heating.

REFERENCE: Chapter 5, 2018 *International Plumbing Code*

KEY POINTS:
- What is the maximum temperature of the water when the water heater is a part of a space heating system? For tankless water heaters?
- Where are drain valves for a water heater to be located? What is their purpose? What are the diameter and thread requirements?
- What are the labeling and marking requirements for water heaters and storage tanks?
- What access dimensions are mandated for water heaters installed in attics?
- When are seismic supports required?
- What access and clearances apply to water heaters? What are the minimum dimensions for working space?
- Where are shut-off valves required for water heaters?
- What safety devices are required for water heaters?
- When are water heater temperature and pressure relief valves required? What are the installation requirements? Approval criteria?
- What limitations are placed on the discharge of the temperature and pressure relief valve? What are the termination requirements?
- When are safety pans required under water heaters?
- What are the minimum dimensions of a water heater pan? What size of drain is required?
- What locations are approved for termination of safety pan drains? When is a drain line not required for a water heater safety pan?

Topic: Water Heater as Space Heater	Category: Water Heaters
Reference: IPC 501.2	Subject: General Provisions

Code Text: *Where a combination potable water heating and space heating system requires water for space heating at temperatures higher than 140°F (60°C), a master thermostatic mixing valve complying with ASSE 1017 shall be provided to limit the water supplied to the potable hot water distribution system to a temperature of 140°F (60°C) or less. The potability of the water shall be maintained throughout the system.*

Discussion and Commentary: When a water heater has a dual purpose of supplying hot water and serving as a heat source for a hot water space heating system, the maximum outlet water temperature for the potable hot water distribution system is limited to 140°F (60°C). A master thermostatic mixing valve conforming to ASSE 1017 must be provided to limit the water temperature to 140° (60°C) or less. These valves are used extensively in applications for domestic service to mix hot and cold water to reduce high service water temperature to the building distribution system. These devices are not intended for final temperature control at fixtures and appliances (see ASSE 1016).

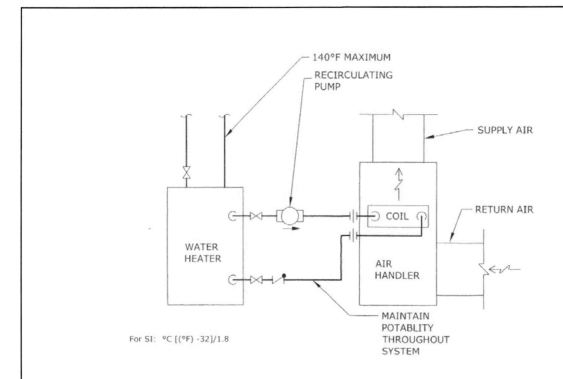

WATER-TO-AIR HEAT EXCHANGER

Chemicals of any type must not be added to the heating system, as this would directly contaminate the potable water supply. Protection of the potable water supply must be in accordance with Section 608.

Topic: Drain Valves	**Category:** Water Heaters
Reference: IPC 501.3	**Subject:** General Provisions

Code Text: *Drain valves for emptying shall be installed at the bottom of each tank-type water heater and hot water storage tank. The drain valve inlet shall be not less than $^3/_4$-inch (19 mm) nominal iron pipe size and the outlet shall be provided with male garden hose threads.*

Discussion and Commentary: A tank-type water heater must be capable of being drained to facilitate service, sediment removal, repair or replacement. Drains require an inlet of $^3/_4$-inch nominal iron pipe size and an outlet equipped with a standard male hose thread.

A water heater is defined as any heating appliance or equipment that heats potable water and supplies such water to the potable hot water distribution system.

Study Session 6

Topic: Water Heater Labeling	Category: Water Heaters
Reference: IPC 501.5	Subject: General Provisions

Code Text: *Water heaters shall be third-party certified.*

Discussion and Commentary: Water heaters must be third-party certified by an approved agency as complying with the applicable and appropriate national standards. Some examples of standards that are used as a basis for testing and certification of water heaters include ANSI Z21.10.1 and ANSI Z21.10.3 for gas-burning water heaters, UL 174 and UL 1453 for domestic electric water heaters, UL 1453 for commercial electric water heaters and UL 732 for oil-burning water heaters.

Reliance upon the certification process to indicate the performance characteristics of the water heater is a fundamental principle of the code. The presence of a certification mark is part of the total information that the code official needs to consider in the approval of the water heater.

Topic: Water Temperature from Tankless Heaters	**Category:** Water Heaters
Reference: IPC 501.6	**Subject:** General Provisions

Code Text: *The temperature of water from tankless water heaters shall be a maximum of 140°F (60°C) when intended for domestic uses. This provision shall not supersede the requirement for protective shower valves in accordance with Section 412.3.*

Discussion and Commentary: The intent of this section is to prevent excessively high water temperatures from reaching plumbing fixtures. Tankless heaters do not have a storage capacity and are often called "instantaneous" because the water is heated at the same time and at the same rate it is used. Instantaneous heaters can discharge an uncertain range of temperatures at any given time, depending on the use. Therefore, some form of temperature control is necessary to protect the user against exposure to excessively hot water discharged from domestic fixtures such as lavatories, kitchen sinks, tubs and laundry trays. This is accomplished with a tempering valve adjusted to deliver water at a maximum temperature of 140°F, or equipping the heater with a temperature-limiting device or thermostat that has a maximum setting of 140°F.

412.3 Individual shower valves. Individual shower and tubshower combination valves shall be balanced-pressure, thermostatic or combination balanced-pressure/thermostatic valves that conform to the requirements of ASSE 1016/ASME A112.1016/CSA B125.16 or ASME A112.18.1/CSA B125.1 and shall be installed at the point of use. Shower and tub-shower combination valves required by this section shall be equipped with a means to limit the maximum setting of the valve to 120°F (49°C), which shall be field adjusted in accordance with the manufacturer's instructions. In-line thermostatic valves shall not be utilized for compliance with this section.

Where pressure-balanced only type shower mixing valves are installed, any change in a tankless water heater temperature setting requires an adjustment of the maximum temperature setting of the mixing valve.

Study Session 6

Topic: Pressure Marking of Storage Tanks **Category:** Water Heaters
Reference: IPC 501.7 **Subject:** General Provisions

Code Text: *Storage tanks and water heaters installed for domestic hot water shall have the maximum allowable working pressure clearly and indelibly stamped in the metal or marked on a plate welded thereto or otherwise permanently attached. Such markings shall be in a position with access on the outside of the tank so as to make inspection or reinspection readily possible.*

Discussion and Commentary: Tank-type water heaters, like all pressure vessels, must be able to withstand the working pressures to which they will be subjected. The maximum working pressure of the water heater must be known so that a properly rated relief valve not exceeding the manufacturer's rated working pressure can be installed. The working pressure must be marked in such a way that it is permanent, not susceptible to damage and legible for the life of the water heater. Therefore, if the relief valve requires replacement, a properly sized valve can be reinstalled.

Allstar Testing

Tested at 300 PSI

Max. operating pressure 150 PSI

Capacity 40 gallons

The marking on the water heater must be located to provide access for inspecting and servicing.

Topic: General Provisions
Reference: IPC 502.1
Category: Water Heaters
Subject: Installation

Code Text: *Water heaters shall be installed in accordance with the manufacturer's instructions. Oil-fired water heaters shall conform to the requirements of this code and the* International Mechanical Code. *Electric water heaters shall conform to the requirements of this code and provisions of NFPA 70. Gas-fired water heaters shall conform to the requirements of the* International Fuel Gas Code. *Solar thermal water heating systems shall conform to the requirements of the* International Mechanical Code *and ICC 900/SRCC 300.*

Discussion and Commentary: In addition to the IPC requirements, all water heaters must be installed in accordance with the manufacturer's instructions and the applicable portions of the referenced codes and standards. The manufacturer's instructions are thoroughly evaluated by the third-party certification agency to ensure safe installation. The certifying agency can require the manufacturer to alter, delete or add information in the installation instructions as necessary to achieve compliance with the applicable standards and code requirements. In effect, the manufacturer's installation instructions become a part of the code and, when followed, ensure that the water heater operates safely in accordance with the applicable standards.

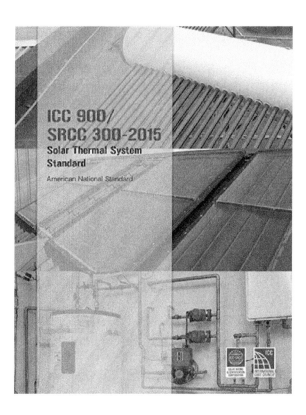

In addition to safety requirements, standard ICC 900/SRCC 300 addresses design, performance, longevity and maintenance of solar thermal water heating systems.

Topic: Elevation and Protection	Category: Water Heaters
Reference: IPC 502.1.1	Subject: Installation

Code Text: *Elevation of water heater ignition sources and mechanical damage protection requirements for water heaters shall be in accordance with the* International Mechanical Code *and the* International Fuel Gas Code.

Discussion and Commentary: The *International Mechanical Code* (IMC) and the *International Fuel Gas Code* (IFGC) contain the referenced provisions for protection of appliances subject to damage from vehicles or other mechanical damage as well as elevation of ignition sources in garages. In addition, IPC Section 305.7 requires protection of plumbing components (which would include water heaters) against damage. To prevent inadvertent ignition of heavier-than-air flammable vapors, IMC Section 304.3 and IFGC Section 305.3 require elevation of ignition sources at least 18 inches above the floor in garages and hazardous locations, unless the appliance is listed as flammable vapor ignition resistant.

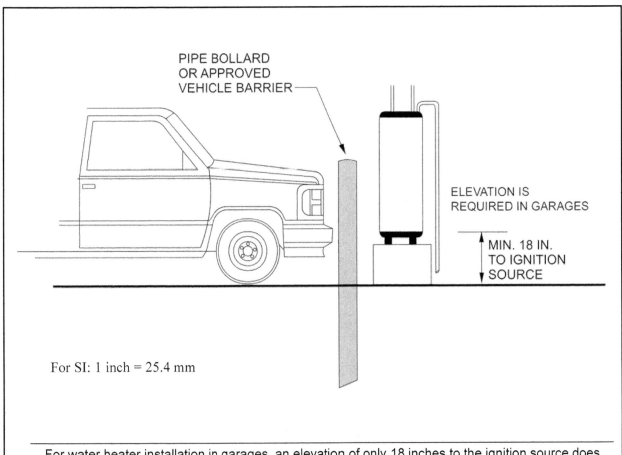

For SI: 1 inch = 25.4 mm

For water heater installation in garages, an elevation of only 18 inches to the ignition source does not provide adequate protection from vehicle impact even if the elevated platform were concrete. Such an installation would require location in an alcove, or protection with curbs, walls, bollards or some other means.

Topic: Seismic Supports
Reference: IPC 502.4
Category: Water Heaters
Subject: Installation

Code Text: *Where earthquake loads are applicable in accordance with the* International Building Code, *water heater supports shall be designed and installed for the seismic forces in accordance with the* International Building Code.

Discussion and Commentary: Chapter 16 of the *International Building Code* (IBC) contains determination of seismic loads based on Seismic Design Category. IPC Section 308.2 requires piping supports to be designed to resist seismic loads. Similarly, this section requires water heater supports to be designed to resist the same seismic loads in accordance with the IBC.

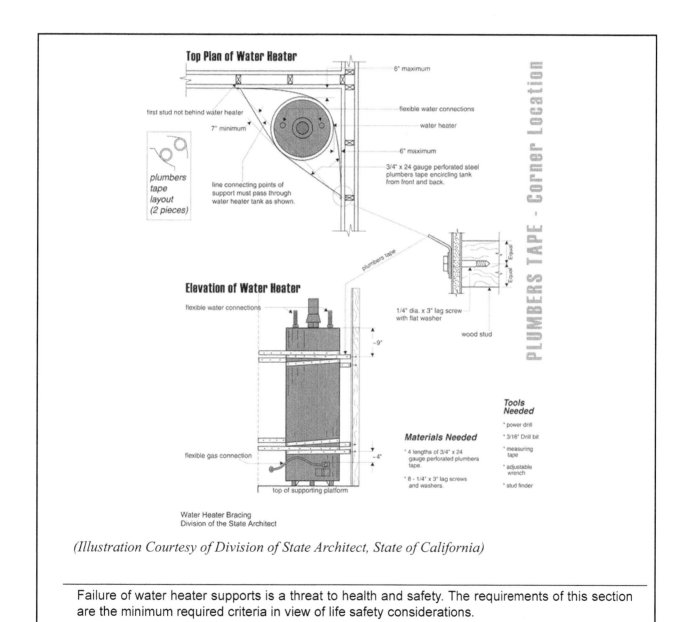

(Illustration Courtesy of Division of State Architect, State of California)

Failure of water heater supports is a threat to health and safety. The requirements of this section are the minimum required criteria in view of life safety considerations.

Topic: Clearances for Maintenance
Reference: IPC 502.5
Category: Water Heaters
Subject: Installation

Code Text: *Appliances shall be provided with access for inspection, service, repair and replacement without disabling the function of a fire-resistance-rated assembly or removing permanent construction, other appliances or any other piping or ducts not connected to the appliance being inspected, serviced, repaired or replaced. A level working space not less than 30 inches in length and 30 inches in width (762 mm by 762 mm) shall be provided in front of the control side to service an appliance.*

Discussion and Commentary: The code requires access to water heaters for observation, inspection, adjustment, servicing, repair and replacement. Access is also necessary to conduct operating procedures such as start-up or shutdown. The prescribed 30-inch by 30-inch level working space provides adequate space for servicing the water heater. In addition, the code prohibits any obstructions such as permanent construction and ducts and piping from other appliances or systems that would impede maintenance or removal and replacement of the water heater. Also, access to the space must be adequate to remove the appliance.

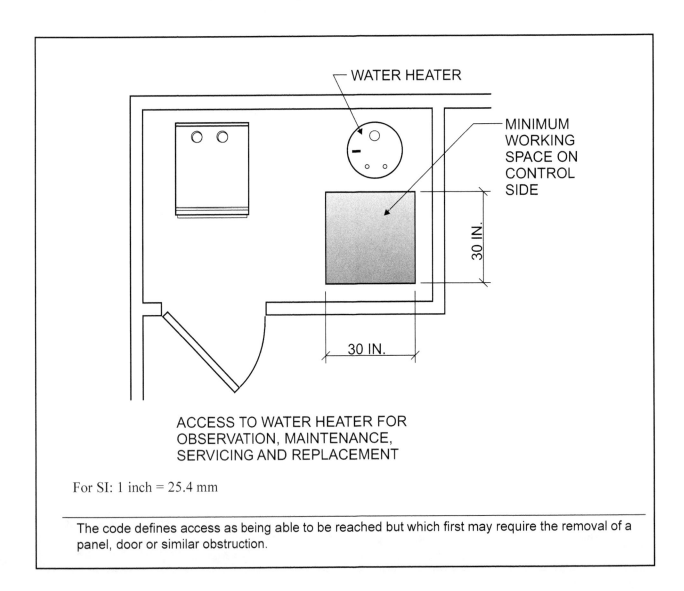

ACCESS TO WATER HEATER FOR OBSERVATION, MAINTENANCE, SERVICING AND REPLACEMENT

For SI: 1 inch = 25.4 mm

The code defines access as being able to be reached but which first may require the removal of a panel, door or similar obstruction.

Topic: Cold Water Line Valve
Reference: IPC 503.1
Category: Water Heaters
Subject: Connections

Code Text: *The cold water branch line from the main water supply line to each hot water storage tank or water heater shall be provided with a valve, located near the equipment and serving only the hot water storage tank or water heater. The valve shall not interfere or cause a disruption of the cold water supply to the remainder of the cold water system. The valve shall be provided with access on the same floor level as the water heater served.*

Discussion and Commentary: A shutoff valve is required on the cold water supply line to each hot water storage tank or water heater and must be located near the equipment. The valve is needed to facilitate service, repair and replacement and to allow for emergency shutoff in the event of a failure. The valve is only to serve the hot water storage tank or water heater, thereby not disrupting the flow of the cold water supply to other portions of the water distribution system when the hot water storage tank or water heater is taken out of service.

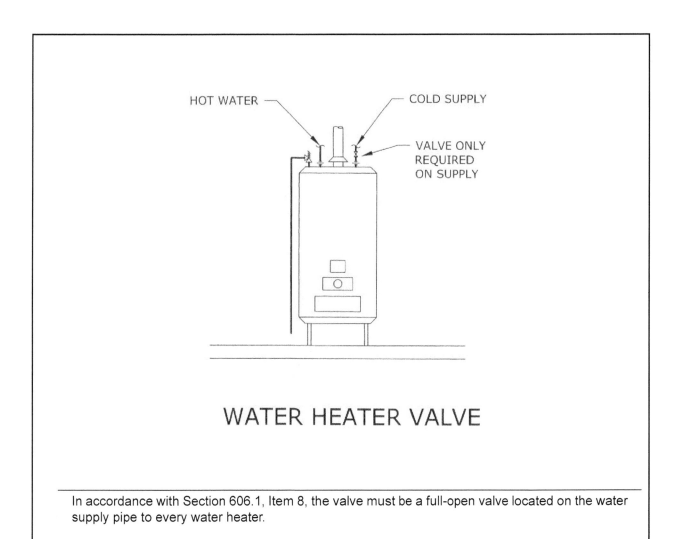

WATER HEATER VALVE

In accordance with Section 606.1, Item 8, the valve must be a full-open valve located on the water supply pipe to every water heater.

Study Session 6

Topic: Antisiphon Devices
Reference: IPC 504.1
Category: Water Heaters
Subject: Safety Devices

Code Text: *An approved means, such as a cold water "dip" tube with a hole at the top or a vacuum relief valve installed in the cold water supply line above the top of the heater or tank, shall be provided to prevent siphoning of any storage water heater or tank.*

Discussion and Commentary: Water heaters are designed to operate only when they are full of water. If some or all of the water is siphoned out of the tank during an interruption in the cold water supply, damage to the water heater from overheating could occur. Typically, water heater designs include a cold water dip tube, which directs the incoming cold water to the bottom of the tank. At the top of the tank, a hole is provided in the dip tube to prevent water from being siphoned from the tank through the tube. ANSI Z21.10.1 and UL 174 both require the dip tube to be provided with a hole located within 6 inches (152 mm) of the top of the tank.

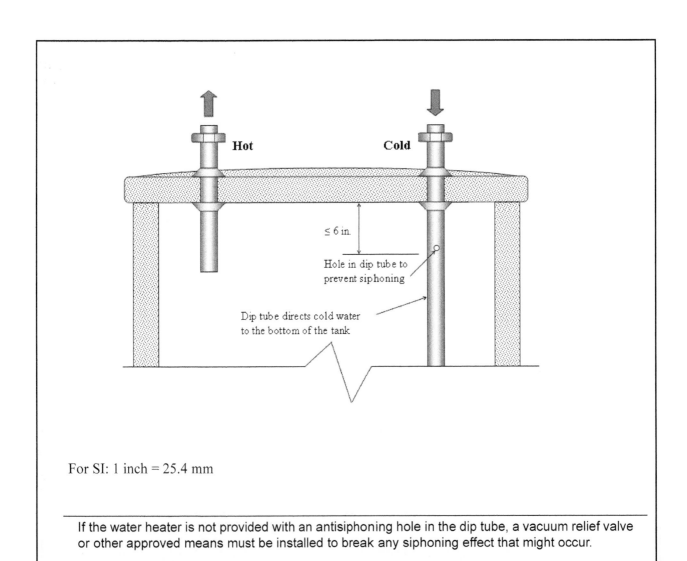

For SI: 1 inch = 25.4 mm

If the water heater is not provided with an antisiphoning hole in the dip tube, a vacuum relief valve or other approved means must be installed to break any siphoning effect that might occur.

Topic: Shutdown	Category: Water Heaters
Reference: IPC 504.3	Subject: Safety Devices

Code Text: *A means for disconnecting an electric hot water supply system from its energy supply shall be provided in accordance with NFPA 70. A separate valve shall be provided to shut off the energy fuel supply to all other types of hot water supply systems.*

Discussion and Commentary: This section parallels NFPA 70 (*National Electrical Code*), the *International Mechanical Code* (IMC) and the *International Fuel Gas Code* (IFGC) by requiring all water heaters to be capable of having the fuel or power supply turned off without affecting other appliances, equipment or systems. The shutoff valves for fuel-fired water heaters and disconnects for electric water heaters are necessary to allow for service, repairs and temporary and emergency shutdown.

Emergency shut-down of water heaters is critically important, as the potential of explosion and severe injury are present in any enclosed system that is heated.

Study Session 6

Topic: Relief Valve
Reference: IPC 504.4
Category: Water Heaters
Subject: Safety Devices

Code Text: *All storage water heaters operating above atmospheric pressure shall be provided with an approved, self-closing (levered) pressure relief valve and temperature relief valve or combination thereof. The relief valve shall conform to ANSI Z21.22. The relief valve shall not be used as a means of controlling thermal expansion.*

Discussion and Commentary: A combination temperature and pressure relief valve, or separate temperature relief and pressure relief valves, protect the occupant and the water heater from unsafe temperatures and excessive pressures that are beyond the rating of the tank. Every water heater except instantaneous point-of-use heaters must have both temperature and pressure relief protection. Water heaters installed without temperature and pressure relief valve protection can produce devastating explosions and have been responsible for deaths and property damage.

Pressure relief valves are designed to relieve excessive pressures that can develop in a closed vessel, tank or system. Temperature relief valves are designed to open in response to excessive temperatures and discharge heated water to limit the temperature of the water in the vessel, tank or system.

Topic: Installation	**Category:** Water Heaters
Reference: IPC 504.4.1	**Subject:** Safety Devices

Code Text: *Such valves shall be installed in the shell of the water heater tank. Temperature relief valves shall be so located in the tank as to be actuated by the water in the top 6 inches (152 mm) of the tank served. For installations with separate storage tanks, the approved, self-closing (levered) pressure relief valve and temperature relief valve or combination thereof conforming to ANSI Z21.22 valves shall be installed on both the storage water heater and storage tank. There shall not be a check valve or shutoff valve between a relief valve and the heater or tank served.*

Discussion and Commentary: Water heaters are typically provided with factory-installed openings that are properly located to receive a relief valve device. Such openings must be used for that purpose. ANSI Z21.10.1 and UL 174 both require a temperature and pressure relief valve to be installed in a location specified by the manufacturer or for the water heater to be provided with a temperature and pressure relief valve. In systems utilizing separate hot water storage tanks, both the water heater and the storage tank require the prescribed relief valves.

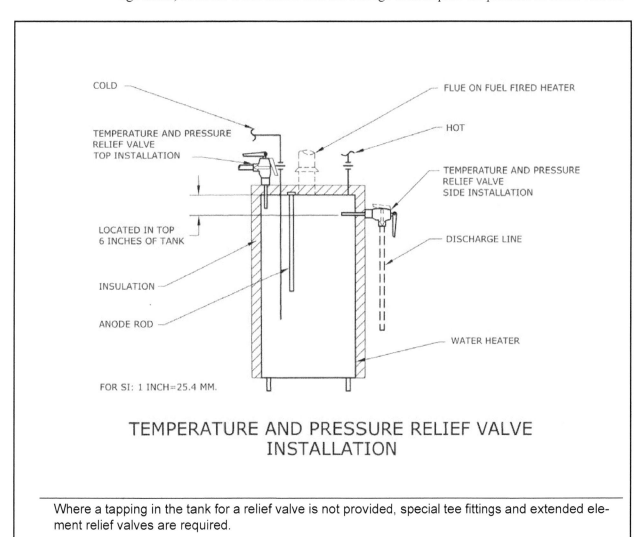

TEMPERATURE AND PRESSURE RELIEF VALVE INSTALLATION

Where a tapping in the tank for a relief valve is not provided, special tee fittings and extended element relief valves are required.

Study Session 6

Topic: Requirements for Discharge Piping **Category:** Water Heaters
Reference: IPC 504.6 **Subject:** Safety Devices

Code Text: *The discharge piping serving a pressure relief valve, temperature relief valve or combination thereof shall:*

1. *Not be directly connected to the drainage system.*
2. *Discharge through an air gap located in the same room as the water heater.*
3. *Not be smaller than the diameter of the outlet of the valve served and shall discharge full size to the air gap.*
4. *Serve a single relief device and shall not connect to piping serving any other relief device or equipment.*
5. *Discharge to the floor, to the pan serving the water heater or storage tank, to a waste receptor or to the outdoors.*
6. *Discharge in a manner that does not cause personal injury or structural damage.*
7. *Discharge to a termination point that is readily observable by the building occupants.*
8. *Not be trapped.*
9. *Be installed so as to flow by gravity.*
10. *Terminate not more than 6 inches (152 mm) above and not less than two times the discharge pipe diameter above the floor or flood level rim of the waste receptor.*
11. *Not have a threaded connection at the end of such piping.*
12. *Not have valves or tee fittings.*
13. *Be constructed of those materials listed in Section 605.4 or materials tested, rated and approved for such use in accordance with ASME A112.4.1*
14. *Be one nominal size larger than the size of the relief valve outlet, where the relief valve discharge piping is installed with insert fittings. The outlet end of such tubing shall be fastened in place.*

Discussion and Commentary: The requirements for relief valve discharge piping are itemized for clear understanding of the provisions. Each item describes the limitations or the needed safety features. In item 4, a discharge pipe must serve only one relief device so that the source of the problem can be immediately identified.

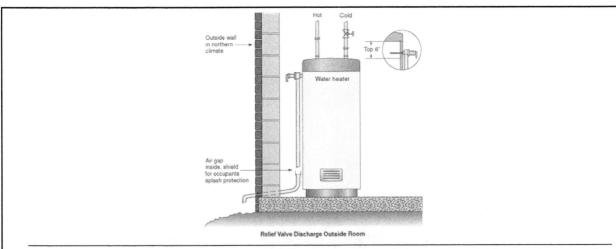

When a discharge takes place, the code intends to protect against personal injury and structural damage, but not necessarily other property damage.

Topic: Pan Size and Drain
Reference: IPC 504.7.1
Category: Water Heaters
Subject: Safety Devices

Code Text: *The pan shall be not less than 1½ inches (38 mm) deep and shall be of sufficient size and shape to receive all dripping or condensate from the tank or water heater. The pan shall be drained by an indirect waste pipe having a minimum diameter of ¾ inch (19 mm). Piping for safety pan drains shall be of those materials listed in Table 605.4.*

Discussion and Commentary: The purpose of a safety pan is to prevent leaking water from damaging the area surrounding or below the storage tank-type water heater or separate storage tank. The pan must be of sufficient size and shape so as to catch all dripping water or condensate. The pan must be drained by an indirect waste pipe having a minimum diameter of ¾ inch. Typically, a pan is required for storage tank-type water heaters installed in attics or on upper floors where leaking water would damage building components such as wood floor framing and sheathing, as well as drywall ceilings in the spaces below.

Pans are not required for tankless water heaters. The intent of a pan installation is to protect the structure from leaks from the tanks of storage type water heaters and hot water storage tanks.

Topic: Pan Drain Termination
Reference: IPC 504.7.2

Category: Water Heaters
Subject: Safety Devices

Code Text: *The pan drain shall extend full-size and terminate over a suitably located indirect waste receptor or floor drain or extend to the exterior of the building and terminate not less than 6 inches (152 mm) and not more than 24 inches (610 mm) above the adjacent ground surface. Where a pan drain was not previously installed, a pan drain shall not be required for a replacement water heater installation.*

Discussion and Commentary: The pan drain must not be reduced in size over its length, as any reduction will act as a restriction and impede the discharge. The pan drain must terminate to an indirect waste receptor, floor drain or extend to the exterior of the building. An air gap or air break must be provided to prevent backflow when the pan drain terminates into an indirect waste receptor or a floor drain. When the pan drain terminates to the exterior of the building, the termination must not be less than 6 inches nor more than 24 inches above the adjacent ground surface.

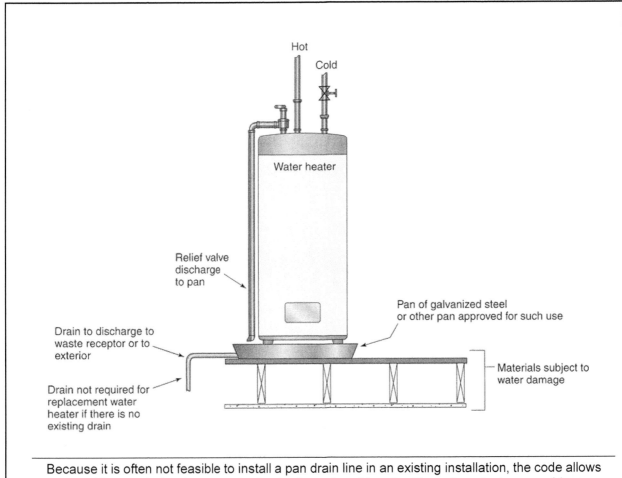

Because it is often not feasible to install a pan drain line in an existing installation, the code allows a pan without a drain when a water heater is replaced in a location where leakage could cause damage. In many cases, the pan will contain the leak for a period of time sufficient for detection by the occupant.

Study Session 6
IPC Chapter 5

1. All of the following are minimum requirements of a water heater installation, except _____.

    a. a valve on the cold water supply to the water heater

    b. a drain valve at the bottom of each tank-type water heater

    c. a means to prevent siphoning of the tank in the event of a negative supply pressure

    d. a means to provide continuous circulation from the piping systems to the heater

    Reference _____

2. Which of the following is required on a bottom-fed water heater?

    a. dip tube   b. circulating pump

    c. vacuum relief valve   d. thermal expansion device

    Reference _____

3. Unless the tank's working pressure is less, the maximum pressure setting for a temperature and pressure relief valve is _____ psi.

    a. 125
    b. 200
    c. 180
    d. 150

    Reference _____

Study Session 6

4. For servicing, a water heater requires a minimum _____ level working space on the control side.

   a. 20-inch by 30-inch
   b. 24-inch by 30-inch
   c. 30-inch by 30-inch
   d. 30-inch by 36-inch

   Reference _____

5. The maximum temperature setting of a temperature and pressure relief valve is _____.

   a. 120°F
   b. 140°F
   c. 180°F
   d. 210°F

   Reference _____

6. A storage tank-type water heater is required to be installed in a pan when _____.

   a. required by the code official
   b. installed in an attic
   c. leakage will cause damage
   d. required by the manufacturer

   Reference _____

7. The drain pipe of a water heater pan shall be not less than _____ inch in diameter.

   a. 3/4
   b. 1/2
   c. 3/8
   d. 1

   Reference _____

8. The temperature and pressure relief valve drain shall not discharge to _____.

   a. a waste receptor
   b. the outdoors
   c. the water heater pan
   d. a point 8 inches above the floor

   Reference _____

9. All of the following are prohibited in a temperature and pressure relief valve drain, except _____.
   a. traps
   b. valves
   c. elbow fittings
   d. threaded ends

   Reference _____

10. The relieving capacity of a temperature relief valve shall not be less than the _____ of the water heater.
    a. heat input
    b. heat output
    c. temperature limit
    d. pressure limit

    Reference _____

11. The termination of a temperature and pressure relief valve discharge pipe shall be _____.
    a. not less than 6 inches above the floor
    b. through an air bank
    c. to a floor drain
    d. readily observable

    Reference _____

12. An unfired hot water storage tank shall have an insulation value not less than _____ (h • ft² • °F)/Btu.
    a. R-7.5
    b. R-10.5
    c. R-12.5
    d. R-14.5

    Reference _____

13. Galvanized steel drain pans for water heaters must be fabricated of material not less than _____ inch in thickness.
    a. 0.036
    b. 0.0149
    c. 0.0236
    d. 0.0478

    Reference _____

14. The maximum allowable water temperature from a tankless-type water heater intended for domestic use is _____.

    a. 120°F b. 140°F
    c. 160°F d. 180°F

    Reference _____

15. The valve on the cold water supply to a water heater shall not _____.

    a. be a full-open type
    b. serve any other fixture
    c. be adjacent to the water heater
    d. be located more than 24 inches from the water heater

    Reference _____

16. A water heater requires _____ certification.

    a. code official b. third-party
    c. manufacturer d. design professional

    Reference _____

17. For a combination water heater and space heating appliance requiring water for space heating at temperatures higher than 140°F, a _____ is required to limit the water temperature of the potable hot water distribution system.

    a. temperature limiting device
    b. combination balanced pressure/thermostatic valve
    c. master thermostatic mixing valve
    d. temperature-actuated flow reduction device

    Reference _____

18. The _____ shall be clearly marked on storage tank water heaters installed for domestic hot water.

    a. pressure test agency b. maximum test pressure
    c. maximum working pressure d. maximum relief pressure

    Reference _____

19. What is the minimum access opening size required for a water heater installed in an attic?
    a. 20 inches by 30 inches
    b. 20 inches by 24 inches
    c. 24 inches by 30 inches
    d. 30 inches by 30 inches

    Reference _____

20. An electric water heater requires a _____.
    a. drain pan
    b. floor drain
    c. vacuum relief valve
    d. disconnecting means

    Reference _____

21. A pan for a water heater shall be not less than _____ inches deep.
    a. 1½
    b. 2
    c. 2½
    d. 3

    Reference _____

22. The pan drain terminating outdoors shall terminate not more than _____ inches above the adjacent ground surface.
    a. 6
    b. 12
    c. 18
    d. 24

    Reference _____

23. Temperature relief valves shall be so located in the tank as to be actuated by the water in the _____ inches.
    a. bottom 6
    b. bottom 12
    c. top 6
    d. top 12

    Reference _____

24. A water heater installed in an attic shall be located no more than _____ feet from the attic access opening.
    a. 12
    b. 20
    c. 24
    d. 32

    Reference _____

25. A passageway to a water heater installed in an attic shall have continuous solid flooring not less than _____ inches wide.

    a. 22   b. 24

    c. 30   d. 36

    Reference _____

Study Session 7

2018 IPC Sections 601 through 605
Water Supply and Distribution I

OBJECTIVE: To develop an understanding of the code provisions related to water supply sources, water supply pipe locations, pumps, joints and fittings.

REFERENCE: Sections 601 through 605, 2018 *International Plumbing Code*

KEY POINTS:
- What rules apply to individual water supplies?
- When is disinfection of the water supply system required?
- What regulations apply to potable water pumps? Pump enclosures?
- How is water service piping sized? What is the minimum size?
- What separation is required between underground water piping and the building sewer?
- What are the other restrictions on water service line locations?
- What design criteria apply to water distribution systems? How are water flow rates and water consumption limited?
- How are fixture supply pipe sizes determined?
- Where water pressure may fluctuate, what is used as the design pressure?
- What measures are required to solve inadequate water pressure? Excessive water pressure?
- How is water hammer prevented?
- How is manifold sizing accomplished for gridded and parallel water distribution systems?
- What identification is needed for individual shutoff valves?
- What are the access requirements for manifolds?
- What are the design criteria and minimum working pressure ratings for water service pipe? Water distribution pipe?
- What materials are permitted for water service pipe? Water distribution pipe? Pipe fittings?

KEY POINTS:
(Cont'd)
- What are the approved methods for joining pipe? For what type of materials is each method approved?
- Which pipe joints are approved for underground use only? Which are approved for above ground use only?
- What limitations apply to the solder used in water piping systems?
- What types of joints are permitted for joining different pipe materials?

Topic: Solar Energy Utilization
Reference: IPC 601.2

Category: Water Supply Distribution
Subject: General Provisions

Code Text: *Solar energy systems used for heating potable water or using an independent medium for heating potable water shall comply with the applicable requirements of this code. The use of solar energy shall not compromise the requirements for cross connection or protection of the potable water supply system required by the International Plumbing Code.*

Discussion and Commentary: Solar systems for heating water consist of two basic types: direct connection and indirect connection. In a direct connection system, the heat transfer fluid is potable water. The *International Mechanical Code* (IMC) contains information on the design and installation of solar heating systems. The potable water source must be protected from possible contamination from piping and joint materials used in the system and from the inadvertent introduction of nonpotable or toxic transfer fluids. In an indirect connection system, a freeze-protected heat transfer fluid is circulated through a closed loop to a heat exchanger. The heat is then transferred indirectly to the potable water. The fluids in these systems are nonpotable and occasionally toxic. The type of heat exchanger used in these systems depends on the exact nature of the transfer fluid used.

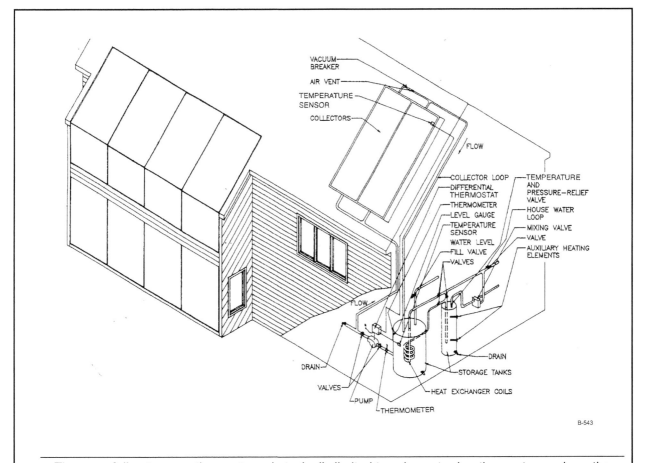

The use of direct connection systems is typically limited to solar water-heating systems where the potable water is heated directly by the solar collector and circulated through the system and is suited for use only in areas where the water in the collectors is not subject to freezing.

Study Session 7

Topic: Existing Piping Used for Grounding
Category: Water Supply and Distribution
Reference: IPC 601.3
Subject: General Provisions

Code Text: *Existing metallic water service piping used for electrical grounding shall not be replaced with nonmetallic pipe or tubing until other approved means of grounding is provided.*

Discussion and Commentary: In many buildings, the underground metal water service piping is used as part of the electrical grounding system of the building. A minimum 10 feet of metal water service pipe in contact with the soil is considered a grounding electrode and is connected to the electrical service panel with a grounding electrode conductor. Replacement of this underground metal piping with nonmetallic piping removes or impairs the grounding system, creating a potential hazard and necessitating a need for another method of grounding the electrical system.

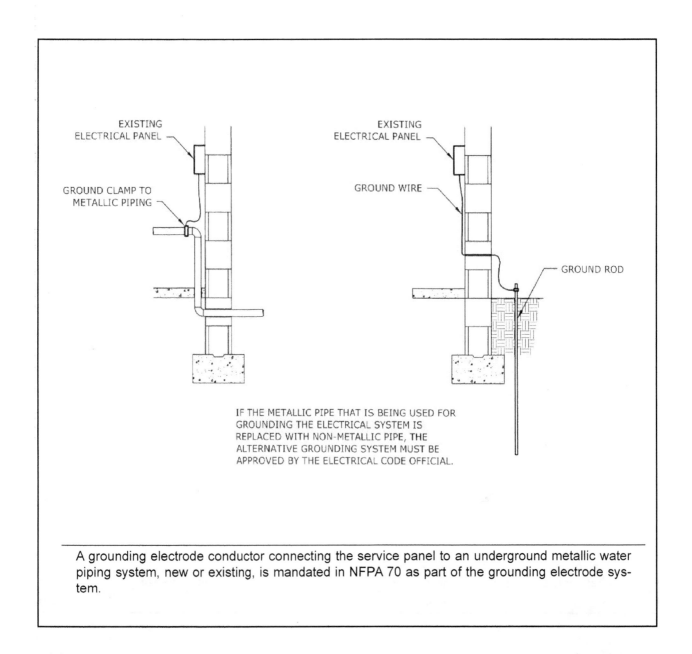

IF THE METALLIC PIPE THAT IS BEING USED FOR GROUNDING THE ELECTRICAL SYSTEM IS REPLACED WITH NON-METALLIC PIPE, THE ALTERNATIVE GROUNDING SYSTEM MUST BE APPROVED BY THE ELECTRICAL CODE OFFICIAL.

A grounding electrode conductor connecting the service panel to an underground metallic water piping system, new or existing, is mandated in NFPA 70 as part of the grounding electrode system.

Topic: Individual Water Supply
Reference: IPC 602.3

Category: Water Supply and Distribution
Subject: Water Required

Code Text: *Where a potable public water supply is not available, individual sources of potable water supply shall be utilized.*

Discussion and Commentary: An individual water supply is only permitted where a public system is unavailable. Individual sources of water supply may include: water wells, cisterns with treatment, reservoirs with treatment and other systems approved by the health department or authority having jurisdiction.

A common method for drilling water wells employs rotary auger equipment mounted on heavy trucks.

Study Session 7

Topic: Sources
Reference: IPC 602.3.1
Category: Water Supply and Distribution
Subject: Water Required

Code Text: *Dependent on geological and soil conditions and the amount of rainfall, individual water supplies are of the following types: drilled well, driven well, dug well, bored well, spring, stream or cistern. Surface bodies of water and land cisterns shall not be sources of individual water supply unless properly treated by approved means to prevent contamination. Individual water supplies shall be constructed and installed in accordance with the applicable state and local laws. Where such laws do not address all of the requirements set forth in NGWA-01, individual water supplies shall comply with NGWA-01 for those requirements not addressed by state and local laws.*

Discussion and Commentary: The sources for an individual water supply include wells, springs, cisterns, streams and surface water impoundments. Wells are probably the most common source of individual water supply used today and consist of a vertical shaft that extends down into the earth to a water-bearing strata. Wells may be bored, drilled, driven or dug. See Section 202 for the definitions of each well type and a cistern. Where state or local ordinances regulating individual water supplies do not exist or are not adequate, the IPC references the water well standard NGWA-01 for individual water supply requirements.

CISTERN. A small covered tank for storing water for a home or farm. Generally, this tank stores rainwater to be utilized for purposes other than in the potable water supply, and such tank is placed underground in most cases.

WELL

Bored. A well constructed by boring a hole in the ground with an auger and installing a casing.

Drilled. A well constructed by making a hole in the ground with a drilling machine of any type and installing casing and screen.

Driven. A well constructed by driving a pipe in the ground. The drive pipe is usually fitted with a well point and screen.

Dug. A well constructed by excavating a large-diameter shaft and installing a casing.

Surface water impoundments always have to be treated if used as a supply of potable water. This may include some form of chlorination or ozone treatment.

Topic: Minimum Quantity
Reference: IPC 602.3.2

Category: Water Supply and Distribution
Subject: Water Required

Code Text: *The combined capacity of the source and storage in an individual water supply system shall supply the fixtures with water at rates and pressures as required by Chapter 6.*

Discussion and Commentary: The amount and quality of water supplied to a building are critical to both the health of the occupants and the safe and efficient use of the plumbing fixtures and drainage system. IPC Section 602.3.2 addresses the minimum quantity of water from the storage and source of individual (well) water supplies.

For an individual water supply the design professional must determine the water demand rate for the building in accordance with the requirements of Section 604, Design of Building Water Distribution System, and in the same manner as if the water were supplied from a public source.

Topic: Disinfection of System	Category: Water Supply and Distribution
Reference: IPC 602.3.4	Subject: Water Required

Code Text: *After construction the individual water supply system shall be purged of deleterious matter and disinfected in accordance with Section 610.*

Discussion and Commentary: A private water supply system must be disinfected after construction. The disinfection procedure must be as prescribed in Section 610, Disinfection of Potable Water System, for all potable water systems.

610.1 General. New potable water systems shall be purged of deleterious matter and disinfected prior to utilization. The method to be followed shall be that prescribed by the health authority or water purveyor having jurisdiction or, in the absence of a prescribed method, the procedure described in either AWWA C651 or AWWA C652, or as described in this section. This requirement shall apply to "on-site" or "in-plant" fabrication of a system or to a modular portion of a system.

1. The pipe system shall be flushed with clean, potable water until dirty water does not appear at the points of outlet.

2. The system or part thereof shall be filled with a water/chlorine solution containing at least 50 parts per million (50 mg/L) of chlorine, and the system or part thereof shall be valved off and allowed to stand for 24 hours; or the system or part thereof shall be filled with a water/chlorine solution containing at least 200 parts per million (200 mg/L) of chlorine and allowed to stand for 3 hours.

3. Following the required standing time, the system shall be flushed with clean potable water until the chlorine is purged from the system.

4. The procedure shall be repeated where shown by a bacteriological examination that contamination remains present in the system.

Potable water is defined as water free from impurities present in amounts sufficient to cause disease or harmful physiological effects and conforming to the bacteriological and chemical quality requirements of the Public Health Service Drinking Water Standards or the regulations of the public health authority having jurisdiction.

Topic: Separation from Building Sewer **Category:** Water Supply and Distribution
Reference: IPC 603.2 **Subject:** Water Service

Code Text: *Where water service piping is located in the same trench with the building sewer, such sewer shall be constructed of materials listed in Table 702.2. Where the building sewer piping is not constructed of materials listed in Table 702.2, the water service pipe and the building sewer shall be horizontally separated by not less than 5 feet (1524 mm) of undisturbed or compacted earth. The required separation distance shall not apply where a water service pipe crosses a sewer pipe, provided the water service is sleeved to a point not less than 5 feet (1524 mm) horizontally from the sewer pipe centerline on both sides of such crossing. The sleeve shall be of pipe materials listed in Table 605.3, 702.2 or 702.3. The required separation distance shall not apply where the bottom of the water service pipe, located within 5 feet (1524 mm) of the sewer, is not less than 12 inches (305 mm) above the highest point of the top of the building sewer.*

Discussion and Commentary: Contamination can occur when there is a leak in the building sewer located near the water service pipe. The soil then becomes contaminated around the water pipe, and, if the water service pipe has a subsequent failure, contamination of the potable water supply could occur. The simplest means of reducing the possibility of soil contamination is to install the building sewer and water service pipe in two trenches separated horizontally by undisturbed or compacted earth. Any contamination will tend to saturate the excavation backfill soil before settling into the undisturbed, compacted earth. As an alternative, water and sewer pipes can be in the same trench if the water pipe is placed at least 12 inches above the sewer pipe.

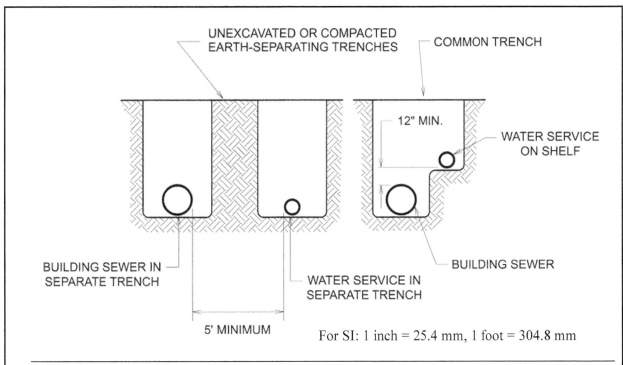

The requirements for separating the water service from the building sewer are intended to reduce the possibility of the sewer contaminating the potable water supply in the event of a failure of the water supply and building sewer pipes.

Topic: Design Criteria
Reference: IPC 604.3

Category: Water Supply and Distribution
Subject: Design of Water Distribution System

Code Text: *The water distribution system shall be designed, and pipe sizes shall be selected such that under conditions of peak demand, the capacities at the fixture supply pipe outlets shall not be less than shown in Table 604.3. The minimum flow rate and flow pressure provided to fixtures and appliances not listed in Table 604.3 shall be in accordance with the manufacturer's installation instructions.*

Discussion and Commentary: The design of the water distribution system is based on fixture capacities during peak demand for the particular occupancy and use of the building. The design takes into consideration the highest anticipated use of fixtures, for example at an intermission or break period. Accepted engineering practice does not necessarily assume that all fixtures are being used at the same time but reflects normal use of the fixtures at the busiest time. The capacity of each fixture is determined by the flow rate and flow pressure values of Table 604.3.

TABLE 604.3
WATER DISTRIBUTION SYSTEM DESIGN CRITERIA REQUIRED CAPACITY AT FIXTURE SUPPLY PIPE OUTLETS

FIXTURE SUPPLY OUTLET SERVING	FLOW RATE[a] (gpm)	FLOW PRESSURE (psi)
Bathtub, balanced-pressure, thermostatic or combination balanced-pressure/thermostatic mixing valve	4	20
Bidet, thermostatic mixing valve	2	20
Combination fixture	4	8
Dishwasher, residential	2.75	8
Drinking fountain	0.75	8
Laundry tray	4	8
Lavatory, private	0.8	8
Lavatory, private, mixing valve	0.8	8
Lavatory, public	0.4	8
Shower	2.5	8
Shower, balanced-pressure, thermostatic or combination balanced-pressure/thermostatic mixing valve	2.5[b]	20
Sillcock, hose bibb	5	8
Sink, residential	1.75	8
Sink, service	3	8
Urinal, valve	12	25
Water closet, blow out, flushometer valve	25	45
Water closet, flushometer tank	1.6	20
Water closet, siphonic, flushometer valve	25	35
Water closet, tank, close coupled	3	20
Water closet, tank, one piece	6	20

For SI: 1 pound per square inch = 6.895 kPa,
1 gallon per minute = 3.785 L/m.

a. For additional requirements for flow rates and quantities, see Section 604.4.
b. Where the shower mixing valve manufacturer indicates a lower flow rating for the mixing valve, the lower value shall be applied.

Table 604.3 is updated periodically through the code development process to reflect current technology and fixture design, and to correspond to the design values of the applicable referenced standards to ensure proper functioning of fixtures.

Topic: Gridded and Parallel System Manifolds **Category:** Water Supply and Distribution
Reference: IPC 604.10 **Subject:** Design of Water Distribution System

Code Text: *Hot water and cold water manifolds installed with gridded or parallel connected individual distribution lines to each fixture or fixture fitting shall be designed in accordance with Sections 604.10.1 through 604.10.3.*

Discussion and Commentary: Gridded and parallel water distribution systems are both permitted to be used by installers. This allows for more flexibility in using the most appropriate system based on the situation and need. A parallel system is also referred to as a "home run" system and is the more common installation. A separate supply line is run from the manifold to each fixture. Gridded systems originated with dwelling fire sprinkler systems in which plumbing fixtures and sprinklers are supplied through a single water distribution system. A grid system is interconnected to provide two or more paths to each fixture supply pipe.

Parallel Water Distribution System Using PEX Piping

Individual fixture shutoff valves installed at the manifold shall be identified as to the fixture being supplied.

Study Session 7

Topic: Soil and Ground Water
Reference: IPC 605.1

Category: Water Supply and Distribution
Subject: Materials, Joints and Connections

Code Text: *The installation of a water service or water distribution pipe shall be prohibited in soil and ground water contaminated with solvents, fuels, organic compounds or other detrimental materials causing permeation, corrosion, degradation or structural failure of the piping material. Where detrimental conditions are suspected, a chemical analysis of the soil and ground water conditions shall be required to ascertain the acceptability of the water service or water distribution piping material for the specific installation. Where detrimental conditions exist, approved alternative materials or routing shall be required.*

Discussion and Commentary: When pipe is buried, the surrounding soil conditions might cause the pipe to degrade or corrode at an accelerated rate. The soil can be evaluated, or knowledge of the historical effects from the soil may be used to determine if additional requirements are necessary to protect the piping material. Most soils are corrosive to galvanized steel pipe. The pipe is either coated and wrapped with coal tar, or an elastomeric or epoxy coating is applied to the exterior of the pipe. Some soils affect copper tubing. Soil with cinders contains acid produced by combining water with sulfur compounds, which will attack unprotected copper pipe. Copper tubing in these instances must be coated with a protective layer.

Although corrosion and degradation for buried water pipe is typically a concern with galvanized steel or copper materials, thermoplastic pipe placed in soil containing heavy concentrations of hydrocarbons is also subject to degradation.

Topic: Lead Content of Drinking Water Pipe
Category: Water Supply and Distribution
Reference: IPC 605.2.1
Subject: Materials, Joints and Connections

Code Text: *Pipe, pipe fittings, joints, valves, faucets and fixture fittings utilized to supply water for drinking or cooking purposes shall comply with NSF 372 and shall have a weighted average lead content of 0.25 percent or less.*

Discussion and Commentary: IPC Section 605.2.1 matches federal law that requires pipe, pipe fittings, joints, valves, faucets and fixture fittings that are used to supply water for drinking or cooking purposes to have not more than 0.25 percent lead content, based on a weighted average of wetted surface areas in accordance with NSF 372. The 0.25 percent limitation does not apply to portions of the water distribution system that do not supply water for drinking or cooking. The existing 8 percent limitation is still in effect for those portions of the system.

Neither NSF 372 nor the federal law requires low-lead compliant products be marked or identified in any particular manner, and identification markings are not standardized between manufacturers or third-party certification agencies. However, the IPC requirements for third-party certification to NSF 372 will make its compliance with the code easier to verify.

Topic: Water Service Pipe	**Category:** Water Supply and Distribution
Reference: IPC 605.3	**Subject:** Materials, Joints and Connections

Code Text: *Water service pipe shall conform to NSF 61 and shall conform to one of the standards listed in Table 605.3. All water service pipe or tubing, installed underground and outside of the structure, shall have a working pressure rating of not less than 160 psi (1100 kPa) at 73.4°F (23°C). Where the water pressure exceeds 160 psi (1100 kPa), piping material shall have a working pressure rating not less than the highest available pressure. Water service piping materials not third-party certified for water distribution shall terminate at or before the full open valve located at the entrance to the structure. All ductile iron water pipe shall be cement mortar lined in accordance with AWWA C104/A21.4.*

Discussion and Commentary: Piping material that comes in contact with potable water is required to conform to the requirements of NSF 61. The intent is to control the potential adverse health effects produced by indirect additives, products and materials that come in contact with potable water. Plastic water pipe tested and labeled in accordance with NSF 14 as potable water pipe also conforms to NSF 61 insofar as NSF 14 makes reference to and requires compliance with NSF 61.

TABLE 605.3
WATER SERVICE PIPE

MATERIAL	STANDARD
Acrylonitrile butadiene styrene (ABS) plastic pipe	ASTM D1527; ASTM D2282
Chlorinated polyvinyl chloride (CPVC) plastic pipe	ASTM D2846; ASTM F441; ASTM F442; CSA B137.6
Chlorinated polyvinyl chloride/aluminum/chlorinated polyvinyl chloride (CPVC/AL/CPVC)	ASTM F2855
Copper or copper-alloy pipe	ASTM B42; ASTM B302
Copper or copper-alloy tubing (Type K, WK, L, WL, M or WM)	ASTM B75; ASTM B88; ASTM B251; ASTM B447
Cross-linked polyethylene (PEX) plastic pipe and tubing	ASTM F876; AWWA C904; CSA B137.5
Cross-linked polyethylene/aluminum/cross-linked polyethylene (PEX-AL-PEX) pipe	ASTM F1281; ASTM F2262; CSA B137.10
Cross-linked polyethylene/aluminum/high-density polyethylene (PEX-AL-HDPE)	ASTM F1986
Ductile iron water pipe	AWWA C151/A21.51; AWWA C115/A21.15
Galvanized steel pipe	ASTM A53
Polyethylene (PE) plastic pipe	ASTM D2239; ASTM D3035; AWWA C901; CSA B137.1
Polyethylene (PE) plastic tubing	ASTM D2737; AWWA C901; CSA B137.1
Polyethylene/aluminum/polethylene (PE-AL-PE) pipe	ASTM F1282; CSA B137.9
Polyethylene of raised temperature (PE-RT) plastic tubing	ASTM F2769; CSA B137.18
Polypropylene (PP) plastic pipe or tubing	ASTM F2389; CSA B137.11
Polyvinyl chloride (PVC) plastic pipe	ASTM D1785; ASTM D2241; ASTM D2672; CSA B137.3
Stainless steel pipe (Type 304/304L)	ASTM A312; ASTM A778
Stainless steel pipe (Type 316/316L)	ASTM A312; ASTM A778

Certain plastic piping materials, including chlorinated polyvinyl chloride (CPVC) and cross-linked polyethylene (PEX), are permitted for both water service and water distribution. For all such materials, a transition or termination of the material would not be required.

Topic: Fittings	Category: Water Supply and Distribution
Reference: IPC 605.5	Subject: Materials, Joints and Connections

Code Text: *Pipe fittings shall be approved for installation with the piping material installed and shall comply with the applicable standards listed in Table 605.5. Pipe fittings utilized in water supply systems shall also comply with NSF 61. Ductile and gray iron pipe and pipe fittings utilized in water service piping systems shall be cement mortar lined in accordance with AWWA C104/A21.4.*

Discussion and Commentary: Each fitting is designed to be installed in a particular system with a given material or combination of materials. Drainage pattern fittings must be installed in drainage systems. Vent fittings are limited to the venting system. Many fittings are intended to be used only for water distribution systems.

TABLE 605.5
PIPE FITTINGS

MATERIAL	STANDARD
Acrylonitrile butadiene styrene (ABS) plastic	ASTM D2468
Cast iron	ASME B16.4
Chlorinated polyvinyl chloride (CPVC) plastic	ASSE 1061; ASTM D2846; ASTM F437; ASTM F438; ASTM F439; CSA B137.6
Copper or copper alloy	ASME B16.15; ASME B16.18; ASME B16.22; ASME B16.26; ASME B16.51; ASSE 1061; ASTM F1476; ASTM F1548
Cross-linked polyethylene/aluminum/high-density polyethylene (PEX-AL-HDPE)	ASTM F1986
Fittings for cross-linked polyethylene (PEX) plastic tubing	ASSE 1061, ASTM F877; ASTM F1807; ASTM F1960; ASTM F2080; ASTM F2098, ASTM F2159; ASTM F2434; ASTM F2735; CSA B137.5
Fittings for polyethylene of raised temperature (PE-RT) plastic tubing	ASSE 1061, ASTM D3261; ASTM F1807; ASTM F2098; ASTM F2159; ASTM F2735; ASTM F2769; CSA B137.18
Gray iron and ductile iron	ASTM F1476; ASTM F1548; AWWA C110/A21.10; AWWA C153/A21.53
Insert fittings for polyethylene/aluminum/polyethylene (PE-AL-PE) and cross-linked polyethylene/aluminum/cross-linked polyethylene (PEX-AL-PEX)	ASTM F1974; ASTM F1281; ASTM F1282; CSA B137.9; CSA B137.10
Malleable iron	ASME B16.3
Metal (brass) insert fittings for polyethylene/aluminum/polyethylene (PE-AL-PE) and cross-linked polyethylene/aluminum/cross-linked polyethylene (PEX-AL-PEX)	ASTM F1974
Polyethylene (PE) plastic pipe	ASTM D2609; ASTM D2683; ASTM D3261; ASTM F1055; CSA B137.1
Polypropylene (PP) plastic pipe or tubing	ASTM F2389; CSA B137.11
Polyvinyl chloride (PVC) plastic	ASTM D2464; ASTM D2466; ASTM D2467; CSA B137.2; CSA B137.3
Stainless steel (Type 304/304L)	ASTM A312; ASTM A778; ASTM F1476; ASTM F1548
Stainless steel (Type 316/316L)	ASTM A312; ASTM A778; ASTM F1476; ASTM F1548
Steel	ASME B16.9; ASME B16.11; ASME B16.28; ASTM F1476; ASTM F1548

Many pipe standards also include fittings. However, there are a number of other standards that strictly regulate pipe fittings. As with all piping materials that come in contact with potable water, water pipe fittings are required to comply with the requirements set forth in NSF 61.

Topic: Polyethylene Plastic Installation
Reference: IPC 605.18.4
Category: Water Supply and Distribution
Subject: Materials, Joints and Connections

Code Text: *Polyethylene pipe shall be cut square, with a cutter designed for plastic pipe. Except where joined by heat fusion, pipe ends shall be chamfered to remove sharp edges. Kinked pipe shall not be installed. The minimum pipe bending radius shall not be less than 30 pipe diameters, or the minimum coil radius, whichever is greater. Piping shall not be bent beyond straightening of the curvature of the coil. Bends shall not be permitted within 10 pipe diameters of any fitting or valve. Stiffener inserts installed with compression-type couplings and fittings shall not extend beyond the clamp or nut of the coupling or fitting.*

Discussion and Commentary: Any properly made pipe joint requires that the pipe ends be cut square for proper alignment, proper insertion depth and adequate surface area for joining. Because polyethylene plastic pipe and tubing can be kinked and stress-weakened, the minimum pipe bending radius is specified so as not to exceed the structural capacity of the material. The minimum bending radius must not be less than the radius of the pipe coil as it came from the manufacturer or 30 pipe diameters, whichever of these two criteria is the largest.

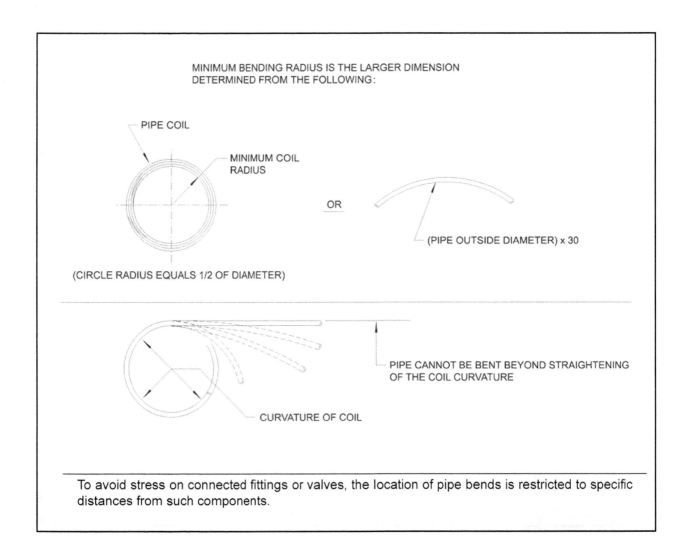

To avoid stress on connected fittings or valves, the location of pipe bends is restricted to specific distances from such components.

Topic: Polyethylene (PP) Plastic
Reference: IPC 605.19.1
Category: Water Supply and Distribution
Subject: Materials, Joints and Connections

Code Text: *Heat-fusion joints for polypropylene pipe and tubing joints shall be installed with socket-type heat-fused polypropylene fittings, butt-fusion polypropylene fittings or electrofusion polypropylene fittings. Joint surfaces shall be clean and free from moisture. The joint shall be undisturbed until cool. Joints shall be made in accordance with ASTM F2389. Mechanical and compression sleeve joints shall be installed in accordance with the manufacturer's instructions.*

Discussion and Commentary: The requirements for mechanical and heat fusion joints are described separately to avoid misunderstanding and confusion. The details and methodology for mechanical and compression joints are governed by the manufacturer's installation instructions, whereas heat-fusion joints must meet certain code performance characteristics.

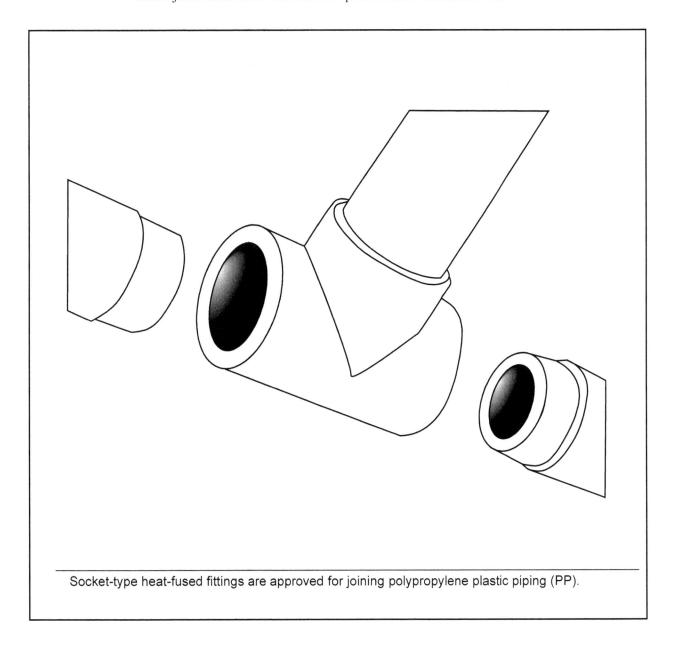

Socket-type heat-fused fittings are approved for joining polypropylene plastic piping (PP).

Topic: PVC Plastic
Reference: IPC 605.21.1
Category: Water Supply and Distribution
Subject: Materials, Joints and Connections

Code Text: *Mechanical joints on waterpipe shall be made with an elastomeric seal conforming to ASTM D3139. Mechanical joints shall not be installed in above-ground systems unless otherwise approved. Joints shall be installed in accordance with the manufacturer's instructions.*

Discussion and Commentary: Mechanical joints for PVC water piping are typically limited to underground applications. A PVC plastic hub pipe is connected using an elastomeric compression gasket. The pipe must be inserted to the full depth of the hub to make a proper joint. PVC piping is approved for water service pipe but is not included as an acceptable material for water distribution piping in Table 605.4.

ASTM
ASTM International
100 Barr Harbor Drive
West Conshohocken, PA 19428-2959

Section	Material	Application	Standard	Title	Applies to IPC Sections
605.22.1	polyvinyl chloride (PVC) plastic pipe	Mechanical joints for underground water piping	ASTM D 3139	Specification for Joints for Plastic Pressure Pipes Using Flexible Elastomeric Seals	605.10.1, 605.22.1

The IPC defines four specific joint types: expansion, flexible, mechanical and slip.

Study Session 7
IPC Sections 601 through 605

1. A _____ is not permitted as a source for an individual water supply unless the water is treated to prevent contamination.

    a. spring   b. cistern

    c. dug well   d. drilled well

    Reference _____

2. The maximum allowable water pressure on the water distribution system is _____.

    a. 25 psi   b. 40 psi

    c. 80 psi   d. 100 psi

    Reference _____

3. When the maximum allowable water pressure within a building is exceeded, a _____ is required.

    a. flow control valve (vented)

    b. pressure reducing valve

    c. in-line pressure balancing valve

    d. pressure relief valve

    Reference _____

4. Where quick-closing valves are utilized in a water distribution system, a _____ shall be installed.
   a. pressure reducing valve
   b. flow control device
   c. water hammer arrestor
   d. pressure relief valve

   Reference _____

5. Joints between polyethylene of raised temperature (PE-RT) plastic tubing and fittings shall be _____ joints.
   a. heat-fusion
   b. mechanical
   c. solvent cemented
   d. threaded

   Reference _____

6. The maximum allowable lead content of water supply pipe and fittings supplying water for cooking or drinking is _____ percent.
   a. 0.02
   b. 8
   c. 2
   d. 0.25

   Reference _____

7. Which of the following is required to be installed with a pressure reducing valve?
   a. strainer
   b. ball valve
   c. check valve
   d. vacuum breaker

   Reference _____

8. Polypropylene (PP) pipe conforming to _____ is approved for water distribution piping.
   a. ASTM D1785
   b. AWWA C151
   c. ASTM F2239
   d. ASTM F2389

   Reference _____

9. Hot water distribution piping and tubing shall have a minimum pressure rating of _____ psi at _____ °F.
   a. 100, 180
   b. 160, 210
   c. 110, 140
   d. 120, 200

   Reference _____

10. Gate valves intended to supply drinking water shall comply with _____.

   a. NSF 18
   b. NSF 61
   c. ASSE 1016
   d. ASSE 1017

   Reference _____

11. Which of the following transition fitting materials is approved for a connection between copper or copper-alloy and galvanized steel piping?

   a. plastic
   b. copper alloy
   c. galvanized steel
   d. stainless steel

   Reference _____

12. The pressure rating of Schedule 80 PVC or CPVC water pipe is reduced by _____ percent when threaded.

   a. 10
   b. 25
   c. 35
   d. 50

   Reference _____

13. Where street main pressures are known to be variable, the _____ available pressure is used as the design criteria for the water distribution system.

   a. mean
   b. maximum
   c. minimum
   d. average

   Reference _____

14. The minimum pressure rating for water service piping is _____ psi at 73.4°F.

   a. 100
   b. 150
   c. 160
   d. 200

   Reference _____

15. A parallel water distribution system has a supply branch from a manifold to a shower that is fifty feet in developed length. The available pressure at the meter is 60 PSI. What is the minimum required size of the fixture supply to the shower?

   a. $1/4$ inch
   b. $3/8$ inch
   c. $1/2$ inch
   d. $5/8$ inch

   Reference _____

16. What is the maximum allowable lead composition in a solder classified as *lead free*?
    a. 0 percent
    b. 0.2 percent
    c. 2 percent
    d. 8 percent

    Reference _____

17. The maximum water consumption flow rate for nonmetered public lavatories is _____ gpm at 60 psi.
    a. 0.25
    b. 0.5
    c. 2
    d. 2.2

    Reference _____

18. The maximum water consumption flow rate for a blow-out type water closet is _____ gallons per flush.
    a. 1.6
    b. 3.5
    c. 1.0
    d. 2.2

    Reference _____

19. Individual water supply system pumps installed in basements shall be mounted not less than _____ inches above the basement floor.
    a. 18
    b. 16
    c. 12
    d. 8

    Reference _____

20. Water service pipe shall be not less than _____ inch(es) in diameter.
    a. $3/4$
    b. $1/2$
    c. 1
    d. $1\,1/4$

    Reference _____

21. In general, water service pipe shall be separated horizontally from the building sewer by a minimum of _____ feet of undisturbed or compacted earth.
    a. 3
    b. 4
    c. 5
    d. 6

    Reference _____

22. Water service pipe is permitted in the same trench as the building sewer, provided the bottom of the water service pipe is not less than _____ inches above the top of the highest point of the sewer.

    a. 24   b. 6
    c. 18   d. 12

    Reference _____

23. In all cases, solvent cement joints of CPVC/AL/CPVC water piping require a primer if the pipe size is greater than _____ inch(es) in diameter.

    a. 1 1/4   b. 1 1/2
    c. 2   d. 1

    Reference _____

24. For underground PVC water service piping, solvent-cement joints require _____ primer.

    a. purple   b. yellow
    c. orange   d. no

    Reference _____

25. A flush valve urinal requires a minimum fixture supply pipe size of _____ inch.

    a. 3/8   b. 1/2
    c. 3/4   d. 1

    Reference _____

Study Session 7

2018 IPC Sections 606 through 613
Water Supply and Distribution II

OBJECTIVE: To develop an understanding of the code provisions related to potable water supply and its protection against contamination. To develop an understanding of the provisions that ensure the supply of adequate cold and hot water to each fixture.

REFERENCE: Sections 606 through 613, 2018 *International Plumbing Code*

KEY POINTS:
- Where are full-open valves required? Shutoff valves?
- What are the access and identification requirements for shutoff and full open valves?
- At what point is a water pressure booster required, and what type of booster system is permitted? What are the installation requirements?
- What are the labeling requirements for water distribution pipes installed in bundles?
- Which fixtures require a hot water supply? Which fixtures may have either hot water or tempered water?
- What limitations are placed on the developed length of hot water piping?
- What controls are placed on thermal expansion?
- Which is the correct side for the installation of hot water to a fixture faucet?
- When is pipe insulation required?
- How is the potable water supply protected from contamination?
- What are the identification requirements for nonpotable water systems?
- What are the various methods of backflow prevention and what applications are approved for each method?
- What methods are approved for protecting the potable water supply at the outlets?
- What is the minimum height of an air gap above the fixture flood level rim?
- What are the connection requirements for automatic sprinkler systems and standpipe systems?
- What are the access, protection and maintenance requirements for backflow prevention assemblies?

KEY POINTS:
(Cont'd)
- What requirements apply to the location and construction of individual water supply wells?
- What water supply and connection requirements apply to health care plumbing?
- When is disinfection of the potable water system required?
- What standards apply to drinking water treatment units?

Topic: Location of Shutoff Valves
Reference: IPC 606.2
Category: Water Supply and Distribution
Subject: Water Distribution System Installation

Code Text: Shutoff valves shall be installed in the following locations:

1. On the fixture supply to each plumbing fixture other than bathtubs and showers in one- and two-family residential occupancies, and other than in individual sleeping units that are provided with unit shutoff valves in hotels, motels, boarding houses and similar occupancies.
2. On the water supply pipe to each sillcock.
3. On the water supply pipe to each appliance or mechanical equipment.

Discussion and Commentary: A shutoff valve, unlike a full-open valve, has no requirements for the cross-sectional area of flow. Therefore, there is a greater pressure drop through a shutoff valve when compared to a full-open valve. Shutoff valves are commonly referred to as *stops* and include globe valves and straight and angle stops.

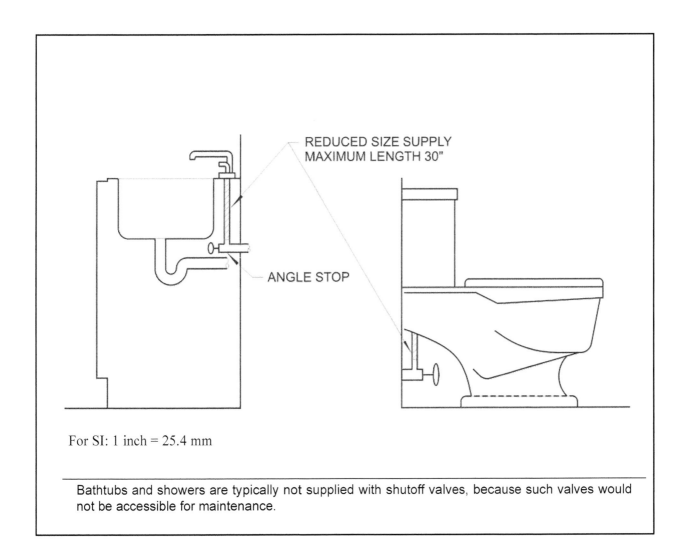

For SI: 1 inch = 25.4 mm

Bathtubs and showers are typically not supplied with shutoff valves, because such valves would not be accessible for maintenance.

Topic: Access to Valves
Reference: IPC 606.3
Category: Water Supply and Distribution
Subject: Water Distribution System Installation

Code Text: *Access shall be provided to all full-open valves and shutoff valves.*

Discussion and Commentary: Valves of full-open type and shutoff valves require access for the purposes of repair and maintenance. This requirement is not based on whether such valves are required by the code. All such valves, required by code or installed by choice, must be accessible.

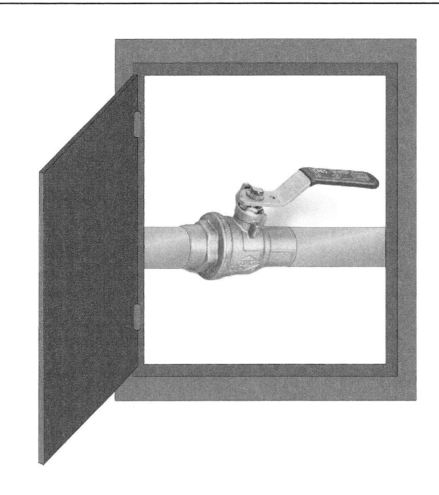

The code permits an access cover such as a panel, door or similar obstruction that must be moved or removed to gain access to the valve.

Topic: Where Required
Reference: IPC 607.1

Category: Water Supply and Distribution
Subject: Hot Water Supply System

Code Text: *In residential occupancies, hot water shall be supplied to all plumbing fixtures and equipment utilized for bathing, washing, culinary purposes, cleansing, laundry or building maintenance. In nonresidential occupancies, hot water shall be supplied for culinary purposes, cleansing, laundry or building maintenance purposes. In nonresidential occupancies, hot water or tempered water shall be supplied for bathing and washing purposes. Tempered water shall be supplied through a water temperature limiting device that conforms to ASSE 1070/ASME A112.1070/CSA B125.70 and shall limit the tempered water to a maximum of 110°F (43°C). This provision shall not supersede the requirement for protective shower valves in accordance with Section 412.3.*

Discussion and Commentary: Hot water is necessary primarily for convenience and the comfort of building occupants. In certain occupancies, tempered water (water ranging in temperature from 85°F to 110°F) (see the definition of tempered water in Section 202) may be supplied in lieu of hot water. For example, in a restaurant, tempered water could be supplied to a hand-washing sink instead of hot water. Tempered water must be supplied to all hand-washing fixtures located in public toilet facilities in accordance with Section 419.5, regardless of the occupancy. A water temperature limiting device is required to limit the tempered water temperature to 110°F. The water heater thermostat control cannot be substituted for required devices for limiting the temperature of hot or tempered water delivered to the fixture.

Hot water must be supplied to service sinks, which are used for cleaning and building maintenance purposes. The code defines hot water as water at a temperature of 110°F or greater.

Study Session 8

Topic: Supply to Fixtures
Reference: IPC 607.2
Category: Water Supply and Distribution
Subject: Hot Water Supply System

Code Text: *The developed length of hot or tempered water piping, from the source of hot water to the fixtures that require hot or tempered water, shall not exceed 50 feet (15 240 mm). Recirculating system piping and heat-traced piping shall be considered to be sources of hot or tempered water.*

Discussion and Commentary: Limiting the distance between hot or tempered water sources and the fixture outlet reduces the length of time it takes for heated water to reach the user, thereby conserving water and the energy necessary to heat the water.

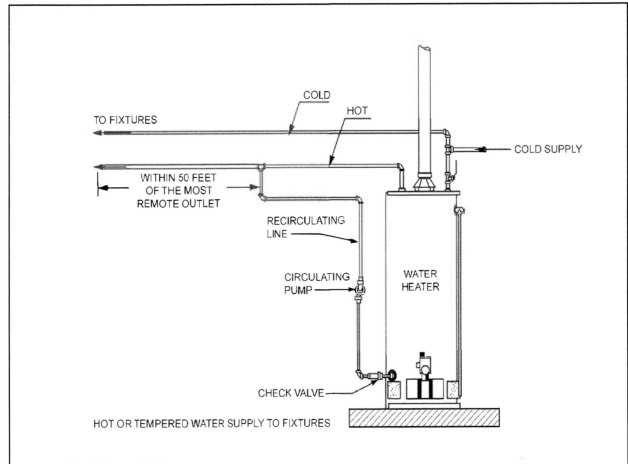

For SI: 1 foot = 304.8 mm

Recirculating system piping and heat-traced piping maintain the temperature of the heated water and are considered sources of hot or tempered water. Therefore, the maximum distance of 50 feet is measured from the connection to the recirculating system or the heat traced piping when available.

Topic: Flow of Hot Water to Fixtures
Reference: IPC 607.4

Category: Water Supply and Distribution
Subject: Hot Water Supply System

Code Text: *Fixture fittings, faucets and diverters shall be installed and adjusted so that the flow of hot water from the fittings corresponds to the left-hand side of the fixture fitting. Exception: Shower and tub/shower mixing valves conforming to ASSE 1016/ASME A112.1016/ CSA B125.16 or ASME A112.18.1/CSA B125.1, where the flow of hot water corresponds to the markings on the device.*

Discussion and Commentary: One of the oldest expressions in plumbing is "Hot on the left, cold on the right." The code mandates that hot corresponds to the left side of the fixture fitting for safety reasons. It has become an accepted practice to equate the left side of the faucet with hot water. The intent is to protect an individual from potential scalding when turning on what is believed to be cold water is actually hot water.

Sinks and other fixtures require hot water controls to be on the left side of the fixture. An exception permits shower and tub/shower mixing valves to have the flow of hot water correspond to the markings on the device.

Study Session 8

Topic: General Provisions
Reference: IPC 608.1

Category: Water Supply and Distribution
Subject: Potable Water Supply Protection

Code Text: *A potable water supply system shall be designed, installed and maintained in such a manner so as to prevent contamination from nonpotable liquids, solids or gases being introduced into the potable water supply through cross-connections or any other piping connections to the system. Backflow preventer applications shall conform to Table 608.1, except as specifically stated in Sections 608.2 through 608.17.10.*

Discussion and Commentary: The most important aspect of a plumbing code is the protection of potable water systems. Documented local and widespread occurrences of sickness and disease have occurred because of inadequate safeguarding of the water supply.

TABLE 608.1
APPLICATION OF BACKFLOW PREVENTERS

DEVICE	DEGREE OF HAZARD[a]	APPLICATION[b]	APPLICABLE STANDARDS
Backflow prevention assemblies:			
Double check backflow prevention assembly and double check fire protection backflow prevention assembly	Low hazard	Backpressure or backsiphonage Sizes $3/8''–16''$	ASSE 1015, AWWA C510, CSA B64.5, CSA B64.5.1
Double check detector fire protection backflow prevention assemblies	Low hazard	Backpressure or backsiphonage Sizes $2''–16''$	ASSE 1048
Pressure vacuum breaker assembly	High or low hazard	Backsiphonage only Sizes $1/2''–2''$	ASSE 1020, CSA B64.1.2
Reduced pressure principle backflow prevention assembly and reduced pressure principle fire protection backflow assembly	High or low hazard	Backpressure or backsiphonage Sizes $3/8''–16''$	ASSE 1013, AWWA C511, CSA B64.4, CSA B64.4.1
Reduced pressure detector fire protection backflow prevention assemblies	High or low hazard	Backsiphonage or backpressure (Fire sprinkler systems)	ASSE 1047
Spill-resistant vacuum breaker assembly	High or low hazard	Backsiphonage only Sizes $1/4''–2''$	ASSE 1056; CSA B64.1.3
Backflow preventer plumbing devices:			
Antisiphon-type fill valves for gravity water closet flush tanks	High hazard	Backsiphonage only	ASSE 1002/ASME A112.1002/CSA B125.12, CSA B125.3
Backflow preventer for carbonated beverage machines	Low hazard	Backpressure or backsiphonage Sizes $1/4''–3/8''$	ASSE 1022
Backflow preventer with intermediate atmospheric vents	Low hazard	Backpressure or backsiphonage Sizes $1/4''–3/4''$	ASSE 1012, CSA B64.3
Dual-check-valve-type backflow preventer	Low hazard	Backpressure or backsiphonage Sizes $1/4''–1''$	ASSE 1024, CSA B64.6
Hose connection backflow preventer	High or low hazard	Low head backpressure, rated working pressure, backpressure or backsiphonage Sizes $1/2''–1''$	ASME A112.21.3, ASSE 1052, CSA B64.2.1.1
Hose connection vacuum breaker	High or low hazard	Low head backpressure or backsiphonage Sizes $1/2''$, $3/4''$, $1''$	ASME A112.21.3, ASSE 1011, CSA B64.2, CSA B64.2.1
Laboratory faucet backflow preventer	High or low hazard	Low head backpressure and backsiphonage	ASSE 1035, CSA B64.7
Pipe-applied atmospheric-type vacuum breaker	High or low hazard	Backsiphonage only Sizes $1/4''–4''$	ASSE 1001, CSA B64.1.1
Vacuum breaker wall hydrants, frost-resistant, automatic-draining type	High or low hazard	Low head backpressure or backsiphonage Sizes $3/4''$, $1''$	ASME A112.21.3, ASSE 1019, CSA B64.2.2
Other means or methods:			
Air gap	High or low hazard	Backsiphonage or backpressure	ASME A112.1.2
Air gap fittings for use with plumbing fixtures, appliances and appurtenances	High or low hazard	Backsiphonage or backpressure	ASME A112.1.3
Barometric loop	High or low hazard	Backsiphonage only	(See Section 608.14.4)

For SI: 1 inch = 25.4 mm.
a. Low hazard—See Pollution (Section 202).
   High hazard—See Contamination (Section 202).
b. See Backpressure, low head (Section 202).
   See Backsiphonage (Section 202).

It is imperative that the potable water supply be maintained in a safe-for-drinking condition at all times and at all outlets.

Topic: Reduced Pressure Backflow Preventer **Category:** Water Supply and Distribution
Reference: IPC 608.14.2 **Subject:** Potable Water Supply Protection

Code Text: *Reduced pressure principle backflow prevention assemblies shall conform to ASSE 1013, AWWA C511, CSA B64.4 or CSA B64.4.1. Reduced pressure detector assembly backflow preventers shall conform to ASSE 1047. These devices shall be permitted to be installed where subject to continuous pressure conditions. The relief opening shall discharge by air gap and shall be prevented from being submerged.*

Discussion and Commentary: A reduced pressure principle backflow preventer is considered to be the most reliable mechanical method for preventing backflow. These devices consist of dual independently acting, spring-loaded check valves that are separated by a chamber or *zone* equipped with a relief valve. The pressure downstream of the device and in the central chamber between the check valves is maintained at a minimum of 2 psi less than the potable water supply pressure at the device inlet, hence the name *reduced pressure principle*. The relief valve located in the central chamber is held closed by the pressure differential between the inlet supply pressure and the central chamber pressure.

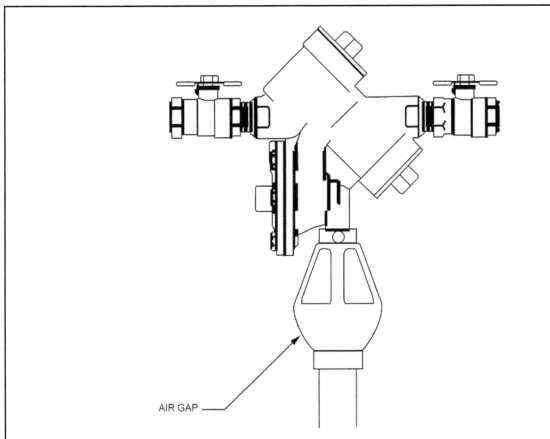

REDUCED PRESSURE PRINCIPLE BACKFLOW PREVENTION ASSEMBLY

In the event of backpressure or negative supply pressure, the relief valve will open to the atmosphere and drain any backflow that has leaked through the check valve. The relief vent will also allow air to enter to prevent any siphonage.

Study Session 8

Topic: Barometric Loop
Reference: IPC 608.14.4

Category: Water Supply and Distribution
Subject: Potable Water Supply Protection

Code Text: *Barometric loops shall precede the point of connection and shall extend vertically to a height of 35 feet (10 668 mm). A barometric loop shall only be utilized as an atmospheric-type or pressure-type vacuum breaker.*

Discussion and Commentary: The code considers a barometric loop to be equivalent to a vacuum breaker and allows it to be installed in any location where a vacuum breaker would otherwise be required.

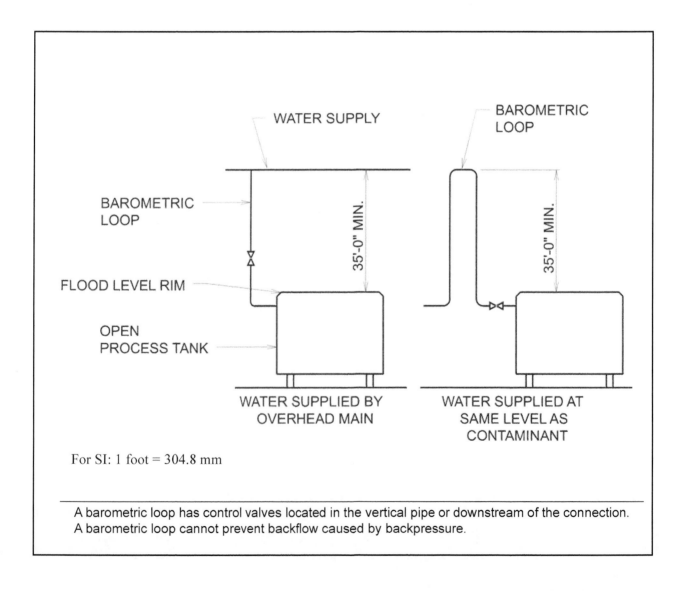

For SI: 1 foot = 304.8 mm

A barometric loop has control valves located in the vertical pipe or downstream of the connection. A barometric loop cannot prevent backflow caused by backpressure.

180   2018 IPC Study Companion

Topic: Atmospheric-Type Vacuum Breakers **Category:** Water Supply and Distribution
Reference: IPC 608.14.6 **Subject:** Potable Water Supply Protection

Code Text: *Pipe-applied atmospheric-type vacuum breakers shall conform to ASSE 1001 or CSA-B64.1.1. Hose-connection vacuum breakers shall conform to ASME A112.21.3, ASSE 1011, ASSE 1019, ASSE 1035, ASSE 1052, CSA B64.2, CSA B64.2.1, CSA B64.2.1.1, CSA B64.2.2 or CSA B64.7. These devices shall operate under normal atmospheric pressure when the critical level is installed at the required height.*

Discussion and Commentary: An atmospheric vacuum breaker is designed to prevent siphonic action from occurring downstream of the device. When siphon action or a vacuum is applied to the water supply, the vacuum breaker opens to the supply inlet of the vacuum breaker, and the disc float drops over the opening. Air enters the atmospheric port opening, allowing the remaining water in the piping downstream from the vacuum breaker to drain.

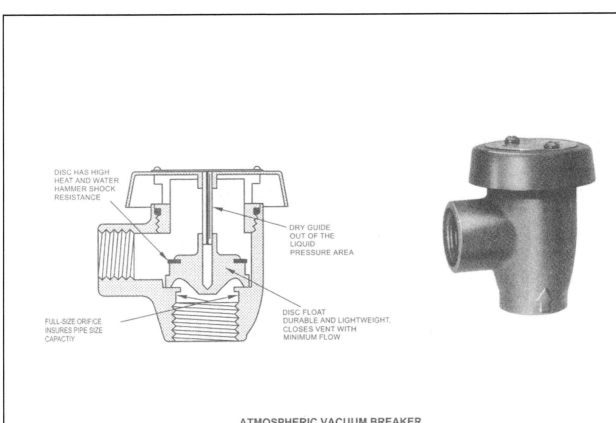

ATMOSPHERIC VACUUM BREAKER
(Illustration courtesy of Watts Regulator Company)

Valves must not be installed downstream of this device, as this would subject the device to supply pressure, thereby rendering it inoperative.

Topic: Double Check-Valve Assemblies
Reference: IPC 608.14.7
Category: Water Supply and Distribution
Subject: Potable Water Supply Protection

Code Text: *Double check backflow prevention assemblies shall conform to ASSE 1015, CSA B64.5, CSA B64.5.1 or AWWA C510. Double check detector fire protection backflow prevention assemblies shall conform to ASSE 1048. These devices shall be capable of operating under continuous pressure conditions.*

Discussion and Commentary: These devices are designed for low-hazard applications subject to backpressure and back-siphonage applications. The devices consist of two independent spring-loaded check valves in series. Test cocks are provided to permit testing of the devices.

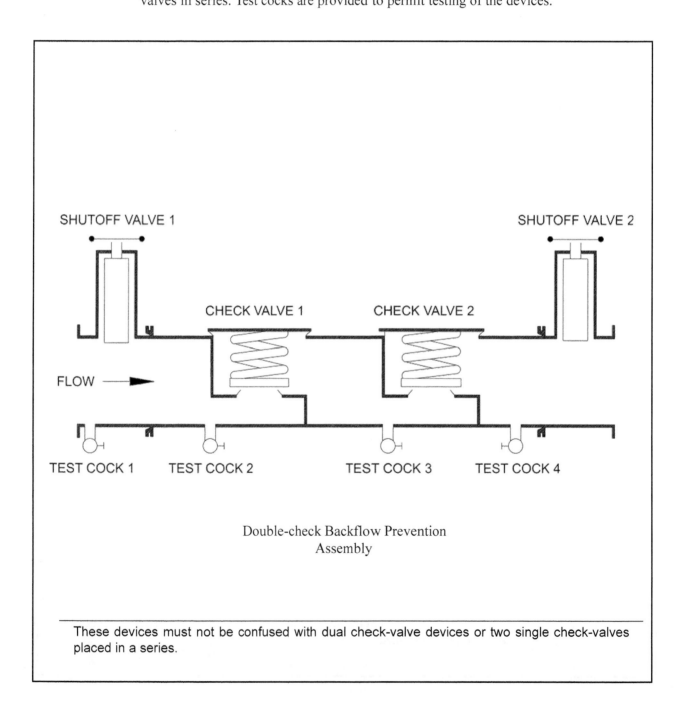

Double-check Backflow Prevention Assembly

These devices must not be confused with dual check-valve devices or two single check-valves placed in a series.

Topic: Protection by Air Gap
Reference: IPC 608.16.1

Category: Water Supply and Distribution
Subject: Potable Water Supply Protection

Code Text: *Openings and outlets shall be protected by an air gap between the opening and the fixture flood level rim as specified in Table 608.16.1. Openings and outlets equipped for hose connection shall be protected by means other than an air gap.*

Discussion and Commentary: An air gap between the fixture supply outlet and the flood level rim is a simple and effective means to prevent backflow and contamination of the water supply. The minimum air gap distance is based on the type of fixture, the diameter of the outlet and the proximity to a wall or a wall corner in accordance with Table 608.16.1. An air gap is not appropriate for an outlet with a hose connection, as occurs at a mop sink, because the hose can become submerged and be a source of contamination to the potable water supply. A vacuum breaker is required for backflow protection at hose connections.

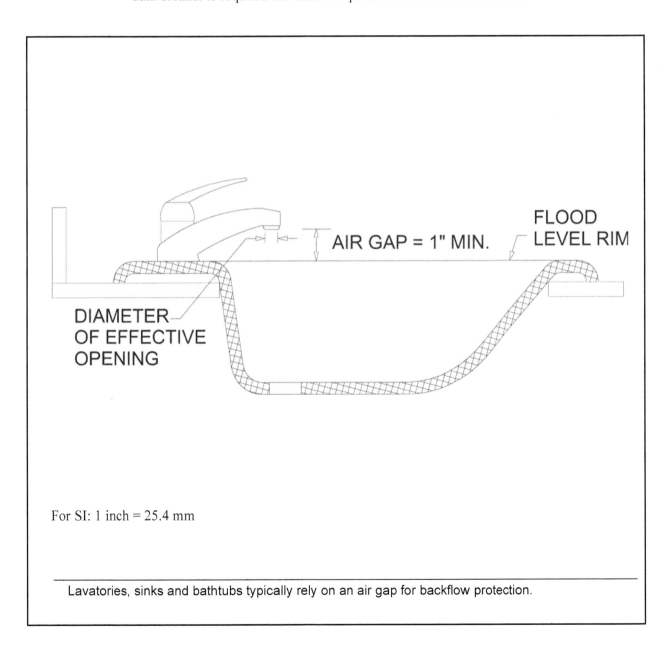

Lavatories, sinks and bathtubs typically rely on an air gap for backflow protection.

Topic: Beverage Dispensers
Reference: IPC 608.17.1
Category: Water Supply and Distribution
Subject: Potable Water Supply Protection

Code Text: *The water supply connection to each carbonated beverage dispenser shall be protected against backflow by a backflow preventer conforming to ASSE 1022 or by an air gap. The portion of the backflow preventer device downstream from the second check valve of the device and the piping downstream therefrom shall not be affected by carbon dioxide gas. The water supply connection to each coffee machine and each noncarbonated beverage dispenser shall be protected against backflow by a backflow preventer conforming to ASSE 1022 or ASSE 1024, or protected by an air gap.*

Discussion and Commentary: When connected to the water distribution system, beverage dispensing machines have the potential for creating cross connection and as such must be protected by a backflow preventer or an integral air gap. An ASSE 1022 backflow preventer, specially designed for carbon dioxide exposure, is approved for a carbonated drink dispenser, and is not required for noncarbonated drink dispensers or coffee machines. Coffee machines and noncarbonated beverage dispensers can be connected to the potable water supply using either an ASSE 1024 or ASSE 22 backflow preventer. The ASSE 1022 device has a vent opening that leaks water when the downstream check valve of the device fails. The leaking water requires a safe point of discharge (a drain). The ASSE 1024 device (which does not have a vent opening) does not need a drain, thus simplifying installations for noncarbonated drink dispensers and coffee machines.

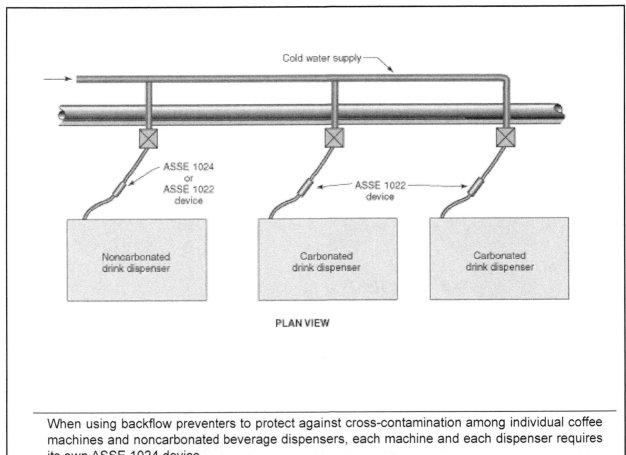

When using backflow preventers to protect against cross-contamination among individual coffee machines and noncarbonated beverage dispensers, each machine and each dispenser requires its own ASSE 1024 device.

Topic: Connections to Fire Sprinkler System **Category:** Water Supply and Distribution
Reference: IPC 608.17.4 **Subject:** Potable Water Supply Protection

Code Text: *The potable water supply to automatic fire sprinkler and standpipe systems shall be protected against backflow by a double check backflow prevention assembly, a double check fire protection backflow prevention assembly or a reduced pressure principle fire protection backflow prevention assembly.* See exceptions for systems installed as a portion of the water distribution system and for deluge, preaction or dry pipe sprinkler systems.

Discussion and Commentary: A double check backflow prevention assembly is the minimum form of backflow prevention required between the potable water supply and an automatic fire sprinkler system or standpipe system. Protection by a double check backflow prevention assembly is permitted only where the sprinkler or standpipe system is filled from a potable water source.

If antifreeze or other chemicals are added to a sprinkler or standpipe system, or if a nonpotable hazardous secondary supply system is involved, the potable water supply must be protected with a reduced pressure principle backflow prevention assembly.

Study Session 8

Topic: Additives or Nonpotable Source
Reference: IPC 608.17.4.1
Category: Water Supply and Distribution
Subject: Potable Water Supply Protection

Code Text: *Where systems under continuous pressure contain chemical additives or antifreeze, or where systems are connected to a nonpotable secondary water supply, the potable water supply shall be protected against backflow by a reduced pressure principle backflow prevention assembly or a reduced pressure principle fire protection backflow prevention assembly. Where chemical additives or antifreeze are added to only a portion of an automatic fire sprinkler or standpipe system, the reduced pressure principle backflow prevention assembly or the reduced pressure principle fire protection backflow prevention assembly shall be permitted to be located so as to isolate that portion of the system. Where systems are not under continuous pressure, the potable water supply shall be protected against backflow by an air gap or an atmospheric vacuum breaker conforming to ASSE 1001 or CSA B64.1.1.*

Discussion and Commentary: A nonpotable secondary water supply for fire sprinkler systems could include above- or below-ground tanks, private wells, ponds, reservoirs and lakes. In the event of loss or inadequacy of the primary potable supply, the secondary nonpotable water source is pumped into the system, thereby contaminating the potable supply in the event backflow occurs. Fire suppression systems that are not under continuous pressure are classified as indirect cross connections. When subject to only backsiphonage, these systems may be protected by an atmospheric-type vacuum breaker conforming to ASSE 1001 or CSA B64.1.1. These devices protect the potable water supply against pollutants or contaminants that could otherwise enter the system because of backsiphonage through the outlet.

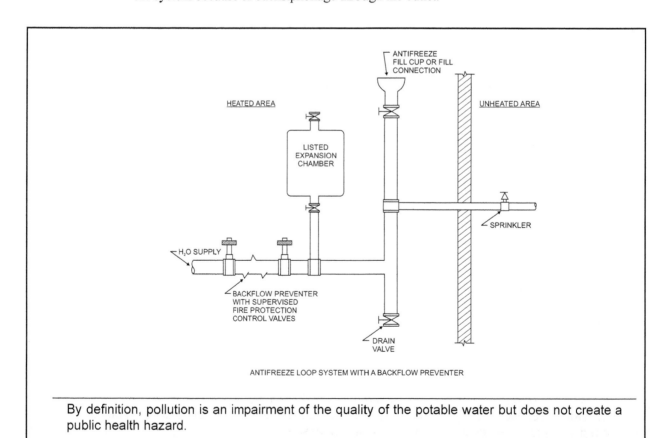

ANTIFREEZE LOOP SYSTEM WITH A BACKFLOW PREVENTER

By definition, pollution is an impairment of the quality of the potable water but does not create a public health hazard.

Topic: Humidifiers
Reference: IPC 608.17.10
Category: Water Supply and Distribution
Subject: Potable Water Supply Protection

Code Text: *The water supply connection to humidifiers that do not have internal backflow protection shall be protected against backflow by a backflow preventer conforming to ASSE 1012 or by an air gap.*

Discussion and Commentary: Humidifiers may have contaminated water that could flow into the potable water system if a backflow event occurs. If the humidifier has an internal backflow device no additional protection is required. Otherwise, protection must be provided with an air gap or an ASSE 1012 backflow preventer.

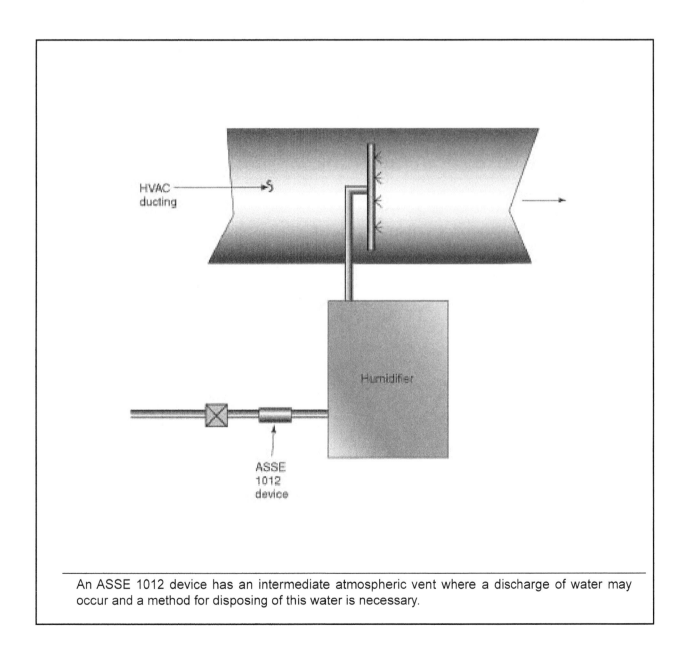

An ASSE 1012 device has an intermediate atmospheric vent where a discharge of water may occur and a method for disposing of this water is necessary.

Topic: Water-Tight Casings
Reference: IPC 608.18.4
Category: Water Supply and Distribution
Subject: Individual Water Supply Protection

Code Text: *Each well shall be provided with a water-tight casing to not less than 10 feet (3048 mm) below the ground surface. Casings shall extend not less than 6 inches (152 mm) above the well platform. Casings shall be large enough to permit installation of a separate drop pipe. Casings shall be sealed at the bottom in an impermeable stratum or extend several feet into the water-bearing stratum.*

Discussion and Commentary: Any contaminant can enter the well with relative ease if the well does not have a proper casing. High-water tables are more susceptible to contamination because of their close proximity to the ground surface.

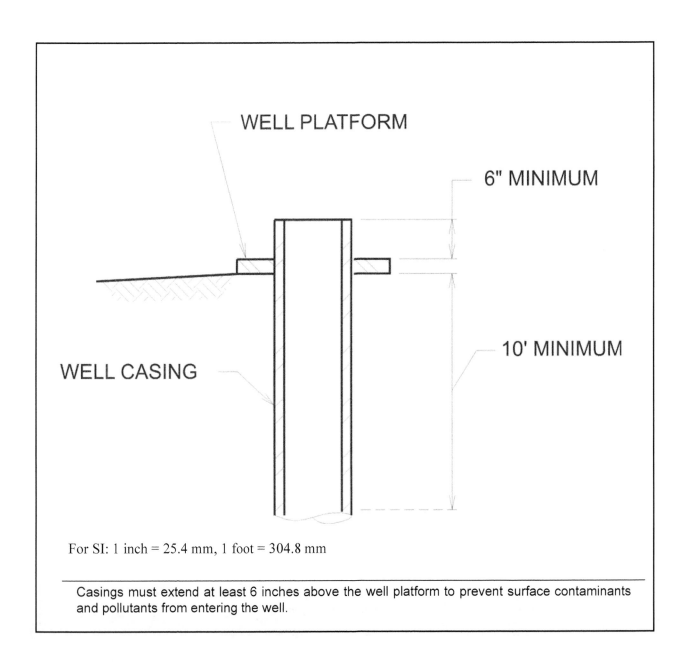

For SI: 1 inch = 25.4 mm, 1 foot = 304.8 mm

Casings must extend at least 6 inches above the well platform to prevent surface contaminants and pollutants from entering the well.

Topic: Cover
Reference: IPC 608.18.7
Category: Water Supply and Distribution
Subject: Individual Water Supply Protection

Code Text: *Potable water wells shall be equipped with an overlapping water-tight cover at the top of the well casing or pipe sleeve such that contaminated water or other substances are prevented from entering the well through the annular opening at the top of the well casing, wall or pipe sleeve. Covers shall extend downward not less than 2 inches (51 mm) over the outside of the well casing or wall. A dug well cover shall be provided with a pipe sleeve permitting the withdrawal of the pump suction pipe, cylinder or jet body without disturbing the cover. Where pump sections or discharge pipes enter or leave a well through the side of the casing, the circle of contact shall be water tight.*

Discussion and Commentary: A cover serves to protect the well water from contamination from an outside source. It must fit firmly to the casing with cracks or openings filled tightly to create a watertight seal.

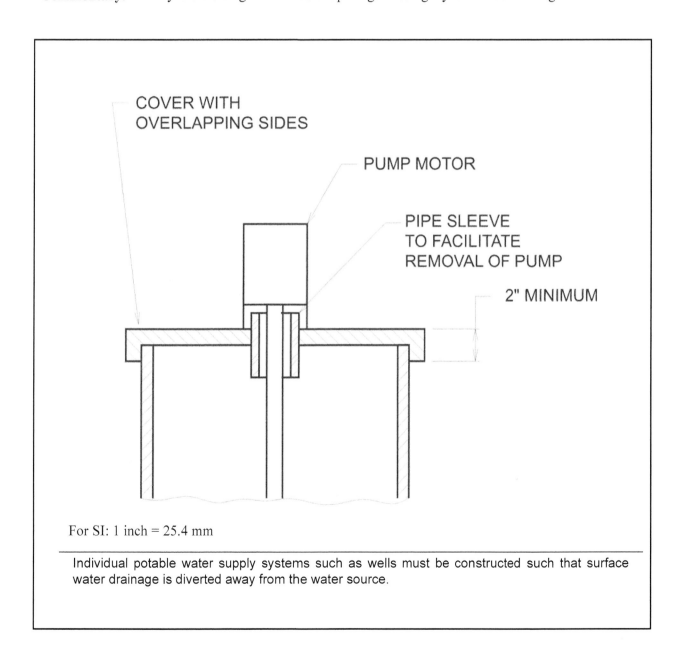

For SI: 1 inch = 25.4 mm

Individual potable water supply systems such as wells must be constructed such that surface water drainage is diverted away from the water source.

Quiz

Study Session 8
IPC Sections 606 through 613

1. In one- and two-family residential occupancies, the water supply to a _____ does not require a shutoff valve.

    a. kitchen sink   b. sillcock

    c. mechanical appliance d. bathtub

    Reference _____

2. Which valves in the distribution system are required to be identified?

    a. all valves

    b. service valves only

    c. sillcock valves, pressure reducing valves and backflow prevention valves

    d. service valves, hose bibb valves and those remote from the fixtures served

    Reference _____

3. In nonresidential occupancies, tempered water for washing purposes shall be limited to not more than _____ °F by a temperature limiting device.

    a. 105   b. 140

    c. 110   d. 120

    Reference _____

4. A water supply tank with a filling capacity of 175 GPM requires a minimum _____ -inch diameter overflow.

    a. 2½   b. 3

    c. 4   d. 6

Reference _____

5. A _____ valve is required on the water supply to a water heater.

    a. globe   b. shutoff

    c. full-open   d. gate

Reference _____

6. Which of the following devices is not approved for isolating a high-hazard cross-connection?

    a. spill-resistant vacuum breaker assembly

    b. double check backflow prevention assembly

    c. hose connection vacuum breaker

    d. reduced pressure principle backflow prevention assembly

Reference _____

7. Nonpotable water distribution piping must be identified by the color _____.

    a. orange   b. red

    c. gray   d. purple

Reference _____

8. A thermal expansion tank is required for a storage water heater having a _____ on the cold water line to the water heater.

    a. low-pressure cutoff

    b. full-open valve

    c. hose bibb

    d. check valve

Reference _____

9. A _____ backflow prevention assembly is not approved for protection of the potable water supply to an automatic fire sprinkler system.

   a. pressure vacuum breaker

   b. reduced-pressure-principle fire protection

   c. double check

   d. double check fire protection

   Reference _____

10. An irrigation system that has been designed for application of chemicals using a pump assisted chemical hopper must be isolated from the potable water supply by a(n) _____.

    a. barometric loop

    b. atmospheric vacuum breaker

    c. pressure vacuum breaker assembly

    d. reduced pressure principle backflow prevention assembly

    Reference _____

11. Within a building, piping for a nonpotable water system must be labeled every _____ feet or less.

    a. 100   b. 50

    c. 25   d. 12

    Reference _____

12. The minimum air gap required for a whirlpool tub filler spout with a 1-inch diameter effective opening that is located away from sidewalls is _____.

    a. 1 inch   b. 1.5 inches

    c. 2 inches   d. 2.5 inches

    Reference _____

13. For nonpotable water piping with a diameter of 4 inches, identification lettering shall be at least _____ inches high and the background field shall be at least _____ inches in length.

    a. 1.25, 12   b. 1.25, 8

    c. 2.5, 12   d. 2.5, 24

Reference _____

14. A private water well shall be located at least _____ feet from a septic tank.

    a. 10   b. 100

    c. 50   d. 25

Reference _____

15. The minimum concentration of chlorine required for disinfection of a potable water supply system is _____ parts per million for 24 hours.

    a. 25   b. 50

    c. 100   d. 200

Reference _____

16. A vacuum breaker serving a bedpan washer is required to be located a minimum of _____ feet above the floor.

    a. 3   b. 4

    c. 5   d. 6

Reference _____

17. Which of the following is required to prevent the collapse of an elevated pressure tank in a water pressure booster system?

    a. check-valve   b. vacuum breaker

    c. vacuum relief valve   d. pressure reducing valve

Reference _____

18. A barometric loop shall extend vertically to a height of _____ feet.
    a. 25   b. 35
    c. 43.3   d. 50

    Reference _____

19. The warning sign at nonpotable water outlets shall have letters not less than _____ inch in height on a contrasting background.
    a. 1   b. 3/4
    c. 1/2   d. 3/8

    Reference _____

20. Freezeproof yard hydrants that drain the riser into the ground _____.
    a. are prohibited
    b. are permitted when identified as nonpotable
    c. are not considered to be stop-and-waste valves
    d. require integral backflow protection

    Reference _____

21. Approved deck mounted vacuum breakers shall be installed with the critical level not less than _____ above the flood level of the rim.
    a. 6 inches   b. 2 inches
    c. 1 inch   d. 1/2 inch

    Reference _____

22. For fixtures that require hot water, the developed length of the hot water piping from the source to the fixture shall not exceed _____ feet.
    a. 75   b. 25
    c. 50   d. 100

    Reference _____

23. Hose bibbs require protection from backflow by a(n) _____.

   a. air gap

   b. vacuum breaker

   c. reduced pressure principle backflow preventer

   d. double check valve

   Reference _____

24. Where located close to the wall, a lavatory outlet with an effective opening of ½ inch diameter requires a minimum _____ -inch air gap.

   a. 1
   b. 1 ½
   c. 2
   d. 2 ½

   Reference _____

25. If a water purveyor were unable to provide a water supply at flow pressures sufficient to supply the minimum required pressures at the fixtures, all of the following would be a suitable resolution, *except* _____.

   a. oversizing the water distribution piping system

   b. a hydropneumatic pressure booster system

   c. a water pressure booster pump system

   d. an elevated supplemental water supply

   Reference _____

2018 IPC Sections 701 through 707
Sanitary Drainage I

OBJECTIVE: To develop an understanding of the overall code provisions that regulate the materials, design and installation of sanitary drainage. To develop an understanding of the specific provisions of the code that apply to joints and fittings in the sanitary drainage system.

REFERENCE: Sections 701 through 707, 2018 *International Plumbing Code*

KEY POINTS:
- Under what circumstances would a building not have to connect to a public sewer?
- When is a building required to have a separate sewer connection?
- What provisions are made to protect the sanitary drainage system from chemical wastes?
- What limitations apply to drainage piping installed in food service areas?
- What type of alignment is required for horizontal drainage piping?
- Is it permitted to reduce the size of drainage pipe in the direction of flow?
- What precautions are necessary when connecting horizontal branches at the base of drainage stacks?
- Whenever filled or unstable ground is present, what materials are permitted for piping in the ground, and which standards apply?
- Are sanitary and storm building sewers or drains permitted to be laid in one trench?
- What is necessary to prove an existing system can be connected to a new system?
- What limitations are placed on the location of a horizontal branch connection in relation to the base of a stack? A stack offset?
- What materials and fittings are suitable for underground installations? Above ground?
- What type and schedule of plastic pipe is permitted to be threaded?
- What types of fittings and joints are approved for the various types of plastic drainage piping materials?
- When is primer not required for solvent cement joints of PVC plastic piping?
- Under what circumstances can heat fusion joints be used?

KEY POINTS:
(Cont'd)

- What types of joints are approved for vertical and horizontal transitions in drainage piping?
- Under what circumstances may heel- or side-inlet fittings be used?
- Which section applies to joints between cast-iron pipe or fittings?
- Are solvent cement joints permitted below ground?
- What type of joint is to be used to join plastic pipe to other piping material?
- What limitations apply to the use of a double sanitary tee?
- What types of joints and connections are prohibited?

Topic: Separate Sewer Connection
Reference: IPC 701.3
Category: Sanitary Drainage
Subject: General Provisions

Code Text: *A building having plumbing fixtures installed and intended for human habitation, occupancy or use on premises abutting on a street, alley or easement in which there is a public sewer shall have a separate connection with the sewer. Where located on the same lot, multiple buildings shall not be prohibited from connecting to a common building sewer that connects to the public sewer.*

Discussion and Commentary: The code prohibits the combining of sewers serving different buildings prior to connection to the public sewer. The only exception is where the sewers to be combined are serving buildings on the same lot or parcel of land. This section does not prohibit the use of adjoining properties that have been included in a dedicated easement approved by the administrative authority. The common building sewer is an extension of the public sewer and under control of the public authority.

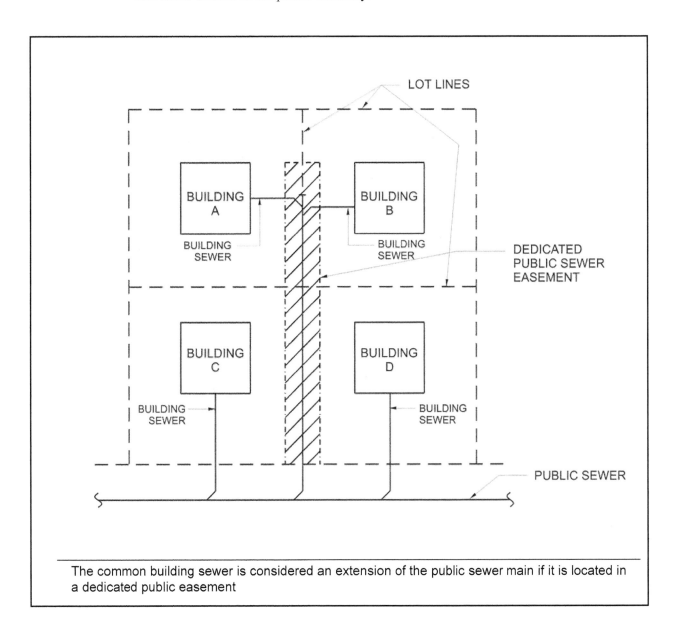

The common building sewer is considered an extension of the public sewer main if it is located in a dedicated public easement

Topic: Chemical Waste System	**Category:** Sanitary Drainage
Reference: IPC 702.6	**Subject:** Materials

Code Text: *A chemical waste system shall be completely separated from the sanitary drainage system. The chemical waste shall be treated in accordance with Section 803.2 before discharging to the sanitary drainage system. Separate drainage systems for chemical wastes and vent pipes shall be of an approved material that is resistant to corrosion and degradation for the concentrations of chemicals involved.*

Discussion and Commentary: There is no universal material available to resist all chemical action. Each pipe has qualities that make it resistant to certain chemical waste systems. An individual analysis of compatibility is required for the installation of a chemical waste and vent system. Piping material such as borosilicate glass or polyolefin plastic is often used for special waste applications. Acid wastes in the vapor state are more corrosive than in the liquid state; therefore, it is important to provide material that resists chemical action for the vent piping as well as for the drainage piping.

803.1 Neutralizing device required for corrosive wastes. Corrosive liquids, spent acids or other harmful chemicals that destroy or injure a drain, sewer, soil or waste pipe, or create noxious or toxic fumes or interfere with sewage treatment processes shall not be discharged into the plumbing system without being thoroughly diluted, neutralized or treated by passing through an approved dilution or neutralizing device. Such devices shall be automatically provided with a sufficient supply of diluting water or neutralizing medium so as to make the contents noninjurious before discharge into the drainage system. The nature of the corrosive or harmful waste and the method of its treatment or dilution shall be approved prior to installation.

803.2 System design. A chemical drainage and vent system shall be designed and installed in accordance with this code. Chemical drainage and vent systems shall be completely separated from the sanitary systems. Chemical waste shall not discharge to a sanitary drainage system until such waste has been treated in accordance with Section 803.1

A measure of the degree of acidity or alkalinity of a liquid is its pH value, which defines the concentration of free hydrogen ions on a scale of 0 to 14. A pH value of 7 is considered neutral.

Topic: Slope of Horizontal Drainage Piping **Category:** Sanitary Drainage
Reference: IPC 704.1 **Subject:** Drainage Piping Installation

Code Text: *Horizontal drainage piping shall be installed in uniform alignment at uniform slopes. The slope of a horizontal drainage pipe shall be not less than that indicated in Table 704.1 except that where the drainage piping is upstream of a grease interceptor, the slope of the piping shall be not less than $^1/_4$ inch per foot (2-percent slope).*

Discussion and Commentary: Optimal drainage piping performance depends on the pipe size and slope, both of which influence the waste velocity within the drain pipe system. If the velocity is too low in a drain pipe that is excessively oversized, the solids tend to drop out of suspension, settling to the bottom of the pipe. This may eventually result in a drain stoppage. A greater velocity is required to move solids at rest than is required to keep moving solids in suspension. In the special case of grease-laden waste, the minimum slope is $^1/_4$ inch per foot. For larger pipe diameters, this is a greater slope than would otherwise be required in Table 704.1 in order to minimize stoppages related to grease.

Prohibited Installation:
Improper slope

The minimum desired velocity in a horizontal drain pipe is approximately 2 feet per second. This velocity is often referred to as the scouring velocity. The *scouring velocity* is intended to keep solids in suspension.

Topic: Reduction in Pipe Size
Reference: IPC 704.2
Category: Sanitary Drainage
Subject: Drainage Piping Installation

Code Text: *The size of the drainage piping shall not be reduced in the direction of the flow. The following shall not be considered as a reduction in size in the direction of flow:*

1. *A 4-inch by 3-inch (102 mm by 76 mm) water closet flange.*
2. *A water closet bend fitting having a 4-inch (102 mm) inlet and a 3-inch (76 mm) outlet provided that the 4-inch leg of the fitting is upright and below, but not necessarily directly connected to, the water closet flange.*
3. *An offset closet flange.*

Discussion and Commentary: One of the fundamental requirements of a drainage system is that piping cannot be reduced in size in the direction of drainage flow. A size reduction would create an obstruction to flow, possibly resulting in a backup of flow, an interruption of service in the drainage system or stoppage in the pipe.

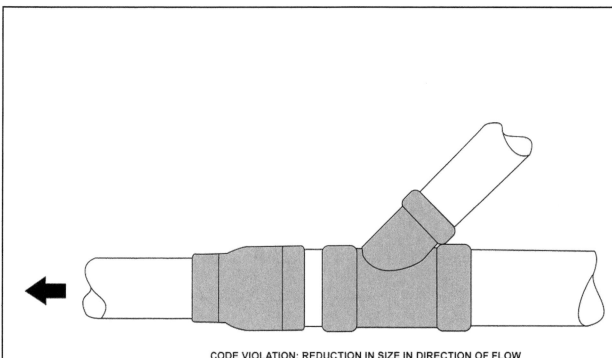

CODE VIOLATION: REDUCTION IN SIZE IN DIRECTION OF FLOW

Water closet flanges, offset bend fittings and offset flanges are specifically listed as exceptions to the provision that drainage piping must not be reduced in size in the direction of flow. These fittings meeting the referenced standards have been used for decades without adverse effects.

Topic: Connections to Stacks
Reference: IPC 704.3
Category: Sanitary Drainage
Subject: Drainage Piping Installation

Code Text: *Horizontal branches shall connect to the bases of stacks at a point located not less than 10 times the diameter of the drainage stack downstream from the stack. Horizontal branches shall connect to horizontal stack offsets at a point located not less than 10 times the diameter of the drainage stack downstream from the upper stack.*

Discussion and Commentary: At the base of every stack, a phenomenon of flow may occur that is commonly called hydraulic jump. Hydraulic jump is the rising in the depth of flow above half full. A horizontal drain designed in accordance with the code is expected to have a normal flow depth of not greater than half full. The rise in flow may be great enough to close off the opening of the pipe, thus creating pressure fluctuations in the system that may affect trap seals. Hydraulic jump occurs within a distance of 10 times the diameter of the drainage stack downstream of the stack connection. To avoid flow interference, backup of flow and extreme pressure fluctuations, horizontal branch connections are prohibited in this area.

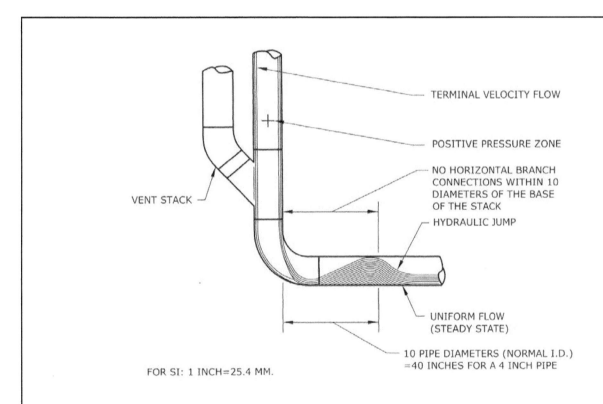

HYDRAULIC JUMP

A horizontal stack offset creates similar flow conditions to those of the horizontal drain at the base of a stack. Therefore, a horizontal branch connecting to the horizontal offset piping also must maintain a distance of 10 pipe diameters from the upper stack.

Topic: Cast Iron Compression Joints
Reference: IPC 705.3.2
Category: Sanitary Drainage
Subject: Joints

Code Text: *Compression gaskets for hub and spigot pipe and fittings shall conform to ASTM C564 and shall be tested to ASTM C1563. Gaskets shall be compressed when the pipe is fully inserted.*

Discussion and Commentary: Compression joints use an elastomeric gasket that is placed in the hub of the cast iron pipe. Lubricant is applied to the inside surface of the gasket material, the spigot end of the connecting pipe is inserted into the gasket, and the pipe sections are pulled together, compressing the gasket and forming a watertight seal. The gaskets must meet the requirements of ASTM C1563.

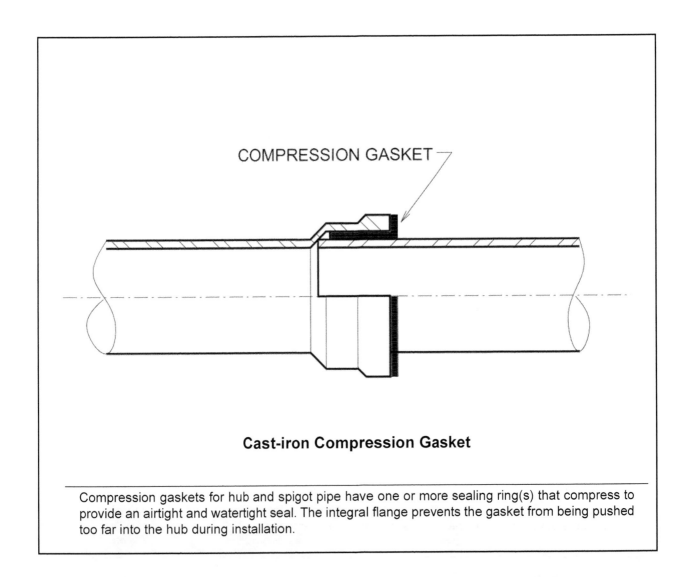

Cast-iron Compression Gasket

Compression gaskets for hub and spigot pipe have one or more sealing ring(s) that compress to provide an airtight and watertight seal. The integral flange prevents the gasket from being pushed too far into the hub during installation.

Topic: Cast Iron Mechanical Joint Coupling **Category:** Sanitary Drainage
Reference: IPC 705.3.3 **Subject:** Joints

Code Text: *Mechanical joint couplings for hubless pipe and fittings shall consist of an elastomeric sealing sleeve and a metallic shield that comply with CISPI 310, ASTM C1277 or ASTM C1540. The elastomeric sealing sleeve shall conform to ASTM C564 or CSA B602 and shall be provided with a center stop. Mechanical joint couplings shall be installed in accordance with the manufacturer's instructions.*

Discussion and Commentary: Mechanical couplings for hubless cast iron pipe have a stainless steel shield, a clamp assembly and an elastomeric sealing sleeve. When the clamp is tightened, the elastomeric material presses against the surface of the pipe to provide an airtight and watertight seal. The sleeve cushions the pipe against shock and vibration. The coupling assembly aligns and protects the pipe joint. The coupling and the elastomeric sleeve must conform to the applicable referenced standard and be installed in accordance with the manufacturer's instructions.

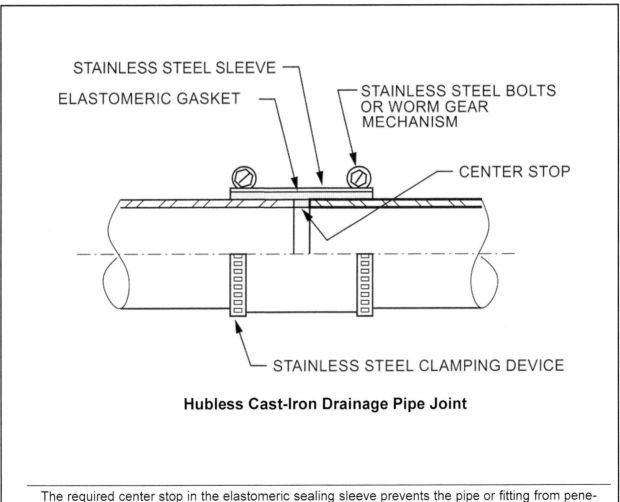

Hubless Cast-Iron Drainage Pipe Joint

The required center stop in the elastomeric sealing sleeve prevents the pipe or fitting from penetrating too far into the coupling and ensures an equal length of elastomeric material on both pipe ends.

Topic: PVC Plastic Mechanical Joints **Category:** Sanitary Drainage
Reference: IPC 705.10.1 **Subject:** Joints

Code Text: *Mechanical joints on drainage pipe shall be made with an elastomeric seal conforming to ASTM C1173, ASTM D3212 or CSA B602. Mechanical joints shall not be installed in above-ground systems, unless otherwise approved. Joints shall be installed in accordance with the manufacturer's instructions.*

Discussion and Commentary: Underground PVC sewer pipe is often installed using a hub pipe connection with an elastomeric compression gasket conforming to ASTM D3212, Standard Specification for Joints for Drain and Sewer Plastic Pipes Using Flexible Elastomeric Seals. The other referenced standards, ASTM C1173, Standard Specification for Flexible Transition Couplings for Underground Piping Systems, and CSA-B602, Mechanical Couplings for Drain, Waste, and Vent Pipe and Sewer Pipe, address flexible and mechanical couplings that may be sleeves or inserts.

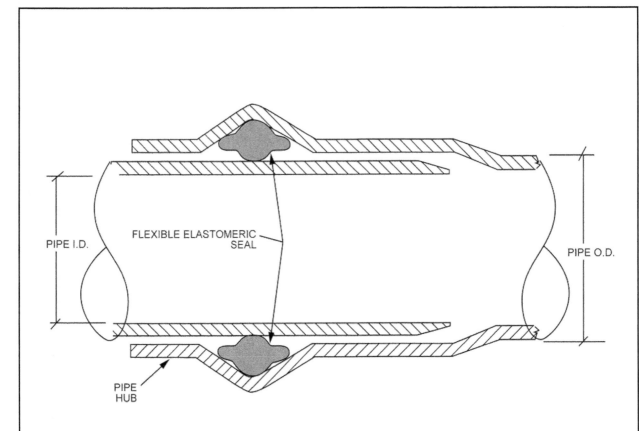

PVC Hub Pipe Joint with Elastomeric Compression Gasket

Mechanical joints for PVC drainage piping are limited to underground use unless otherwise approved by the code official. Installation must follow the manufacturer's instructions.

Topic: PVC Plastic Solvent Cementing
Reference: IPC 705.10.2
Category: Sanitary Drainage
Subject: Joints

Code Text: *Joint surfaces shall be clean and free from moisture. A purple primer that conforms to ASTM F656 shall be applied. Solvent cement not purple in color and conforming to ASTM D2564, CSA B137.3, CSA B181.2 or CSA B182.1 shall be applied to all joint surfaces. The joint shall be made while the cement is wet and shall be in accordance with ASTM D2855. Solvent-cement joints shall be permitted above or below ground.* **Exception:** *A primer is not required where both of the following conditions apply: 1) The solvent cement used is third-party certified as conforming to ASTM D2564. 2) The solvent cement is used only for joining PVC drain, waste and vent pipe and fittings in non-pressure applications in sizes up to and including 4 inches (102 mm) in diameter.*

Discussion and Commentary: PVC solvent cement works by softening the surface of the plastic pipe and fitting to create a strong bond often referred to as "solvent welding." The cement is applied to both the socket of the fitting and the surface of the pipe. While the cement is still wet, the pipe end is inserted into the socket in a twisting motion until it reaches the full depth of the socket and is held in place until the cement sets sufficiently. This method of joining PVC pipe is governed by ASTM D2564, Specification for Solvent Cements for Poly (Vinyl Chloride) (PVC) Pipe and Fittings. The code also requires a two-step process including the application of purple primer for larger diameter pipe and pressure installations.

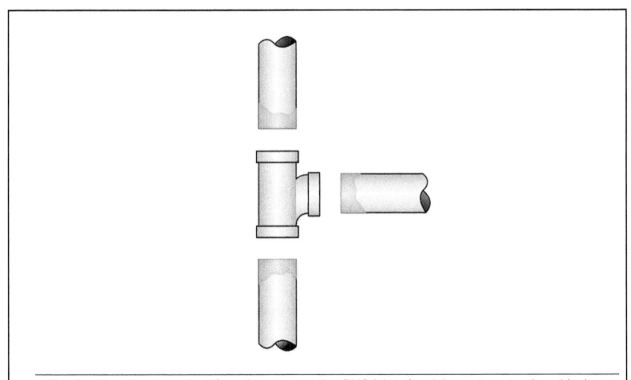

Purple primer is not required for solvent-cementing PVC joints for piping not greater than 4 inches in diameter provided it serves a gravity drainage system. In this case, the solvent cement alone provides sufficient bonding to resist the forces of such a system and often exceeds the pipe and fitting rated pressure capacity.

Topic: Polyethylene Plastic Pipe **Category:** Sanitary Drainage
Reference: IPC 705.12 **Subject:** Joints

Code Text: *Joints between polyethylene plastic pipe and fittings shall be underground. Heat-fusion joint surfaces shall be clean and free from moisture. Joint surfaces shall be cut, heated to melting temperature and joined using tools specifically designed for the operation. Joints shall be undisturbed until cool. Joints shall be made in accordance with ASTM D2657 and the manufacturer's instructions. Mechanical joints in drainage piping shall be made with an elastomeric seal conforming to ASTM C1173, ASTM D3212 or CSA B602. Mechanical joints shall be installed in accordance with the manufacturer's instructions.*

Discussion and Commentary: Polyethylene pipe joints are required to be covered for protection from damage. Requirements for heat fusion and mechanical joints are covered in separate sections. Heat fusion joints are created using special clamping fixtures to maintain alignment and heating devices to soften and fuse the materials.

ASTM
ASTM International
100 Barr Harbor Drive
West Conshohocken, PA 19428-2959

Section	Material	Application	Standard	Title	Applies to IPC Sections
705.12	polyethylene (PE) plastic pipe (SDR-PR)	building sewer pipe	ASTM F714	Specification for Polyethylene (PE) Plastic Pipe (SDR-PR) based on Outside Diameter	Table 702.3

Polyethylene pipe is a plastic pipe that comes in various densities and has a broad range of applications for underground piping systems.

Topic: Installation of Fittings
Reference: IPC 706.3

Category: Sanitary Drainage Piping and Fixture
Subject: Connections between Piping and Fittings

Code Text: *Fittings shall be installed to guide sewage and waste in the direction of flow. Change in direction shall be made by fittings installed in accordance with Table 706.3. Change in direction by combination fittings, side inlets or increasers shall be installed in accordance with Table 706.3 based on the pattern of flow created by the fitting. Double sanitary tee patterns shall not receive the discharge of back-to-back water closets and fixtures or appliances with pumping action discharge.* See exception for back-to-back water closets connecting to a double sanitary tee.

Discussion and Commentary: Drainage fittings and connections must provide a smooth transition of flow without creating obstructions or causing interference. The use of proper fittings helps to maintain the required flow velocities and reduces the possibility of stoppage in the drainage system. Combination fittings are commonly used in drainage systems and must be evaluated for their pattern of flow. Combination fittings include two or more fittings, such as combination wye and eighth bends or tee-wyes. A double sanitary tee (cross) cannot be used for connections to fixtures and appliances with pumping action, as such a fitting has a short pattern for change of direction and could cause backflow to the fixture draining from the opposite side.

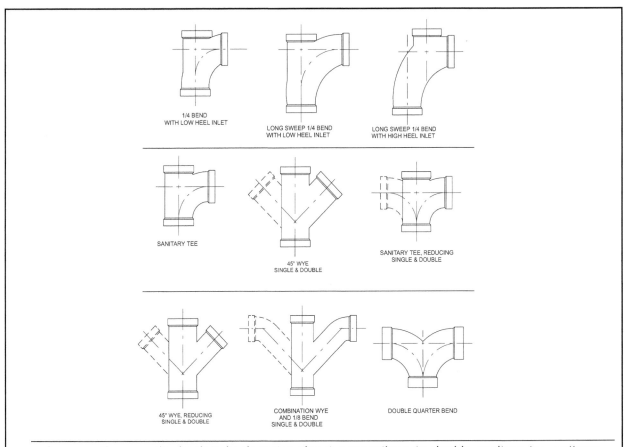

An exception permits back-to-back water closet connections to double sanitary tee patterns where the horizontal developed length between the outlet of the water closet and connection to the double sanitary tee pattern is 18 inches or greater.

Topic: Heel- or Side-Inlet Quarter Bends
Reference: IPC 706.4
Category: Sanitary Drainage
Subject: Connections between Piping and Fittings

Code Text: *Heel-inlet quarter bends shall be an acceptable means of connection, except where the quarter bend serves a water closet. A low-heel inlet shall not be used as a wet-vented connection. Side-inlet quarter bends shall be an acceptable means of connection for drainage, wet venting and stack venting arrangements.*

Discussion and Commentary: Low heel inlets on a quarter bend can become flooded and therefore should not be utilized as wet-vented connections to the drainage system. Because side inlet quarter bends normally do not become flooded on branches without water closets, they can be utilized as a wet vented connection.

NO LIMITATIONS BY SECTION 706.4

NOT ALLOWED FOR WATER CLOSET DRAINS

NOT ALLOWED FOR WATER CLOSET DRAINS AND NOT ALLOWED FOR CONNECTION OF A WET-VENTED FIXTURE DRAIN

¼ BEND WITH SIDE INLET

¼ BEND WITH HIGH-HEEL INLET

¼ BEND WITH LOW-HEEL INLET

FIGURE 706.4
HEEL AND SIDE-INLET QUARTER BENDS

Wet venting is a system where the drain pipe of one fixture serves as the vent for another. The code provides specific limitations on where this method can be used.

Study Session 9
IPC Sections 701 through 707

1. When is a common building sewer connecting more than one building to the public sewer allowed?

    a. when the building tenants agree to the shared use of the sewer

    b. when the city sewer system does not extend to the property line

    c. when the common sewer is controlled by a property owners association

    d. when all buildings using the common sewer are located on the same property

    Reference _____

2. Where the wastewater temperature will exceed _____ °F, the drainage piping material must be rated for the highest temperature of the wastewater.

    a. 110   b. 120

    c. 140   d. 160

    Reference _____

3. A solvent-cement joint between ABS and PVC plastic piping is _____.

    a. prohibited

    b. permitted in above ground locations only

    c. permitted with yellow primer complying with ASTM D3138

    d. permitted only where the building drain connects to the building sewer

    Reference _____

Study Session 9   211

4. All of the following materials are approved for both above ground and below ground installations of the building drainage system *except* _____.

   a. polyolefin   b. polyethylene
   c. polyvinyl chloride   d. stainless steel

   Reference _____

5. A chemical waste piping system requires _____.

   a. dilution of the chemicals involved
   b. resistance to the undiluted chemicals involved
   c. complete separation from the sanitary drainage system
   d. schedule 80 weight pipe or equivalent

   Reference _____

6. Mechanical and _____ joints are approved for polyethylene plastic pipe installed underground.

   a. threaded   b. caulked
   c. solvent-cemented d. heat-fusion

   Reference _____

7. The make-up of a solvent cement joint in 6-inch PVC DWV piping requires application of _____.

   a. purple primer
   b. combination primer/solvent cement conforming to ASTM F493
   c. purple primer or solvent cement that is yellow in color
   d. purple primer or solvent cement that is purple in color

   Reference _____

8. A _____ fitting is approved for connecting copper pipe to galvanized steel pipe.

   a. copper converter   b. copper alloy
   c. threaded galvanized d. soldered copper

   Reference _____

9. Which of the following joints is approved for connecting stainless steel drainage pipe to other material types?

   a. welded joints   b. threaded fittings
   c. mechanical couplings   d. red brass caulking ferrules

   Reference _____

10. Which of the following pipe materials is not suitable for joining by a heat fusion method?

    a. polyethylene   b. polyolefin
    c. polyvinylidene fluoride d. borosilicate

    Reference _____

11. The fixture drain of a(n) _____ shall not connect to a double sanitary tee pattern fitting.

    a. laundry sink   b. kitchen sink
    c. automatic clothes washer d. combination tub/shower

    Reference _____

12. A(n) _____ fitting is prohibited for a horizontal-to-horizontal change in direction of a 2-inch fixture drain to a horizontal branch drain.

    a. quarter-bend   b. sanitary tee
    c. short sweep   d. eighth-bend

    Reference _____

13. Which fixture is prohibited from discharging through a quarter bend that has a heel inlet?

    a. lavatory   b. shower
    c. urinal   d. water closet

    Reference _____

14. The minimum required slope for a 2-inch fixture drain from an automatic clothes washer is _____.

    a. $1/16$ inch per foot   b. $1/8$ inch per foot
    c. $1/4$ inch per foot   d. $1/2$ inch per foot

    Reference _____

15. Horizontal branches connecting to horizontal stack offsets shall connect at a point located not less than _____ stack diameters downstream from the upper stack.

    a. 10   b. 20
    c. 30   d. 40

    Reference _____

16. Where a storm sewer is installed in the same trench as the building sewer, the two pipes _____.

    a. may be laid side-by-side
    b. require a 24-inch horizontal separation
    c. require a 12-inch vertical separation
    d. must be of materials approved for underground inside a building

    Reference _____

17. A 4-inch by 3-inch water closet flange is _____.

    a. not considered a reduction in size
    b. prohibited
    c. an offset fitting
    d. required

    Reference _____

18. Four-inch horizontal drainage piping shall be installed at a minimum slope of _____ inch per foot

    a. $5/16$ b. $1/4$
    c. $3/16$ d. $1/8$

    Reference _____

19. Solvent-cement joints for ABS plastic fittings are permitted _____.

    a. above or below ground   b. only above ground
    c. only below ground   d. below ground if approved

    Reference _____

20. Mechanical joints in PVC pipe are permitted _____.
    a. above or below ground   b. only above ground
    c. only below ground   d. below ground if approved

    Reference _____

21. A _____ joint is permitted to join plastic pipe and cast-iron hub pipe.
    a. TFE seal adapter   b. caulked
    c. slip   d. fitting adapter

    Reference _____

22. Caulking ferrules shall be _____.
    a. copper alloy   b. lead
    c. copper   d. stainless steel

    Reference _____

23. _____ shall be of the recessed drainage type.
    a. Saddle-type fittings
    b. Cement or concrete joints
    c. Threaded drainage pipe fittings
    d. Coextruded pipe fittings

    Reference _____

24. A _____ is not permitted for a vertical to horizontal change of direction.
    a. sixth bend
    b. sanitary tee
    c. long sweep
    d. combination wye and eighth bend

    Reference _____

25. For a 3-inch diameter branch drain, a _____ fitting is permitted for a horizontal to horizontal change of direction.
    a. quarter bend   b. sanitary tee
    c. short sweep   d. wye

    Reference _____

Study Session

10

2018 IPC Sections 708 through 716
Sanitary Drainage II

OBJECTIVE: To develop an understanding of the overall code provisions that regulate the materials, design and installation of sanitary drainage. To develop an understanding of the specific provisions of the code that apply to cleanouts, sumps and ejectors.

REFERENCE: Sections 708 through 716, 2018 *International Plumbing Code*

KEY POINTS:
- Cleanout plugs may be of what materials?
- When are countersunk square heads required on cleanout plugs?
- What is the maximum spacing of cleanouts on horizontal drains?
- How is the maximum spacing measured for cleanouts on building sewers?
- When are additional cleanouts required for a change in direction of a horizontal drain?
- When is it permitted to omit the cleanout at the junction of the building sewer and building drain?
- What requirements apply to manholes used as cleanouts?
- How is the minimum size of a cleanout determined?
- What is the minimum clearance for accessing a cleanout?
- What do drainage fixture unit values designate, and how are they used?
- How are drainage fixture unit values determined for fixtures that do not appear in the tables?
- How are drainage fixture unit values determined for continuous flow and semi-continuous flow pump discharge to the drainage system?
- How is drainage piping sized?
- What requirements apply to sump pits and sewage ejector pumps?
- At what locations are pumps permitted to connect to the sanitary drainage system, and what fittings must be used?
- What portions of the sanitary drainage system must discharge to the sewer by gravity?

KEY POINTS:
(cont'd)
- When are backwater valves required and where are they prohibited?
- What special requirements apply to vacuum drainage systems?
- What limitations apply to pipe-bursting methods for replacing building sewers and building drains?
- What inspection requirements apply to pipe-bursting methods?

Topic: Horizontal Drains and Building Drains **Category:** Sanitary Drainage
Reference: IPC 708.1.1 **Subject:** Cleanouts

Code Text: *Horizontal drainage pipes in buildings shall have cleanouts located at intervals of not more than 100 feet (30 480 mm). Building drains shall have cleanouts located at intervals of not more than 100 feet (30 480 mm) except where manholes are used instead of cleanouts, the manholes shall be located at intervals of not more than 400 feet (122 m). The interval length shall be measured from the cleanout or manhole opening, along the developed length of the piping to the next drainage fitting providing access for cleaning, the end of the horizontal drain or the end of the building drain.* See the exception for fixture drains serving nonremovable traps.

Discussion and Commentary: Cleanout spacing is limited to facilitate cleaning any portion of the drainage system. This distance is based on the use of modern-day cleaning equipment and attempts to minimize the inconvenience and health hazard associated with creating a mess inside the building as a result of removing a blockage. In very large buildings, manholes may be used as cleanouts. Because a manhole improves the ease of access to the piping, and the additional space facilitates the set up and operation of drain cleaning equipment, the distance is increased to 400 feet between manholes serving building drains.

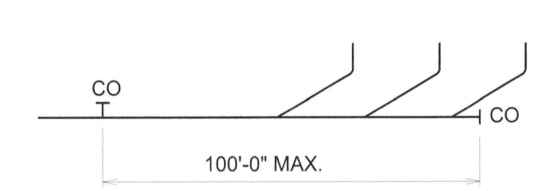

Horizontal Drains within Buildings

For SI: 1 inch = 25.4 mm, 1 foot = 304.8 mm

Increased cleanout spacing may make the use of excessively long rodding cables necessary, which complicates the task and increases the likelihood that the rodding cable will jam or break inside the pipe. Every horizontal drain must have at least one cleanout, regardless of the length.

Topic: Building Sewers
Reference: IPC 708.1.2
Category: Sanitary Drainage
Subject: Cleanouts

Code Text: *Building sewers smaller than 8 inches (203 mm) shall have cleanouts located at intervals of not more than 100 feet (30 480 mm). Building sewers 8 inches (203 mm) and larger shall have a manhole located not more than 200 feet (60 960 mm) from the junction of the building drain and building sewer and at intervals of not more than 400 feet (122 m). The interval length shall be measured from the cleanout or manhole opening, along the developed length of the piping to the next drainage fitting providing access for cleaning, a manhole or the end of the building sewer.*

Discussion and Commentary: For building sewers less than 8 inches in diameter, the maximum spacing for cleanouts matches the 100-foot limit for horizontal drains and building drains inside the building. When a building sewer is 8 inches or larger, manholes are required as cleanouts, and the distance from the junction of the building drain and the building sewer to the first manhole cannot exceed 200 feet. Because the ease of access is improved with manholes, the distance is increased to 400 feet between additional manholes serving building sewers.

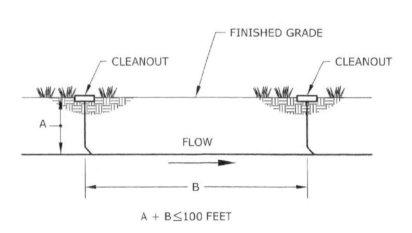

Limitations on Cleanouts in Building Sewers

For SI: 1 foot = 304.8 mm

Outdoor cleanouts for sewers must be brought up to grade for access. Cleanout spacing is measured along the entire developed length of piping between the cleanout access openings.

| **Topic:** Changes of Direction | **Category:** Sanitary Drainage |
| **Reference:** IPC 708.1.4 | **Subject:** Cleanouts |

Code Text: *Where a horizontal drainage pipe, a building drain or a building sewer has a change of horizontal direction greater than 45 degrees (0.79 rad), a cleanout shall be installed at the change of direction. Where more than one change of horizontal direction greater than 45 degrees (0.79 rad) occurs within 40 feet (12 192 mm) of developed length of piping, the cleanout installed for the first change of direction shall serve as the cleanout for all changes in direction within that 40 feet (12 192 mm) of developed length of piping.*

Discussion and Commentary: The requirement for a cleanout at a change in direction greater than 45 degrees is for an individual fitting, not a combination of fittings. If a 90-degree change in direction is accomplished with a single fitting, such as a sweep or combination tee-wye, a cleanout is required. If the same change in direction is accomplished with two one-eighth bends, a cleanout is not required.

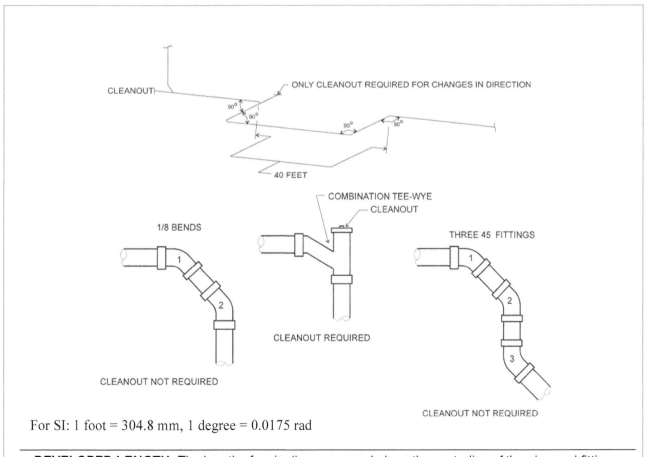

For SI: 1 foot = 304.8 mm, 1 degree = 0.0175 rad

DEVELOPED LENGTH: The length of a pipeline measured along the centerline of the pipe and fittings.

Topic: Cleanout Plugs
Reference: IPC 708.1.6
Category: Sanitary Drainage
Subject: Cleanouts

Code Text: *Cleanout plugs shall be of copper-alloy, plastic or other approved materials. Cleanout plugs for borosilicate glass piping systems shall be of borosilicate glass. Copper-alloy cleanout plugs shall conform to ASTM A74 and shall be limited for use only on metallic piping systems. Plastic cleanout plugs shall conform to the referenced standards for plastic pipe fittings, as indicated in Table 702.4. Cleanout plugs shall have a raised square head, a countersunk square head or a countersunk slot head. Where a cleanout plug will have a trim cover screw installed into the plug, the plug shall be manufactured with a blind end threaded hole for such purpose.*

Discussion and Commentary: Metallic cleanout plugs must be copper alloy such as brass to provide for easy removal. If the cleanout plug is corroded in place, the brass plug is a soft enough material to be chiseled out. Brass cleanout plugs are limited to metallic fittings because the metal plug threads may damage the softer plastic threads of a fitting. Plastic plugs are intended for use with plastic fittings; however, this section does not prohibit the use of plastic plugs with metallic fittings. Like brass plugs, plastic plugs are less likely to seize in metallic fittings. The cleanout plug must have a raised or countersunk square turning surface or a countersunk slot to allow for ease of removal while minimizing the possibility of marring or stripping the surface during removal.

Threaded plastic plugs are suitable for plastic pipe cleanouts. A raised square head is one approved option for a turning surface.

Topic: Manholes
Reference: IPC 708.1.7

Category: Sanitary Drainage
Subject: Cleanouts

Code Text: *Manholes and manhole covers shall be of an approved type. Manholes located inside of a building shall have gas-tight covers that require tools for removal.*

Discussion and Commentary: Where a manhole is provided to serve as a cleanout for a building drain, such manhole is required to have a secured, gas-tight cover. This requirement is to prevent the escape of sewer gas and to reduce the possibility of unauthorized access to the manhole.

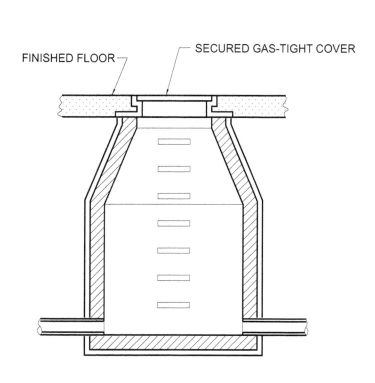

Manholes located inside buildings and used as cleanouts for the building drain must comply with the maximum spacing requirement of 400 feet in accordance with Section 708.1.1.

Study Session 10

Topic: Required Clearance
Reference: IPC 708.1.9
Category: Sanitary Drainage
Subject: Cleanouts

Code Text: *Cleanouts for 6-inch (153 mm) and smaller piping shall be provided with a clearance of not less than 18 inches (457 mm) from, and perpendicular to, the face of the opening to any obstruction. Cleanouts for 8-inch (203 mm) and larger piping shall be provided with a clearance of not less than 36 inches (914 mm) from, and perpendicular to, the face of the opening to any obstruction.*

Discussion and Commentary: The code is very specific on the requirements related to providing drainage piping cleanouts. The usability of these cleanouts is not to be compromised by their placement in the building. The clearances are considered the minimum that will allow the cleanout to serve its purpose. Additional clearance is desirable whenever possible.

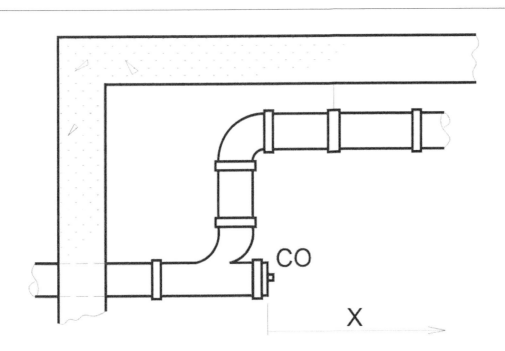

MINIMUM CLEARANCE:
X = MINIMUM 18" FOR 6" AND SMALLER PIPES
X = MINIMUM 36" FOR 8" AND LARGER PIPES

For SI: 1 inch = 25.4 mm

The greater clearance distance for larger pipes is necessary to accommodate larger rodding equipment, as well as other needed equipment.

Topic: Cleanout Access
Reference: IPC 708.1.10
Category: Sanitary Drainage
Subject: Cleanouts

Code Text: *Required cleanouts shall not be installed in concealed locations. For the purposes of this section, concealed locations include, but are not limited to, the inside of plenums, within walls, within floor/ceiling assemblies, below grade and in crawl spaces where the height from the crawl space floor to the nearest obstruction along the path from the crawl space opening to the cleanout location is less than 24 inches (610 mm). Cleanouts with openings at a finished wall shall have the face of the opening located within 1 $\frac{1}{2}$ inches (38 mm) of the finished wall surface. Cleanouts located below grade shall be extended to grade level so that the top of the cleanout plug is at or above grade. A cleanout installed in a floor or walkway that will not have a trim cover installed shall have a countersunk plug installed so the top surface of the plug is flush with the finished surface of the floor or walkway.*

Discussion and Commentary: Because a cleanout is designed to provide access into the drainage system, the cleanout itself must be accessible and cannot be placed in a concealed location. Cleanouts are permitted in a crawl space if the minimum height of 24 inches is maintained for access. For cleanouts serving piping in a concealed location, the cleanout is required to extend up to and flush with the finished floor level or outside grade. At finished wall surfaces, the cleanout opening must be located within 1 $\frac{1}{2}$ inches of the finished surface. Cleanouts located on walking surfaces must be countersunk to minimize the tripping hazard and to protect the cleanout from damage.

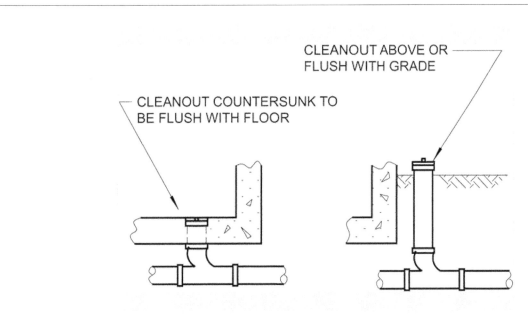

Cleanout Installations

Cleanouts located in driveways or other areas subject to vehicular traffic must be of the type that are able to support vehicle loads in accordance with the referenced standard ASME A112.36.2M.

Topic: Prohibited Use
Reference: IPC 708.1.11
Category: Sanitary Drainage
Subject: Cleanouts

Code Text: *The use of a threaded cleanout opening to add a fixture or to extend piping shall be prohibited except where another cleanout of equal size is installed with the required access and clearance.*

Discussion and Commentary: In existing structures, cleanouts provide a convenient opening for the connection of new piping in remodeling, addition and alteration work. The cleanout fitting is commonly removed to allow a new connection; however, a substitute cleanout must be provided to serve in the same capacity as the cleanout that was eliminated. Many threaded cleanout openings have only a few threads and, therefore, are not intended to receive threaded pipe or male adapters.

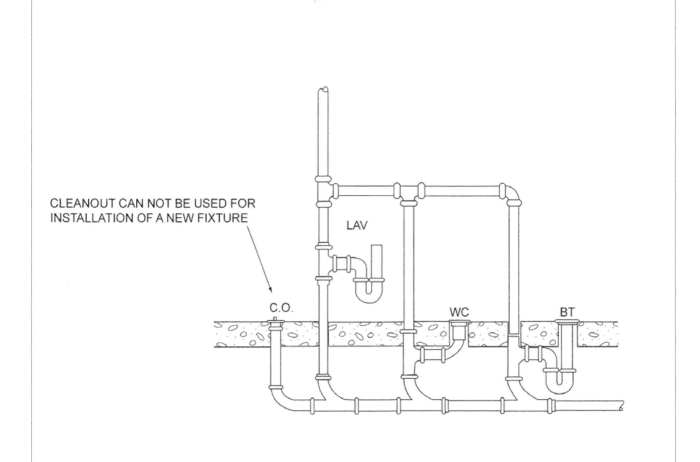

The practice of converting a floor cleanout to serve as a floor drain without a trap is prohibited because floor drains require a trap seal to prevent sewer gases entering the building interior.

Topic: Values for Fixtures
Reference: IPC 709.1

Category: Sanitary Drainage
Subject: Fixture Units

Code Text: *Drainage fixture unit values as given in Table 709.1 designate the relative load weight of different kinds of fixtures that shall be employed in estimating the total load carried by a soil or waste pipe, and shall be used in connection with Tables 710.1(1) and 710.1(2) of sizes for soil, waste and vent pipes for which the permissible load is given in terms of fixture units.*

Discussion and Commentary: Each plumbing fixture is assigned a drainage fixture unit (dfu) value based on the anticipated discharge to the sanitary drainage system. The sizing of piping in the drainage system is based on the capacity of each diameter of pipe expressed in total drainage fixture units. This maximum capacity or "load" is shown in the referenced tables for building drains, branches that connect to the building drain, and building sewers based on the slope of the pipe [Table 710.1(1)] and for horizontal fixture branch drains and stacks [Table 710.1(2)].

TABLE 709.1 (excerpt)
DRAINAGE FIXTURE UNITS FOR FIXTURES AND GROUPS

FIXTURE TYPE	DRAINAGE FIXTURE UNIT VALUE AS LOAD FACTORS	MINIMUM SIZE OF TRAP (inches)
Shower (based on the total flow rate through showerheads and body sprays)		
Flow rate:		
5.7 gpm or less	2	1½
Greater than 5.7 gpm to 12.3 gpm	3	2
Greater than 12.3 gpm to 25.8 gpm	5	3
Greater than 25.8 gpm to 55.6 gpm	6	4

For SI: 1 gallon per minute = 3.785 L/m

Showers sometimes contain multiple shower heads, and the volume of water draining through the waste outlet varies. The drainage fixture unit value, the minimum trap size and drain pipe size is based on the total flow rate through the showerheads and body sprays when operating simultaneously.

Topic: Fixtures Not Listed in Table 709.1 **Category:** Sanitary Drainage
Reference: IPC 709.2 **Subject:** Fixture Units

Code Text: *Fixtures not listed in Table 709.1 shall have a drainage fixture unit load based on the outlet size of the fixture in accordance with Table 709.2. The minimum trap size for unlisted fixtures shall be the size of the drainage outlet but not less than 1.25 inches (32 mm).*

Discussion and Commentary: When a specific plumbing fixture is not listed in Table 709.1, the dfu value is based on the outlet size of the fixture. A $1\frac{1}{4}$-inch drain is the minimum acceptable size to permit proper open channel flow in the pipe for sanitary drainage. The minimum trap size is based on this pipe size.

TABLE 709.2
DRAINAGE FIXTURE UNITS FOR FIXTURE DRAINS OR TRAPS

FIXTURE DRAIN OR TRAP SIZE (inches)	DRAINAGE FIXTURE UNIT VALUE
$1\frac{1}{4}$	1
$1\frac{1}{2}$	2
2	3
$2\frac{1}{2}$	4
3	5
4	6

For SI: 1 inch = 25.4 mm.

Floor drains, floor sinks and hub drains that receive clear waste from refrigerated displays and freezers have a dfu value of only $\frac{1}{2}$. See Section 709.4.1.

Topic: Conversion of GPM Flow to DFU Values **Category:** Sanitary Drainage
Reference: IPC 709.3 **Subject:** Fixture Units

Code Text: *Where discharges to a waste receptor or to a drainage system are only known in gallons per minute (liters per second) values, the drainage fixture unit values for those flows shall be computed on the basis that 1 gpm (0.06 L/s) of flow is equivalent to two drainage fixture units.*

Discussion and Commentary: Equipment that discharges either continuously or semicontinuously, such as pumps, ejectors, air-conditioning equipment, commercial laundries and commercial dishwashers, are assigned two fixture units for each gpm of discharge rate. For example, a continuously operating pump with a discharge rate of 20 gpm (78 L/min) would have a dfu value of 40. Because a dfu is based on probability, only whole numbers are utilized to express fixture unit values.

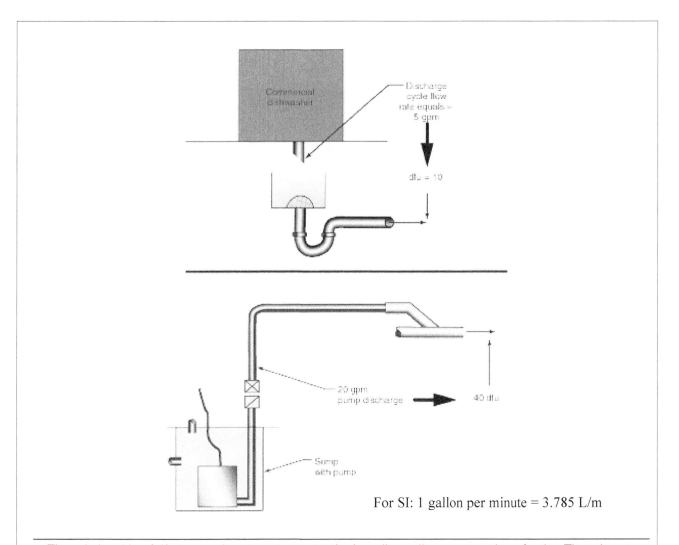

For SI: 1 gallon per minute = 3.785 L/m

The relationship of dfu to gpm is not a constant ratio that allows direct conversion of units. Thus, it cannot be determined that a dfu value of 40 would yield a continuous flow of 20 gpm.

Topic: Sump Pit
Reference: IPC 712.3.2
Category: Sanitary Drainage
Subject: Sumps and Ejectors

Code Text: *The sump pit shall be not less than 18 inches (457 mm) in diameter and not less than 24 inches (610 mm) in depth, unless otherwise approved. The pit shall be provided with access and shall be located such that all drainage flows into the pit by gravity. The sump pit shall be constructed of tile, concrete, steel, plastic or other approved materials. The pit bottom shall be solid and provide permanent support for the pump. The sump pit shall be fitted with a gastight removable cover that is installed not more than 2 inches (51 mm) below grade or floor level. The cover shall be adequate to support anticipated loads in the area of use. The sump pit shall be vented in accordance with Chapter 9.*

Discussion and Commentary: The minimum dimensions of 18 inches in diameter and 24 inches in depth are required, unless the designer or manufacturer can present calculations and other supporting data that will allow the code official to determine that other dimensions work for the situation being addressed. The sump pit is required to be constructed of a durable material, such as tile, concrete, steel, plastic or other approved materials. The bottom of the sump pit must be solid and structurally capable of supporting the sump pump. The sump pit is required to have a gas-tight removable cover to prevent the escape of sewer gas.

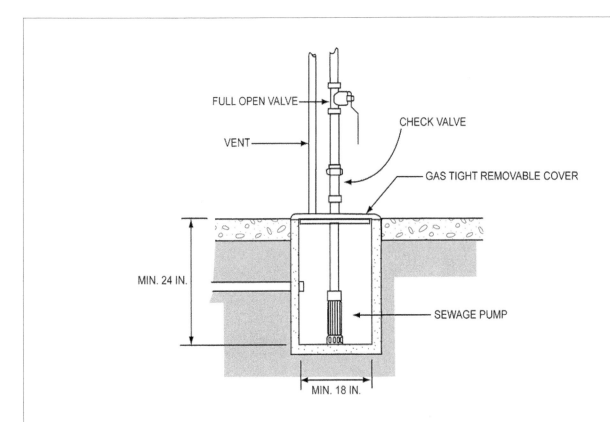

For SI: 1 inch = 25.4 mm

The gastight removable cover must be installed no more than 2 inches below the finished floor surface. While many sump covers are installed flush or project above the finish floor level, allowing a recessed elevation provides flexibility during the rough-in stage of construction.

Topic: Pump Connection to Drainage System
Reference: IPC 712.3.5

Category: Sanitary Drainage
Subject: Sumps and Ejectors

Code Text: *Pumps connected to the drainage system shall connect to a building sewer, building drain, soil stack, waste stack or horizontal branch drain. Where the discharge line connects into horizontal drainage piping, the connection shall be made through a wye fitting into the top of the drainage piping and such wye fitting shall be located not less than 10 pipe diameters from the base of any soil stack, waste stack or fixture drain.*

Discussion and Commentary: The pump discharge piping is permitted to connect to any soil or waste stack and any horizontal sanitary drainage, such as the building sewer, building drain and horizontal branch drain. Connections to horizontal drainage piping must be through a wye fitting into the top of the drain. A wye fitting is appropriate for this vertical to horizontal connection as the best method of directing the pump discharge into the horizontal drain in the direction of flow. In addition, the wye fitting must be located a minimum of 10 pipe diameters away from the base of any stack or fixture drain. This is to reduce the likelihood that discharge from the pump/ejector will interfere with the gravity flow in the drainage system. This separation distance based on the diameter of the horizontal drain will allow the pumped waste flow to settle in the invert of the horizontal drainage piping without creating backups and pressure surges.

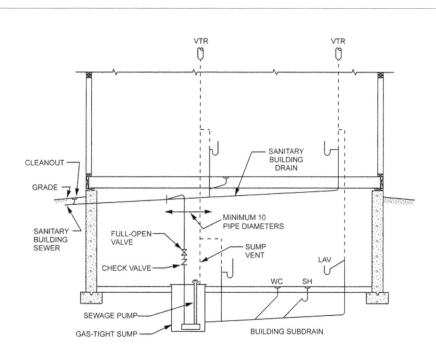

Grinder type sewage pumps are those that include a grinding mechanism for cutting solid and semisolid waste. Such systems reduce clogging and therefore allow smaller diameter pipes to be used.

Topic: Sewage Backflow	**Category:** Sanitary Drainage
Reference: IPC 714.1	**Subject:** Backwater Values

Code Text: *Where plumbing fixtures are installed on a floor with a finished floor elevation below the elevation of the manhole cover of the next upstream manhole in the public sewer, such fixtures shall be protected by a backwater valve installed in the building drain, or horizontal branch serving such fixtures. Plumbing fixtures installed on a floor with a finished floor elevation above the elevation of the manhole cover of the next upstream manhole in the public sewer shall not discharge through a backwater valve. See the exception for existing buildings.*

Discussion and Commentary: A backwater valve is required in areas where the public sewer may back up into the building through the sanitary drainage system serving fixtures located on a floor that is below the elevation of the next upstream manhole cover. Public sewers occasionally become blocked or overloaded, which results in sewage backing up into manholes and any laterals (taps) connected to the sewer system.

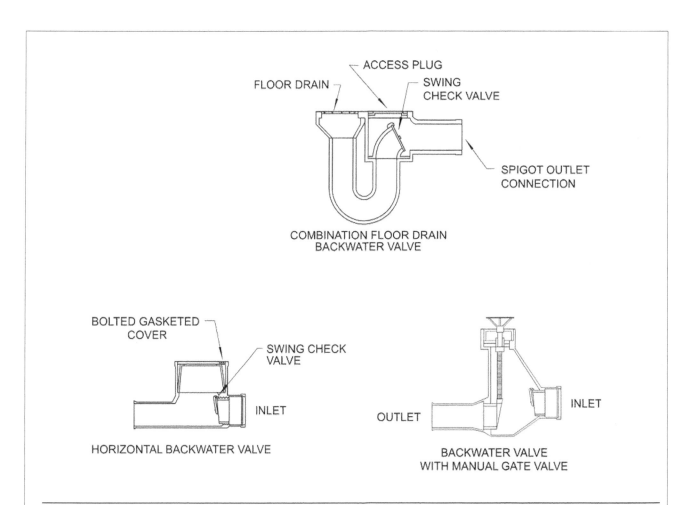

To limit sewer backup through fixtures on the lower floor when the backwater valve is activated, and to limit wear and tear on the backwater valve during normal operation, fixtures located on upper floors that do not require a backwater valve are not permitted to drain through a backwater valve. This rule does not apply to existing buildings because it is not feasible to separate the drainage system for upper and lower fixtures when installing a backwater valve in an existing building.

Topic: System Design	**Category:** Sanitary Drainage
Reference: IPC 715.2	**Subject:** Vacuum Drainage Systems

Code Text: *Vacuum drainage systems shall be designed in accordance with the vacuum drainage system manufacturer's instructions. The system layout, including piping layout, tank assemblies, vacuum pump assembly and other components necessary for proper function of the system shall be in accordance with the manufacturer's instructions. Plans, specifications and other data for such systems shall be submitted to the code official for review and approval prior to installation.*

Discussion and Commentary: Vacuum drainage systems have been commonly used to transport wastewater flows in ships and in prisons. These systems are less prone to clogging than gravity drainage systems and are not required to have conventional trap venting systems or carefully sloped drainage piping. In recent years, vacuum drainage systems have been receiving greater attention as an alternative to gravity drainage systems for all types of buildings because the low water flows from fixtures caused by water-conservation practices are creating solid-waste transport problems in gravity-type drainage systems.

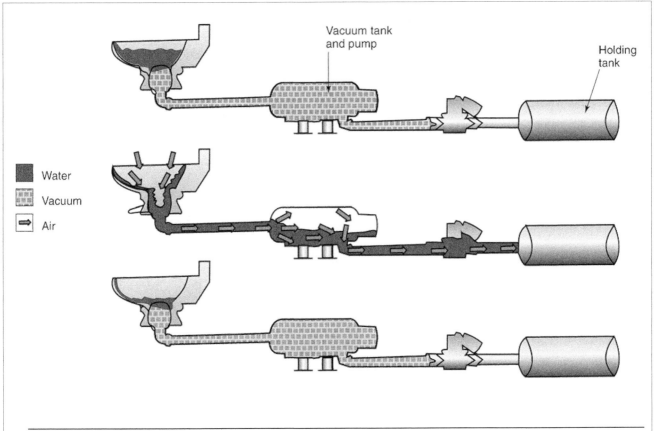

Vacuum drainage systems' technology and design are well proven over many years of use in a variety of applications. Design and installation of these systems must be in accordance with the manufacturer's instructions.

Study Session 10

Topic: Applicability	Category: Sanitary Drainage
Reference: IPC 716.2	Subject: Replacement by Pipe-Bursting Methods

Code Text: *The replacement of building sewer and building drain piping by pipe-bursting methods shall be limited to gravity drainage piping of sizes 6 inches (152 mm) and smaller. The replacement piping shall be of the same nominal size as the existing piping.*

Discussion and Commentary: This section governs the replacement of existing building sewer and building drain piping by pipe-bursting methods and limits its use to the replacement of pipes that are 6 inches and smaller. The method uses an expanding mandrel that is attached to the end of the replacement pipe. The mandrel (with the replacement pipe in tow) is pulled by a cable through the existing sewer line. The mandrel has a hydraulically activated expanding shell that expands and breaks (bursts) the existing pipe to make room for the new pipe as it is pulled into position. The replacement piping is limited to high-density polyethylene (HDPE) plastic pipe having an SDR 17 wall thickness in accordance with ASTM F714. This pipe is an outer-diameter- and wall-thickness-controlled product. SDR 17 provides for an inside diameter that is very close to the inside diameter of PVC and cast iron sewer piping of the same size.

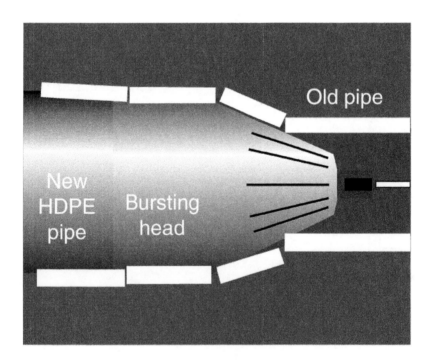

An internal video camera survey is required of the existing system prior to replacement and of the completed installation. The post-installation video must be reviewed and approved by the code official prior to pressure testing of the replacement piping system.

Study Session 10
IPC Sections 708 through 716

1. Where a floor drain receives only clear-water waste from coolers and freezers, the floor drain is assigned a value of _____ drainage fixture unit(s).

    a. 1/2
    b. 0
    c. 1
    d. 2

    Reference _____

2. A 4-inch diameter building drain installed with a slope of 1/4 inch per foot has a capacity to receive the discharge of no more than _____ drainage fixture units (dfus).

    a. 180
    b. 216
    c. 250
    d. 160

    Reference _____

3. For a 2-inch horizontal branch drain less than 30 feet long, a _____ connected upstream of the drain is permitted to serve as a cleanout for the drain.

    a. 1 1/4-inch slip joint P-trap
    b. 1 1/2-inch bathtub overflow outlet
    c. 1 1/2-inch slip joint P-trap
    d. 2-inch shower waste outlet

    Reference _____

4. The drainage fixture unit load from a clinical sink with a 3-inch fixture outlet is _____.

   a. 1 b. 2
   c. 3 d. 5

   Reference _____

5. A sump pump with a discharge capacity of 10 GPM that discharges to the drainage system through a 2-inch indirect waste receptor has a computed drainage fixture unit value of _____.

   a. 3 b. 10
   c. 20 d. 42

   Reference _____

6. A private bathroom with a 1.6 gpf water closet, lavatory, shower, bidet and floor drain has a total drainage fixture unit value of _____.

   a. 5 b. 7
   c. 9 d. 10

   Reference _____

7. The minimum size of any building drain serving a water closet is _____ inches.

   a. 3 b. 4
   c. 2 d. 2½

   Reference _____

8. A vertical distance of _____ feet or more between the connections of horizontal branches to a drainage stack is a branch interval.

   a. 7 b. 8
   c. 9 d. 10

   Reference _____

9. In a building with a basement subdrain sump, _____ is prohibited from discharging to the sump.
    a. subsoil drainage
    b. drainage from soil pipes
    c. waste from laundry fixtures
    d. drainage above the gravity sewer

    Reference _____

10. A _____ is not required for a sewage sump and ejector.
    a. pump alarm   b. vent
    c. check valve   d. full open valve

    Reference _____

11. The ejector pump cut-on control shall be set to prevent the effluent in the sump from rising to within _____ inches of the invert of the gravity drain inlet.
    a. 1½   b. 2
    c. 3   d. 4

    Reference _____

12. The minimum dimensions of a sump pit are _____ inches in diameter and _____ inches deep.
    a. 16, 20   b. 18, 20
    c. 18, 24   d. 20, 24

    Reference _____

13. The discharge pipe of a sewage ejector connecting to horizontal drainage piping shall be connected through a _____.
    a. wye fitting into the side of the drainage piping
    b. sanitary tee into the side of the drainage piping
    c. sanitary tee into the top of the drainage piping
    d. wye fitting into the top of the drainage piping

    Reference _____

14. Sewage grinder pumps that receive the discharge of water closets shall have a minimum discharge opening of _____ inch(es).

    a. 3/4
    b. 1 1/2
    c. 1 1/4
    d. 2

    Reference _____

15. What is the minimum required capacity of a 2-inch sewage pump?

    a. 15 gpm
    b. 21 gpm
    c. 30 gpm
    d. 46 gpm

    Reference _____

16. Unless otherwise approved, cleanout plugs for cast iron piping shall be _____.

    a. cast iron
    b. plastic
    c. copper alloy
    d. plastic or copper alloy

    Reference _____

17. The sump pump discharge piping requires a _____.

    a. backwater valve and shut off valve
    b. ball valve and relief valve
    c. check valve and full open valve
    d. air admittance valve and globe valve

    Reference _____

18. What is the minimum required slope of a 2-inch horizontal drain when part of an approved computerized drainage system design?

    a. 1/16 inch per foot
    b. 1/8 inch per foot
    c. 1/4 inch per foot
    d. 1/2 inch per foot

    Reference _____

19. The cover on a sump pit shall be installed _____.
    a. not more than 2 inches above floor level
    b. not more than 2 inches below floor level
    c. level with grade or finished floor
    d. above grade or finish floor level

    Reference_____

20. Fixtures above the elevation of the next upstream manhole cover in a public sewer are permitted to discharge through a backwater valve when the backwater valve is installed _____.
    a. in an existing building
    b. below the elevation of the next upstream manhole cover
    c. outside the building
    d. at the lowest part of the building drain

    Reference_____

21. When a pipe-bursting method is used for replacing an existing gravity building sewer, the pipe size is limited to a maximum of _____ inches in diameter.
    a. 8   b. 6
    c. 4   d. 3

    Reference_____

22. All horizontal drains shall be provided with cleanouts located not more than _____ feet apart.
    a. 40   b. 60
    c. 80   d. 100

    Reference_____

23. Where more than one change of direction exceeding 45 degrees occurs in a run of piping, only one cleanout shall be required for each _____ feet of developed length.
    a. 40   b. 60
    c. 80   d. 100

    Reference_____

24. A cleanout is required within _____ of the building drain and building sewer junction.

    a. 20 inches on the upstream side

    b. 10 pipe diameters on the downstream side

    c. 10 feet on the upstream side

    d. 20 feet on the downstream side

Reference_____

25. A minimum clearance of _____ inches is required in front of a cleanout for a 2-inch drainage pipe.

    a. 12   b. 18

    c. 24   d. 30

Reference_____

2018 IPC Chapter 8
Indirect/Special Waste

OBJECTIVE: To develop an understanding of the code provisions for indirect connections to the sanitary drainage system. To develop an understanding of how the code provisions for indirect connections prevent sewage from backing up into the indirect waste pipe. To develop an understanding of the code provisions regulating special waste that contains hazardous chemicals.

REFERENCE: Chapter 8, 2018 *International Plumbing Code*

KEY POINTS:
- What type of appliance or equipment is required to discharge through an indirect waste pipe? What is the purpose?
- When are fixtures required to be directly connected to the plumbing system?
- Equipment associated with food is required to discharge through an indirect waste pipe by what means?
- What is required for the waste line serving a floor drain that is located in an area subject to freezing?
- What provisions apply to health care fixtures?
- Devices and equipment discharging potable water to the building drainage system shall be through what type of waste pipe and through what separation?
- What type of protection is required for the discharge of wastewater from swimming pools?
- What type of indirect waste is required for devices and equipment discharging non-potable water to the building drainage system?
- What are the various options for the discharge of a domestic dishwasher?
- What two methods are permitted for the discharge from a commercial dishwashing machine?
- What requirements apply to sinks used for washing utensils, dishes, pots or pans?
- When is indirect waste piping required to be trapped?

KEY POINTS:
(Cont'd)

- What is the difference between an air break and an air gap? When is each required?
- What limitations are placed on the location of waste receptors, and what type of access is required?
- What determines the size of a waste receptor?
- What height is required for the hub or pipe of an indirect waste receptor above the floor?
- What dimension, trap and access requirements apply to standpipes?
- What special restrictions apply to corrosive or hazardous wastes?

Topic: Protection	Category: Indirect/Special Waste
Reference: IPC 801.2	Subject: General Provisions

Code Text: *All devices, appurtenances, appliances and apparatus intended to serve some special function, such as sterilization, humidification, distillation, processing, cooling, or storage of ice or foods, and that discharge to the drainage system, shall be provided with protection against backflow, flooding, fouling, contamination and stoppage of the drain.*

Discussion and Commentary: This section requires appliances and specialized equipment to be protected against contamination resulting from backflow. Similar to backflow protection of the potable water system in Chapter 6, backflow protection in this case addresses potential contamination of the contents, products or surfaces of the appliance or apparatus from the drainage system.

When draining to the sanitary drainage system, ice machines and other clear water waste sources must discharge through an indirect waste pipe and air gap to protect the contents from possible contamination.

Topic: Where Required	**Category:** Indirect/Special Waste
Reference: IPC 802.1	**Subject:** Indirect Wastes

Code Text: *Food-handling equipment, in other than dwelling units, clear-water waste, humidifiers, dishwashing machines and utensils, pots, pans and dishwashing sinks shall discharge through an indirect waste pipe as specified in Sections 802.1.1 through 802.1.8. Fixtures not required to be indirectly connected by this section and the exception to Section 301.6 shall be directly connected to the plumbing system in accordance with Chapter 7.*

Discussion and Commentary: The requirements for indirect wastes are described in Sections 802.1.1 through 802.1.8. Fixtures not required to be indirectly connected by Chapter 8 are required to be directly connected to the plumbing system in accordance with Section 301.3 and Chapter 7.

By definition, an indirect waste pipe is a waste pipe that does not connect directly with the drainage system but that discharges into the drainage system through an air break or air gap into a trap, fixture, receptor or interceptor.

| **Topic:** Food Handling | **Category:** Indirect/Special Waste |
| **Reference:** IPC 802.1.1 | **Subject:** Indirect Wastes |

Code Text: *Equipment and fixtures utilized for the storage, preparation and handling of food shall discharge through an indirect waste pipe by means of an air gap. Each well of a multiple-compartment sink shall discharge independently to a waste receptor.*

Discussion and Commentary: All food must be protected from possible contamination caused by the sanitary drainage system. The requirement for indirect waste connections extends to all storage, cooking and preparation equipment, including vegetable sinks, food washing sinks, refrigerated cases and cabinets, ice boxes, ice-making machines, steam kettles, steam tables, potato peelers, egg boilers, coffee urns and brewers, drink dispensers and similar types of equipment and fixtures. Food stored in walk-in coolers and freezers is specifically addressed in Section 802.1.2. These provisions do not apply to kitchen sinks in dwelling units.

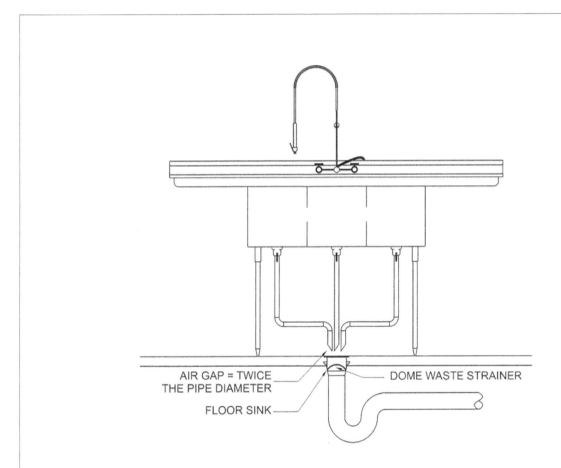

To prevent cross contamination, each well of a multi-compartment food-handling sink must discharge independently to the waste receptor. If the outlets of each well were connected together into a common drain manifold before discharging to the waste receptor, the flow from one well of the sink could backflow into the adjacent well.

Topic: Potable Clear-Water Waste	Category: Indirect/Special Waste
Reference: IPC 802.1.3	Subject: Indirect Wastes

Code Text: *Where devices and equipment, such as sterilizers and relief valves, discharge potable water to the building drainage system, the discharge shall be through an indirect waste pipe by means of an air gap.*

Discussion and Commentary: An indirect waste connection by means of an air gap is required for potable clear-water waste. An air gap prevents possible contamination of the potable water source and the contents of appliances such as sterilizers.

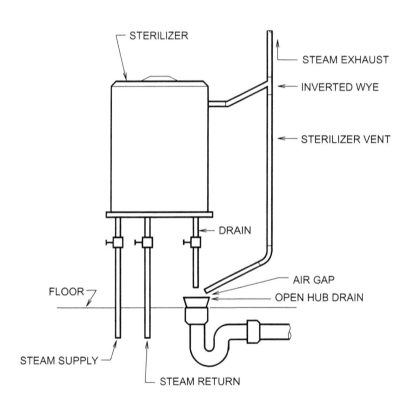

Clear-water waste includes all of the various condensate drains plus sterilizers and relief valves. Clear-water waste is not required to discharge to the sanitary drainage system.

Topic: Nonpotable Clear-Water Waste
Reference: IPC 802.1.5
Category: Indirect/Special Waste
Subject: Indirect Wastes

Code Text: *Where devices and equipment such as process tanks, filters, drips and boilers discharge nonpotable water to the building drainage system, the discharge shall be through an indirect waste pipe by means of an air break or an air gap.*

Discussion and Commentary: Where there is no possibility of contaminating the potable water, the indirect waste may be by means of an air gap or air break. An air break is often preferred to reduce any splashing that may occur. This section does not require the devices and equipment listed to discharge to the drainage system; it only indicates the method of discharge if they do connect.

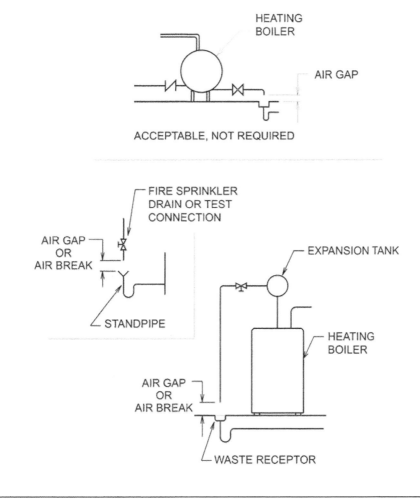

An air break is a piping arrangement in which a drain from a fixture, appliance or device discharges indirectly into another fixture, receptacle or interceptor at a point below the flood level rim and above the trap seal.

Study Session 11 247

Topic: Installation
Reference: IPC 802.3

Category: Indirect/Special Waste
Subject: Indirect Wastes

Code Text: *Indirect waste piping shall discharge through an air gap or air break into a waste receptor. Waste receptors shall be trapped and vented and shall connect to the building drainage system. Indirect waste piping that exceeds 30 inches (762 mm) in developed length measured horizontally, or 54 inches (1372 mm) in total developed length, shall be trapped.* See exception for a clear-water waste receptor that does not connect to the sanitary drainage system.

Discussion and Commentary: To minimize bacterial growth and odor in indirect waste piping, a trap is required when the piping exceeds 30 inches in developed length measured horizontally or 54 inches in total developed length. The trap requirement applies only to fixtures or devices that are open ended. It does not apply to an indirect waste pipe making a direct connection to a device such as a water heater relief valve.

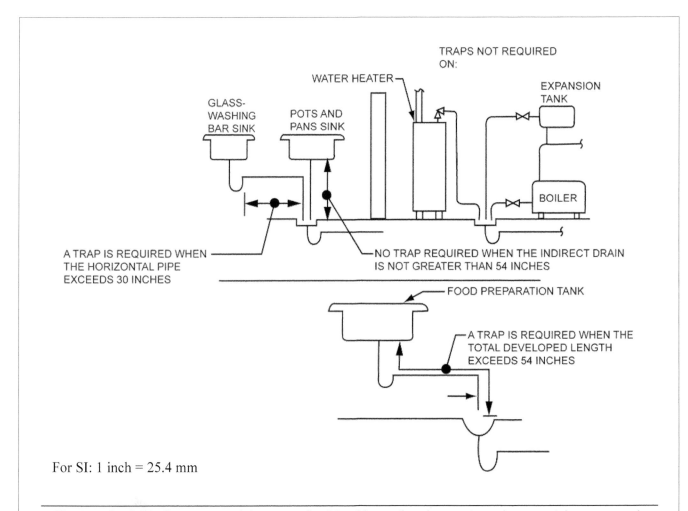

For SI: 1 inch = 25.4 mm

The trap for the indirect waste piping prescribed by this section does not require a vent, because such trap does not serve the same purpose as other traps in the drainage system.

Topic: Air Gap
Reference: IPC 802.3.1
Category: Indirect/Special Waste
Subject: Indirect Wastes

Code Text: *The air gap between the indirect waste pipe and the flood level rim of the waste receptor shall be not less than twice the effective opening of the indirect waste pipe.*

Discussion and Commentary: An air gap is a separation of the drainage pipe that terminates above the flood level rim of the waste receptor. To be completely effective in accomplishing its intended purpose, the physical separation from the waste pipe to the flood level rim of the waste receptor must be at least twice the pipe's inside diameter. This type of indirect waste connection offers a high level of protection by not allowing any possibility for backsiphoning of waste or sewage.

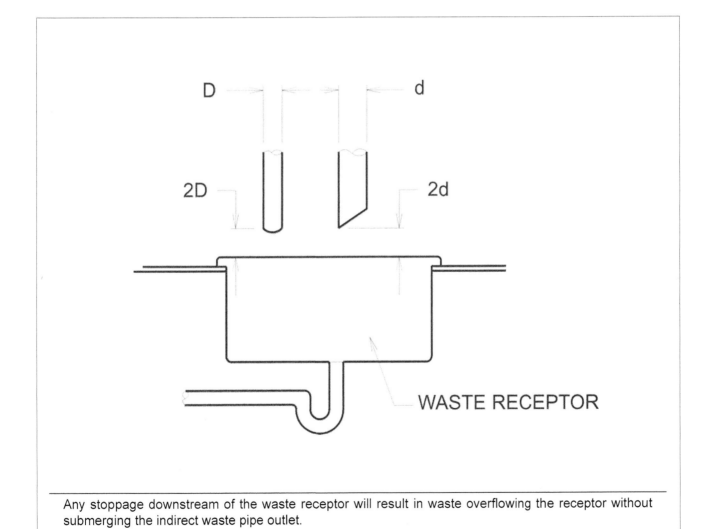

Any stoppage downstream of the waste receptor will result in waste overflowing the receptor without submerging the indirect waste pipe outlet.

Topic: Air Break
Reference: IPC 802.3.2
Category: Indirect/Special Waste
Subject: Indirect Wastes

Code Text: *An air break shall be provided between the indirect waste pipe and the trap seal of the waste receptor.*

Discussion and Commentary: Unlike an air gap, an air break occurs when the termination point of the indirect waste pipe is below the flood level rim of the waste receptor. The air break is the vertical space between the indirect pipe termination and the liquid trap seal. A common installation of this arrangement is a clothes washing machine discharge line that terminates inside the standpipe below the top of the pipe. Under normal operation, the indirect drain termination does not come into contact with backflow from the sanitary drainage system.

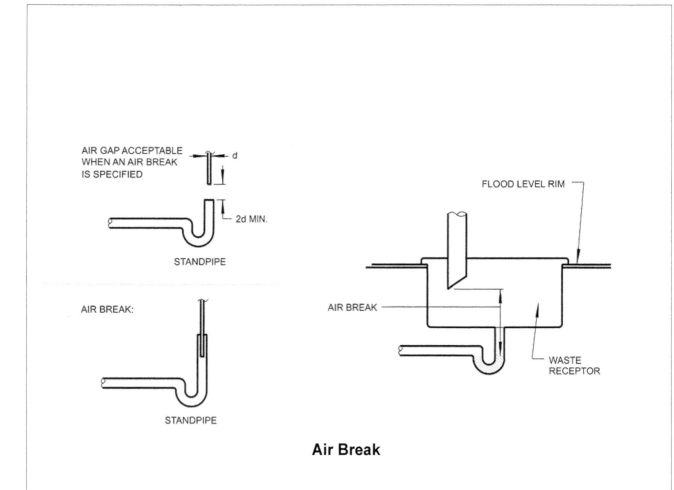

Air Break

An air break is a piping arrangement in which a drain from a fixture, appliance or device discharges indirectly into another fixture, receptacle or interceptor at a point below the flood level rim and above the trap seal.

Topic: Waste Receptors
Reference: IPC 802.4
Category: Indirect/Special Waste
Subject: Indirect Wastes

Code Text: *For other than hub drains that receive only clear-water waste and standpipes, a removable strainer or basket shall cover the outlet of waste receptors. Waste receptors shall not be installed in concealed spaces. Waste receptors shall not be installed in plenums, crawl spaces, attics, interstitial spaces above ceilings and below floors. Ready access shall be provided to waste receptors.*

Discussion and Commentary: There are no specific standards regulating waste receptors. They may be identified by various names, including floor drain, open hub drain, floor sink and waste sink. Floor sinks are specialized sinks designed to be installed in the floor. Manufacturers produce a special line of fixtures designed to be used as waste receptors, some of which look like kitchen sinks.

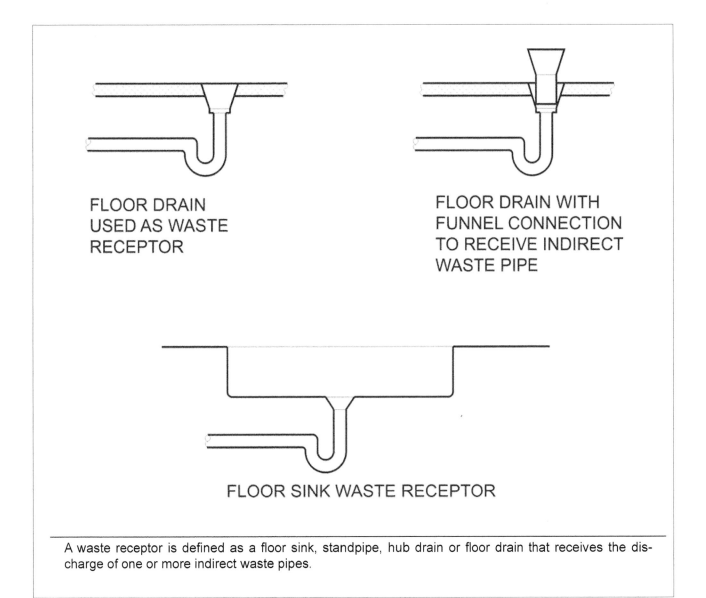

A waste receptor is defined as a floor sink, standpipe, hub drain or floor drain that receives the discharge of one or more indirect waste pipes.

Topic: Size of Receptors
Reference: IPC 802.4.1

Category: Indirect/Special Waste
Subject: Indirect Wastes

Code Text: *A waste receptor shall be sized for the maximum discharge of all indirect waste pipes served by the receptor. Receptors shall be installed to prevent splashing or flooding.*

Discussion and Commentary: Sizing a waste receptor is based on the probability of simultaneous discharge of the various fixtures connecting to the same waste receptor. Two major problems in the design and sizing of a waste receptor are splashing and flooding. Both must be minimized to avoid creating an insanitary condition. Both the shape of the waste receptor and the discharge rate of the indirect waste pipe affect the amount of splashing and flooding involved. The receptor must be capable of accepting all of the discharge without overflowing. While accepting the discharge of an indirect waste pipe, the receptor is simultaneously discharging to the drainage system at a rate based on the size of its drain pipe.

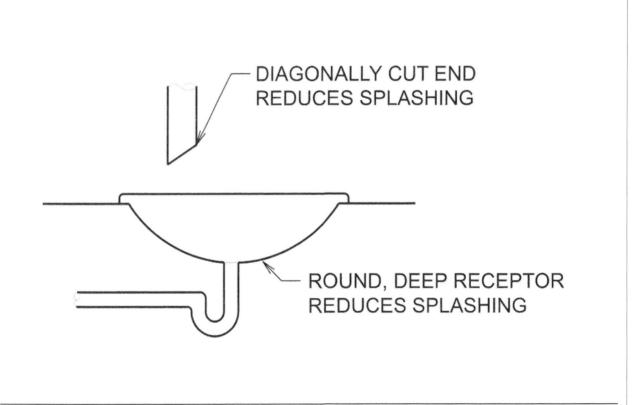

The code does not specify a method for sizing receptors; however, it would be logical to size the drain for the receptor based on the total drainage fixture units (dfus) that discharge to the receptor.

Topic: Hub Drains
Reference: IPC 802.4.2
Category: Indirect/Special Waste
Subject: Indirect Wastes

Code Text: *A hub drain shall be in the form of a hub or pipe extending not less than 1 inch (25.4 mm) above a water-impervious floor.*

Discussion and Commentary: An open hub drain is a common method of providing a waste receptor in water-impervious floors. It eliminates the need to provide a separate fixture with a strainer. A hubbed drain pipe or plain-end section of pipe serves as the receptor for receiving indirect waste. Section 802.3 permits hub drains without strainers provided they receive only clear-water waste.

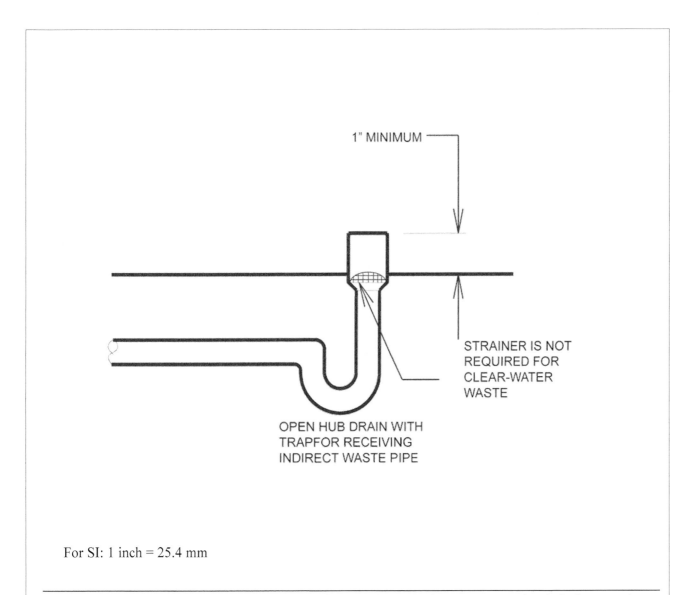

For SI: 1 inch = 25.4 mm

The pipe or hub is required to be a minimum of 1 inch above the floor to prevent the drain from serving as a floor drain.

Study Session 11

Topic: Standpipes
Reference: IPC 802.4.3
Category: Indirect/Special Waste
Subject: Indirect Wastes

Code Text: *Standpipes shall be individually trapped. Standpipes shall extend not less than 18 inches (457 mm) but not greater than 42 inches (1066 mm) above the trap weir. Access shall be provided to all standpipes and drains for rodding.*

Discussion and Commentary: By definition, a standpipe is considered an indirect waste receptor. The minimum dimension for the height of the receptor is intended to provide minimal retention capacity and head pressure to prevent an overflow. This is especially necessary when an indirect waste pipe receives a high rate of discharge, such as the pumped discharge of a clothes washer. The maximum height requirement is intended to control the waste flow velocity at the trap inlet. Excessive inlet velocity can promote trap siphonage.

The trap weir is the bottom surface of the trap outlet pipe that connects to the drain. At this elevation, the water surface is at the same level on both sides of the trap.

Topic: Laundry Tray to Standpipe
Reference: IPC 802.4.3.1
Category: Indirect/Special Waste
Subject: Indirect Wastes

Code Text: *As an alternative for a laundry tray fixture connecting directly to a drainage system, a laundry tray waste line without a fixture trap shall connect to a standpipe for an automatic clothes washer drain. The standpipe shall extend not less than 30 inches (732 mm) above the weir of the standpipe trap and shall extend above the flood level rim of the laundry tray. The outlet of the laundry tray shall not be greater than 30 inches (762 mm) horizontal distance from the side of the standpipe.*

Discussion and Commentary: In typical residential occupancies, a laundry tub is located directly adjacent to a clothes washer. To provide for economy in installing plumbing systems, the code offers an alternative for connecting a laundry tub drain to the clothes washer standpipe rather than a typical fixture trap and drain connection. In this case, the standpipe trap serves as the trap for the laundry tub and an additional trap is not allowed on the fixture drain. The horizontal distance is also limited to 30 inches between the laundry tub and the connection to the standpipe.

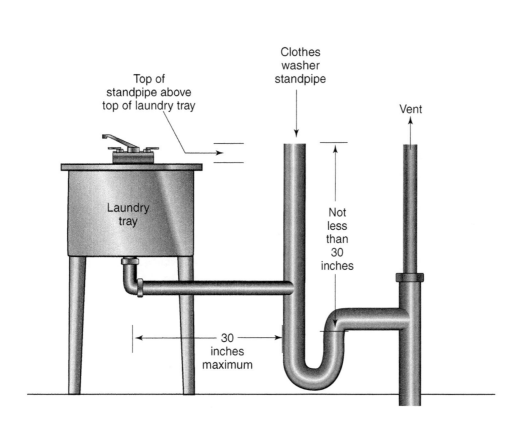

For SI: 1 inch = 25.4 mm

The standpipe is required to extend at least 30 inches above the standpipe trap weir and to extend above the flood level rim of the laundry tub.

Study Session 11

Topic: Corrosive Wastes
Reference: IPC 803.1
Category: Indirect/Special Waste
Subject: Indirect Wastes

Code Text: *Corrosive liquids, spent acids or other harmful chemicals that destroy or injure a drain, sewer, soil or waste pipe, or create noxious or toxic fumes or interfere with sewage treatment processes shall not be discharged into the plumbing system without being thoroughly diluted, neutralized or treated by passing through an approved dilution or neutralizing device. Such devices shall be automatically provided with a sufficient supply of diluting water or neutralizing medium so as to make the contents noninjurious before discharge into the drainage system. The nature of the corrosive or harmful waste and the method of its treatment or dilution shall be approved prior to installation.*

Discussion and Commentary: A special waste system must treat any deleterious waste and reduce the threat to an acceptable level before being discharged to the sanitary drainage system. Special waste systems are associated with atypical plumbing systems, including laboratories, chemical plants, processing plants and hospitals. Treatment generally involves dilution of the chemical waste to an acceptable level.

The code does not specify what is an acceptable level of dilution, because it varies by pipe material and type of waste.

Topic: System Design
Reference: IPC 803.2

Category: Indirect/Special Waste
Subject: Special Wastes

Code Text: *A chemical drainage and vent system shall be designed and installed in accordance with this code. Chemical drainage and vent systems shall be completely separated from the sanitary systems. Chemical waste shall not discharge to a sanitary drainage system until such waste has been treated in accordance with Section 803.1*

Discussion and Commentary: When a chemical drainage system is installed, the drainage and vent piping must still conform to all code requirements. The pipe sizing and installation would have to conform to the requirements of Chapters 7 and 9, and other chapters as applicable.

The code requires a completely separate vent system because of the uncertainty of the nature of fumes and vapors in a chemical waste system. The gases in the chemical drain, waste and vent (DWV) system could be incompatible with the piping materials and gases in the normal DWV system.

Study Session 11

Quiz

Study Session 11
IPC Chapter 8

1. A _____ is required to discharge indirectly through an air gap to the sanitary drainage system.

    a. food-preparation sink

    b. pots-and-pans sink

    c. domestic dishwashing machine

    d. commercial dishwashing machine

    Reference _____

2. A _____ is allowed to discharge through an air break into an indirect waste receptor.

    a. swimming pool deck drain

    b. food-preparation sink

    c. commercial dishwashing machine

    d. sterilizer

    Reference _____

3. Floor drains in walk-in refrigerators of food establishments shall be _____.

    a. directly connected to the drainage system

    b. directly connected to the drainage system when protected with a backwater valve

    c. indirectly connected to the drainage system by means of an air gap

    d. indirectly connected to the drainage system by means of an air break

    Reference _____

4. Fixtures that discharge through an indirect waste connection are required to be trapped when the fixture drain exceeds _____ inches in horizontal developed length.

    a. 36   b. 72

    c. 30   d. 48

Reference _____

5. An indirect waste receptor must be sized based on the _____ of the fixtures served.

    a. largest indirect waste pipe   b. maximum discharge

    c. fixture units   d. function

Reference _____

6. A hub drain receiving the discharge from an ice storage bin through an air gap and connected to the sanitary drainage system is not required to _____.

    a. be trapped and vented

    b. be equipped with a removable strainer

    c. be designed and installed to prevent splashing

    d. extend a minimum of 1 inch above the surrounding floor

Reference _____

7. Corrosive liquids that may harm drainage piping are prohibited from being discharged to the sanitary drainage system unless first _____.

    a. permitted for discharge by state and federal agencies

    b. filtered through a diatomaceous earth filtration system

    c. diluted by water or passed through a neutralizing medium

    d. tested to determine that they are not corrosive to the piping system

Reference _____

8. Indirect waste receptors require _____.

    a. a splash guard   b. ready access

    c. an air gap   d. a deep seal trap

Reference _____

9. Chemical drainage systems require _____.
   a. separation from the sanitary drainage and vent system
   b. installation above ground
   c. piping materials of borosilicate glass, polyvinylidene plastic, polyethylene plastic or polyolefin plastic
   d. installation underground

   Reference _____

10. Automatic clothes washer standpipes are limited to a maximum height of _____ inches above the trap weir.
    a. 18   b. 24
    c. 30   d. 42

    Reference _____

11. The waste line of a commercial dishwashing machine is permitted to discharge through _____.
    a. an air gap or air break
    b. a wye fitting on a sink tail piece
    c. a food waste disposer
    d. an air gap only

    Reference _____

12. Indirect waste receptors shall not be installed in _____.
    a. boiler rooms   b. crawl spaces
    c. pantries   d. soiled linen utility rooms

    Reference _____

13. Swimming pool deck drains that drain to the building's sanitary drainage system shall discharge through a(n) _____.
    a. direct connection
    b. direct waste pipe by means of an air gap
    c. indirect waste pipe by means of an air break or an air gap
    d. indirect waste pipe by means of an air gap

    Reference _____

14. Indirect waste piping that exceeds 54 inches in total developed length shall be _____.

    a. prohibited   b. readily accessible
    c. trapped   d. provided with a relief vent

    Reference _____

15. Standpipes shall extend a minimum of _____ inches above the trap weir.

    a. 6   b. 12
    c. 16   d. 18

    Reference _____

16. A laundry tray is permitted to discharge to the automatic clothes washer standpipe provided the laundry tray waste line _____.

    a. has a fixture trap and drains through an air break
    b. is without a trap and connects directly to the standpipe
    c. does not exceed 24 inches in developed length
    d. discharges to the standpipe at a point not less than 30 inches above the weir of the standpipe trap

    Reference _____

17. A _____ used as an indirect waste receptor does not require a removable strainer.

    a. standpipe
    b. floor sink
    c. floor drain
    d. laundry sink

    Reference _____

18. Hub drains shall be permitted in the form of a hub or pipe extending not less than _____ inch(es) above a water-impervious floor.

    a. $3/4$ b. 2
    c. $1 1/2$ d. 1

    Reference _____

19. The air gap between the indirect waste pipe and the flood level rim of the waste receptor shall be a minimum of _____ times the effective opening of the indirect waste pipe.

    a. 1
    b. 2
    c. 3
    d. 4

Reference_____

20. Special function sterilization, humidification, distillation, processing, cooling and food storage equipment shall be provided with protection against _____.

    a. splashing
    b. fouling
    c. damage
    d. displacement

Reference_____

21. When fixtures discharging to the drainage system are not required to be indirectly connected and do not meet the conditions for on-site nonpotable water reuse systems, they _____.

    a. shall be directly connected
    b. are permitted to be directly connected
    c. are permitted to be indirectly connected
    d. may be directly connected if approved

Reference_____

22. In a walk-in food storage freezer, the waste line serving the floor drain shall _____.

    a. be trapped
    b. not be trapped
    c. be protected from freezing
    d. be directly connected to the drainage system

Reference_____

23. An indirect waste pipe that discharges through an air break must terminate above the _____ of the waste receptor.

    a. flood level rim
    b. trap seal
    c. critical level
    d. strainer dome

Reference_____

24. A neutralizing device for corrosive wastes shall make the contents _____ before discharge into the drainage system.

    a. neutral   b. harmless

    c. nontoxic   d. noninjurious

Reference_____

25. A three-compartment food preparation sink requires indirect connection by means of _____.

    a. three separate indirect waste pipes

    b. an air gap or air break

    c. a drain manifold with a trap

    d. waste piping to a floor sink

Reference_____

Study Session

12

2018 IPC Sections 901 through 909
Vents I

OBJECTIVE: To gain an understanding of the code requirements related to trap seal protection, common vents, wet venting and vent termination.

REFERENCE: Sections 901 through 909, 2018 *International Plumbing Code*

KEY POINTS:
- Vent piping prevents what from occurring in the system?
- What traps and trapped fixtures are required to be vented?
- What special restrictions apply to the vent system for a chemical waste system?
- Can the vent system be used for purposes other than the venting of the plumbing?
- Is testing required for the venting system?
- Open vents through roofs are required to extend above the roof how many inches?
- What measures are taken to prevent frost closure of vents extending through a roof or wall?
- When do the frost closure provisions apply?
- What protection is required to prevent water intrusion when a vent penetrates the roof?
- What minimum distance is required from an open vent terminal in regard to windows, doors and air intakes?
- What clearances are required above grade and away from property lines for vent terminations?
- How many vent pipes must extend to the outdoors?
- Vent piping must drain by what means?
- What are the vent connection requirements in relation to the flood level rims of fixtures?
- When is a vent required for a future fixture?
- How is vent piping sized?
- When is a sump vent required and how is it sized?

KEY POINTS (CONT'D)
- What venting requirements apply to stack offsets?
- When is a relief vent required?
- How is the maximum length of a fixture vent determined?
- What is the maximum fall in a fixture drain?
- What is a crown vent and when is it permitted?

Topic: Roof Extension
Reference: IPC 903.1
Category: Vents
Subject: Vent Terminals

Code Text: *All open vent pipes that extend through a roof shall be terminated not less than [NUMBER] inches (mm) above the roof. Where a roof is to be used for assembly or as a promenade, observation deck, sunbathing deck or similar purposes, open vent pipes shall terminate not less than 7 feet (2134 mm) above the roof.*

Discussion and Commentary: Where the roof is occupied, such as for recreational or assembly purposes, plumbing vents must extend at least 7 feet above the roof to prevent harmful sewer gases from concentrating in the breathing zone of the area. The sewer gases will tend to disperse into the air, rather than accumulate near the roof surface. Otherwise, the minimum termination height must be determined by the local jurisdiction based on snowfall rates.

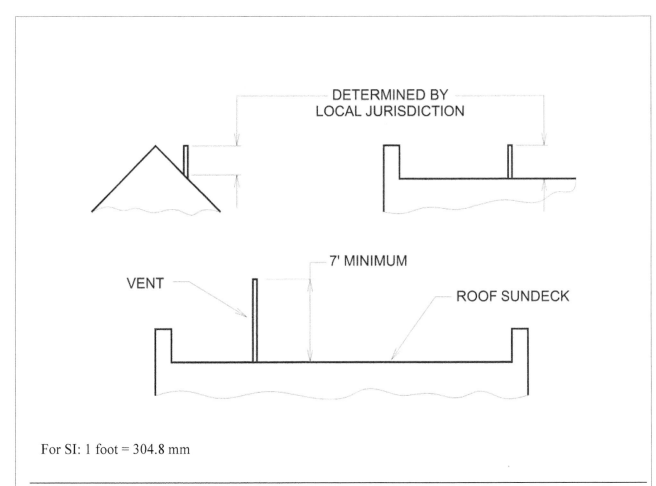

For SI: 1 foot = 304.8 mm

A termination height of 6 inches above the roof is typically used to allow for proper roof flashing. In areas with snow, the termination is typically not less than 6 inches above the anticipated snow accumulation.

Topic: Frost Closure
Reference: IPC 903.2

Category: Vents
Subject: Vent Terminals

Code Text: *Where the 97.5-percent value for outside design temperature is 0°F (-18°C) or less, vent extensions through a roof or wall shall be not less than 3 inches (76 mm) in diameter. Any increase in the size of the vent shall be made not less than 1 foot (305 mm) inside the thermal envelope of the building.*

Discussion and Commentary: In very cold weather, warm, moist air rising to the vent termination condenses on the inside of the pipe and freezes. Over a prolonged period of freezing weather, this frost can accumulate to the point of completely closing the vent, particularly for 1½- and 2-inch vent pipes at the roof termination. Where the 97.5-percent value for outside design temperature is 0°F or less, the code requires not less than 3-inch diameter vent terminals. Smaller diameter vent pipes must transition to the 3-inch diameter starting at not less than 1 foot inside the building's thermal envelope (in the heated space).

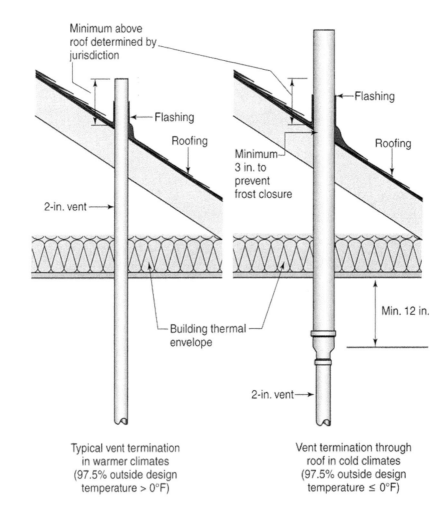

For SI: 1 inch = 25.4 mm

The 97.5-percent value for outside design temperature for major cities in the United States is found in Appendix D of the IPC.

Topic: Location of Vent Terminal
Reference: IPC 903.5
Category: Vents
Subject: Vent Terminals

Code Text: *An open vent terminal from a drainage system shall not be located directly beneath any door, openable window, or other air intake opening of the building or of an adjacent building, and any such vent terminal shall not be within 10 feet (3048 mm) horizontally of such an opening unless it is 3 feet (914 mm) or more above the top of such opening.*

Discussion and Commentary: The vent terminal must be located away from any building air intake opening (gravity or mechanical) to reduce the possibility of sewer gases entering a building. A 10-foot horizontal separation is deemed adequate to allow sewer gases to dissipate into the outdoor atmosphere. For vent terminals that do not meet the horizontal separation requirements, a 3-foot vertical separation above openings ensures the safe discharge of sewer gases.

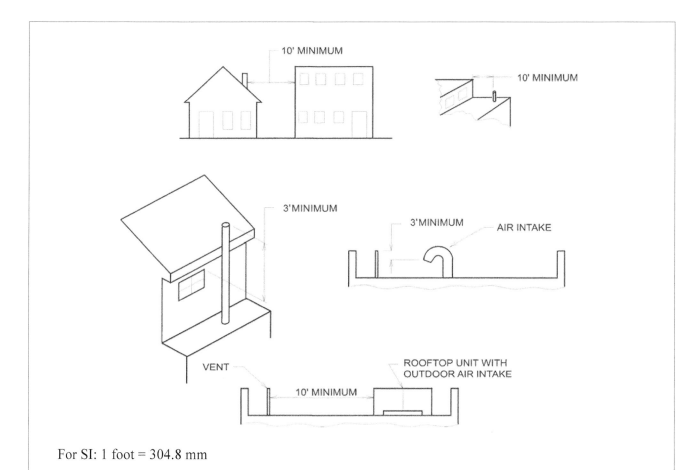

For SI: 1 foot = 304.8 mm

The code does not regulate separation or termination height for vent terminals near nonopenable windows.

Topic: Required Vent Extension
Reference: IPC 904.1
Category: Vents
Subject: Outdoor Vent Extensions

Code Text: *The vent system serving each building drain shall have at least one vent pipe that extends to the outdoors.*

Discussion and Commentary: At least one vent pipe must extend to the outside to ensure that pressures are equalized on each side of the fixture traps in the drain, waste and vent system to preserve the trap seal in each trap. The alternative to venting to the outdoor air is to use air admittance valves, which are mechanical devices that typically open to the inside air when the fixture is draining, thereby preserving the trap seal. Although air admittance valves are permitted in many locations, they are not permitted to provide all of the venting for the DWV system.

Vents extending to the outdoors typically terminate at the roof of the building through flashings that preserve the weather resistance of the roof assembly.

Topic: Vent Stack Required
Reference: IPC 904.2
Category: Vents
Subject: Outdoor Vent Extensions

Code Text: *A vent stack shall be required for every drainage stack that is five branch intervals or more. See the exception for waste stack vents in accordance with Section 913.*

Discussion and Commentary: If a drainage stack is five or more branch intervals in height, a vent stack is required. If the drainage stack is less than five branch intervals in height, a vent stack is not required because the pressures in the drainage stack are not likely to create a pressure differential at the trap seals in excess of 1 inch of water column. A stack vent is typically utilized as a collection point for vent pipes so that a single roof penetration can be made.

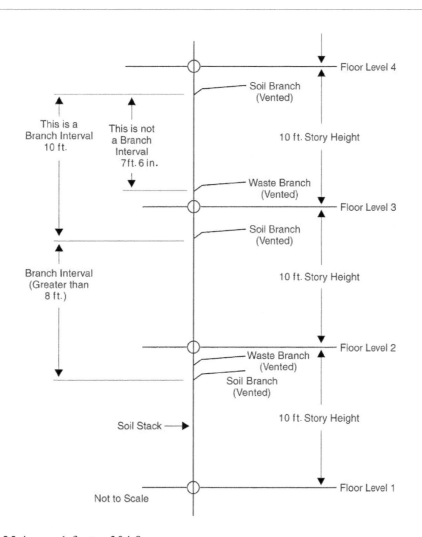

For SI: 1 inch = 25.4 mm, 1 foot = 304.8 mm

BRANCH INTERVAL: A vertical measurement of distance, 8 feet (2438 mm) or more in developed length, between the connections of horizontal branches to a drainage stack. Measurements are taken down the stack from the highest horizontal branch connection.
VENT STACK: A vertical vent pipe installed primarily for the purpose of providing circulation of air to and from any part of the drainage system.

Topic: Vent Termination
Reference: IPC 904.3
Category: Vents
Subject: Outdoor Vent Extensions

Code Text: *Vent stacks and stack vents shall terminate outdoors to the open air or to a stack-type air admittance valve in accordance with Section 918.*

Discussion and Commentary: A vent stack or stack vent cannot terminate in an attic, cupola, open parking structure or any other space within a building envelope, regardless of how well such space is ventilated. The vent must extend to the outdoors to permit gases, vapors and odors from the drainage system to escape into the atmosphere away from the building. If air admittance valves are to be used, they must be stack-type air admittance valves.

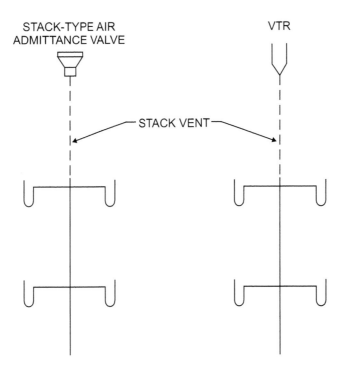

EVERY STACK VENT OR VENT STACK MUST TERMINATE TO OPEN AIR OR STACK-TYPE AIR ADMITTANCE VALVE

AIR ADMITTANCE VALVE: One-way valve designed to allow air to enter the plumbing drainage system when negative pressures develop in the piping system. The device shall close by gravity and seal the vent terminal at zero differential pressure (no flow conditions) and under positive internal pressures.

Topic: Vent Connection at Base
Reference: IPC 904.4
Category: Vents
Subject: Outdoor Vent Extensions

Code Text: *Vent stacks shall connect to the base of the drainage stack. The vent stack shall connect at or below the lowest horizontal branch. Where the vent stack connects to the building drain, the connection shall be located downstream of the drainage stack and within a distance of 10 times the diameter of the drainage stack.*

Discussion and Commentary: A drainage stack of five or more branch intervals must be vented at or below the lowest branch connection to relieve the positive pressure developed in the stack. The connection can be to the stack or to the building drain downstream of the stack and within a distance of 10 times the drainage stack diameter.

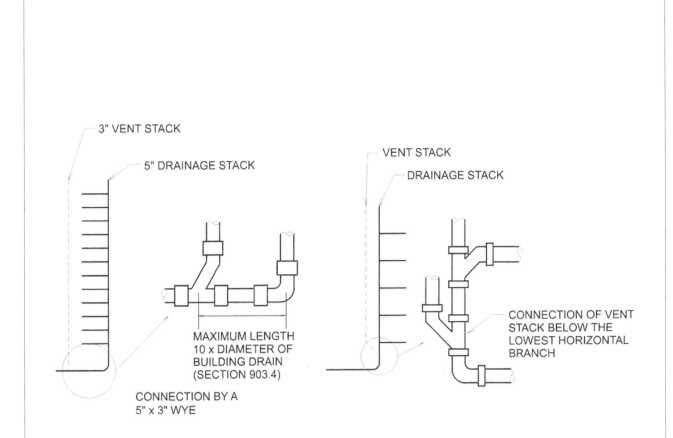

For SI: 1 inch = 25.4 mm

The size of the vent connection to the drainage system must not be less than the size required for the vent stack. Vent stacks are sized in accordance with Section 906.1, based on the size of the drainage stack at its base.

Topic: Grade
Reference: IPC 905.2
Category: Vents
Subject: Vents Connections and Grades

Code Text: *All vent and branch vent pipes shall be so graded and connected as to drain back to the drainage pipe by gravity.*

Discussion and Commentary: Vents convey water vapor from the drainage system and such vapor may condense in the vent piping. Also, rainwater can enter a vent system at the vent termination; therefore, the vent must be sloped to the drainage system, thus preventing any accumulation of condensate or rainwater. The slope of a vent pipe does not affect the movement of air inside the pipe. Vent piping must be adequately supported to maintain slope and prevent sagging.

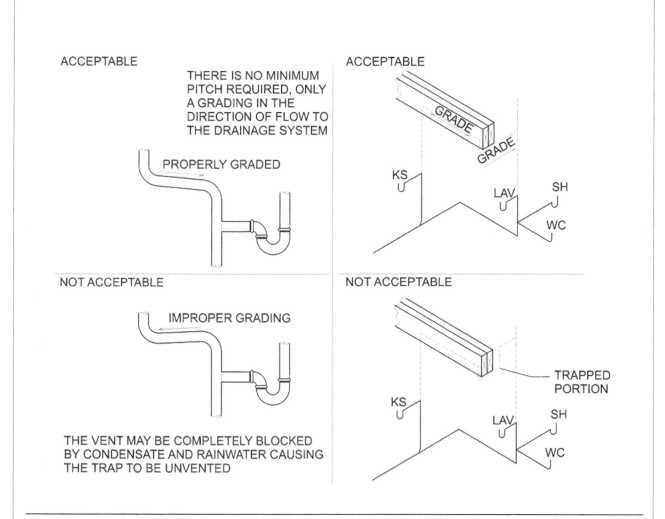

It makes no difference if the vent piping slopes to drain back to the drain piping served by the vent or if the vent piping slopes to drain to a vent stack or stack vent, provided that water will not stand in any portion of the venting system.

Topic: Vent Connection to Drainage System **Category:** Vents
Reference: IPC 905.3 **Subject:** Vent Connections and Grades

Code Text: *Every dry vent connecting to a horizontal drain shall connect above the centerline of the horizontal drain pipe.*

Discussion and Commentary: To avoid possible blockages, the vent must connect to horizontal drains above the centerline. The intent is to prevent waste from entering a dry vent by connecting the vent above the flow line of the drain. Such connections will result in vent piping that forms a 45-degree angle or greater with the horizontal.

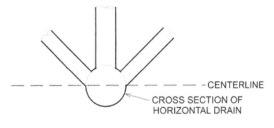

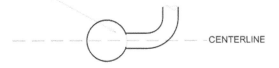

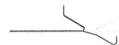

VENT SYSTEM: A pipe or pipes installed to provide a flow of air to or from a drainage system, or to provide a circulation of air within such system to protect trap seals from siphonage and backpressure.

Topic: Vent for Future Fixtures	Category: Vents
Reference: IPC 905.6	Subject: Vent Connections and Grades

Code Text: *Where the drainage piping has been roughed-in for future fixtures, a rough-in connection for a vent shall be installed. The vent size shall be not less than one-half the diameter of the rough-in drain to be served. The vent rough-in shall connect to the vent system, or shall be vented by other means as provided for in this chapter. The connection shall be identified to indicate that it is a vent.*

Discussion and Commentary: Section 710.2 addresses the installation of drainage pipe for future plumbing fixtures. Where future fixture rough-in piping occurs, vent piping must also be installed. The vent pipe is simply roughed-in in such a manner as to remain accessible for future connection when plumbing fixtures are installed. The vent rough-in must be tied in to the vent system, as required by Section 905.1, or it must extend to a vent terminal in the outside air.

710.2 Future fixtures. Where provision is made for the future installation of fixtures, those provided for shall be considered in determining the required sizes of drain pipes.

Where the installation of a future fixture will require making a connection to the vent rough-in, such connection must be identified as a vent so that the purpose of the original installation is evident when the future fixture is installed.

Topic: Where Required
Reference: IPC 908.1
Category: Vents
Subject: Relief Vents—Stacks

Code Text: *Soil and waste stacks in buildings having more than 10 branch intervals shall be provided with a relief vent at each tenth interval installed, beginning with the top floor.*

Discussion and Commentary: This section requires a method of relieving pressure conditions in drainage stacks more than 10 branch intervals in height. The flow in a drainage stack creates both negative and positive pressures. The vent system is designed to equalize the air pressures at the trap seal. A relief vent is required to assist the fixture venting and the venting at the base of the stack by providing midpoint connections to the stack. The relief vent prevents excessive pressure from being created by emitting or admitting air at specified points within the stack.

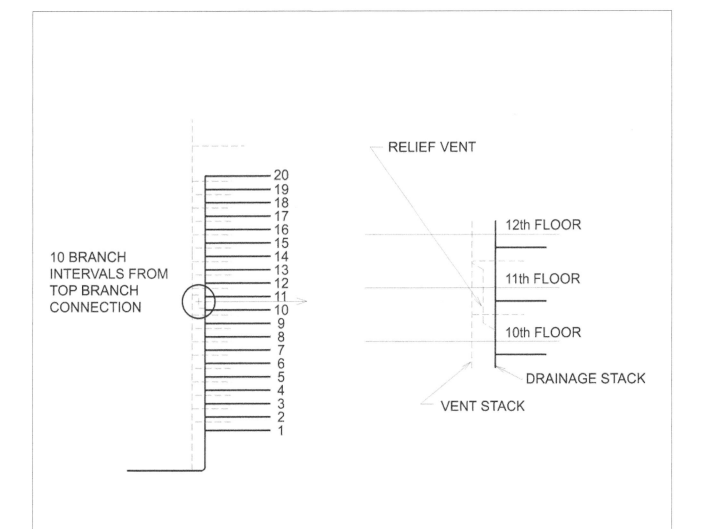

A relief vent must be located every 10 branch intervals, measured from the highest horizontal drainage branch, which is typically the top floor. The interval breaks are then calculated downward to the base of the stack.

Topic: Size and Connection
Reference: IPC 908.2
Category: Vents
Subject: Relief Vents—Stacks

Code Text: *The size of the relief vent shall be equal to the size of the vent stack to which it connects. The lower end of each relief vent shall connect to the soil or waste stack through a wye below the horizontal branch serving the floor, and the upper end shall connect to the vent stack through a wye not less than 3 feet (914 mm) above the floor.*

Discussion and Commentary: This section requires the size of the relief vent to be at least equal to the size of the vent stack to which it connects. This is considered the minimum necessary to provide sufficient venting capacity in both the relief vent and the stack vent to which it is connected.

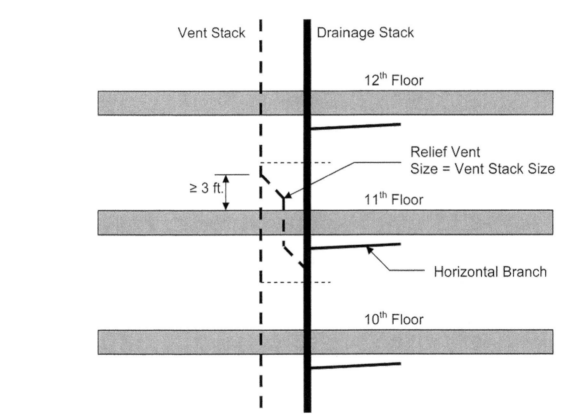

For SI: 1 foot = 304.8 mm

RELIEF VENT: A vent whose primary function is to provide circulation of air between drainage and vent systems. **STACK:** A general term for any vertical line of soil, waste, vent or inside conductor piping that extends through at least one story with or without offsets. **SOIL PIPE:** A pipe that conveys sewage containing fecal matter to the building drain or building sewer.

Topic: Distance of Trap from Vent **Category:** Vents
Reference: IPC 909.1 **Subject:** Fixture Vents

Code Text: *Each fixture trap shall have a protecting vent located so that the slope and the developed length in the fixture drain from the trap weir to the vent fitting are within the requirements set forth in Table 906.1. See the exception for self-siphoning fixtures such as water closets.*

Discussion and Commentary: The distance from every trap to its vent is limited to reduce the possibility of the trap self-siphoning. Self-siphoning of a trap is the siphoning caused by the discharge from the fixture the trap serves. Studies have been done to address whether the trap-to-vent distance for a water closet should be limited. Because the water closet relies on self-siphonage to operate properly, and the trap is resealed after each use, there is no need for limiting the distance from the water closet to a vent.

TABLE 909.1
MAXIMUM DISTANCE OF FIXTURE TRAP FROM VENT

SIZE OF TRAP (inches)	SLOPE (inch per foot)	DISTANCE FROM TRAP (feet)
$1\frac{1}{4}$	$\frac{1}{4}$	5
$1\frac{1}{2}$	$\frac{1}{4}$	6
2	$\frac{1}{4}$	8
3	$\frac{1}{8}$	12
4	$\frac{1}{8}$	16

For SI: 1 inch = 25.4 mm, 1 foot = 304.8 mm, 1 inch per foot = 83.3 mm/m.

The water closet must be vented in all cases, but limiting the distance between the vent connection and the water closet is not necessary. This exception applies to all self-siphoning fixtures.

Topic: Venting of Fixture Drains
Reference: IPC 909.2
Category: Vents
Subject: Fixture Vents

Code Text: *The total fall in a fixture drain due to pipe slope shall not exceed the diameter of the fixture drain, nor shall the vent connection to a fixture drain, except for water closets, be below the weir of the trap.*

Discussion and Commentary: This section reinforces the previous requirement in Section 909.1. The trap weir must stay below the highest inlet to the vent except for fixtures with integral traps. The fixture drain cannot offset or drop vertically, other than the required slope, between the trap and its vent connection.

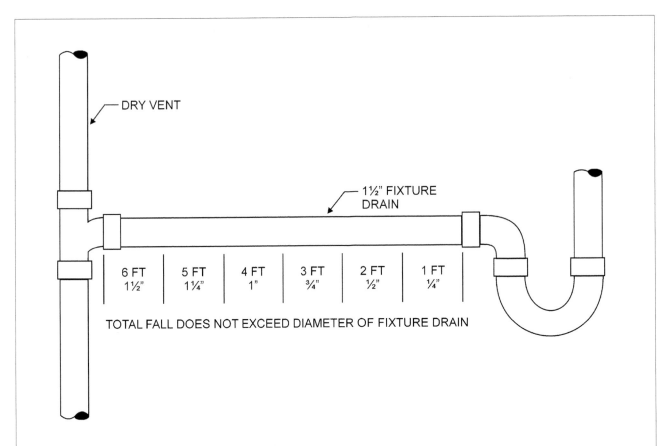

For SI: 1 inch = 25.4 mm, 1 foot = 304.8 mm

FIXTURE DRAIN: The drain from the trap of a fixture to a junction with any other drain pipe.

Topic: Crown Vent
Reference: IPC 909.3
Category: Vents
Subject: Fixture Vents

Code Text: *A vent shall not be installed within two pipe diameters of the trap weir.*

Discussion and Commentary: Without proper venting distance, the vent opening becomes blocked. The blockage is a result of the action of the drainage flowing through the trap. The flow direction and velocity will force waste up into the vent connection, eventually clogging it with debris. It has been determined that the vent connection must be a minimum of two pipe diameters downstream from the trap weir to prevent the vent from becoming blocked.

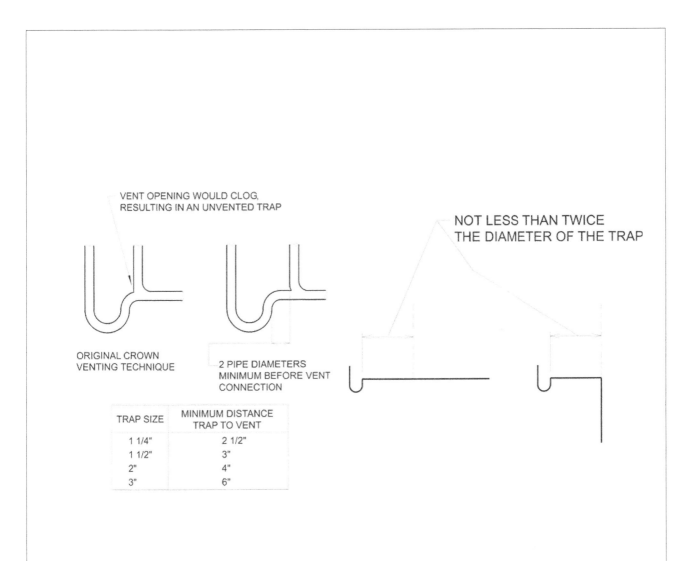

For SI: 1 inch = 25.4 mm

Crown venting is any arrangement where a vent connects at the top of the weir (crown) of a trap.

Study Session 12
IPC Sections 901 through 909

1. The main purpose of venting is for _____.
   a. exhaust of sewer gases
   b. trap seal protection
   c. decreasing flow rates
   d. increasing flow rates

   Reference _____

2. A vent piping system is necessary to prevent pressure differentials of more than _____ against the trap seal of any fixture.
   a. 1 inch of water column
   b. 1 foot of head
   c. 1 PSI
   d. 0.433 PSI

   Reference _____

3. The vent system for a chemical waste system must _____.
   a. connect to the sanitary vent system above the highest fixture
   b. terminate through a wall to the outdoors
   c. be independent of the sanitary vent system
   d. terminate in a stack-type air admittance valve

   Reference _____

4. Prefabricated lead flashings for vent pipe penetrations must have a sheet weight of not less than _____ pounds per square foot.
   a. 3.5
   b. 2.5
   c. 1.25
   d. 0.75

   Reference _____

5. In a sanitary drainage system, what is the minimum number of vent pipes that are required to extend to the outdoors?

   a. one

   b. two

   c. one for each air admittance valve

   d. one for each vent stack or stack vent

   Reference _____

6. A vent stack connection to the base of a stack is required to connect_____.

   a. above the lowest horizontal branch

   b. to the building drain

   c. at or below the lowest horizontal branch

   d. a minimum of 10 pipe diameters away from the stack

   Reference _____

7. Where required to be protected against frost closure, the vent extension through the roof shall be not less than _____ inches in diameter beginning not less than _____ inches inside the thermal envelope.

   a. 4, 12   b. 3, 12

   c. 3, 18   d. 4, 6

   Reference _____

8. Frost closure protection for vent terminals is required in which of the following locations?

   a. Denver, Colorado   b. Juneau, Alaska

   c. Goodland, Kansas   d. South Bend, Indiana

   Reference _____

9. What is the minimum required height of a vent terminal located on a roof that serves as a sun deck?

    a. 1 foot
    b. 2 feet
    c. 7 feet
    d. 10 feet

    Reference _____

10. A vent shall terminate a minimum of _____ feet horizontally from or at least _____ feet above a window opening.

    a. 8, 3
    b. 10, 3
    c. 8, 4
    d. 10, 4

    Reference _____

11. What is the minimum required height above average grade for a vent terminating through the side wall of a building?

    a. 2 feet
    b. 7 feet
    c. 8 feet
    d. 10 feet

    Reference _____

12. Vent pipes installed on the exterior of a building must be protected against freezing if the 97.5-percent value for outside design temperature is _____.

    a. less than 5°F
    b. 5°F or less
    c. 0°F or less
    d. less than 0°F

    Reference _____

13. A dry vent is prohibited from offsetting horizontally until the vertical rise of the vent is _____.

    a. above the highest fixture branch connected to the building drain
    b. above the flood level rim of the highest fixture connecting to the building drain
    c. 6 inches above the connection of the stack vent to a drainage stack
    d. 6 inches above the flood rim of the highest trap or trapped fixture being vented

    Reference _____

14. A kitchen sink with a 1 1/2-inch fixture drain must be vented within a developed length of _____ feet from the trap weir to the vent fitting.

    a. 3
    b. 5
    c. 6
    d. 8

    Reference _____

15. Which fixture is allowed to have a vent connection to the fixture drain below the weir of the trap?

    a. shower drain
    b. laundry sink
    c. floor drain
    d. water closet

    Reference _____

16. What is the maximum developed length of the fixture drain from the trap weir of a water closet to the vent fitting?

    a. 8 feet
    b. 12 feet
    c. 16 feet
    d. unlimited

    Reference _____

17. In no case shall the diameter of stack vents and vent stacks be less than one-half the diameter of the drain served or less than _____ inches.

    a. 1 1/4
    b. 1 1/2
    c. 2
    d. 3

    Reference _____

18. Branch vents exceeding _____ feet in developed length shall be increased by one nominal size for the entire developed length of the vent pipe.

    a. 25
    b. 30
    c. 35
    d. 40

    Reference _____

19. For waste stacks having more than 10 branch intervals, the relief vent must be not less than _____.

    a. 2 inches in diameter
    b. the size of the vent stack
    c. one-half the diameter of the vent stack
    d. one pipe size smaller than the vent stack

    Reference_____

20. Where venting is required for a drainage stack offset, a vent shall connect to the stack _____ the offset.

    a. above
    b. not less than 12 inches above
    c. above or below
    d. above and below

    Reference_____

21. Individual and branch vent pipes exceeding 40 feet in developed length are required to be_____.

    a. not less than 2 inches in diameter
    b. one-half the diameter of the drain served
    c. not less than 2 pipe sizes smaller than the largest drain served
    d. one pipe size greater than otherwise required

    Reference_____

22. When a $1^1/_4$-inch diameter vent pipe serves the sump of a sewage ejector pump with a discharge capacity of 40 gpm, the maximum developed length of the vent is _____ feet.

    a. unlimited
    b. 40
    c. 72
    d. 160

    Reference_____

23. A relief vent is required for a waste stack having more than _____ branch intervals.

    a. 16
    b. 5
    c. 8
    d. 10

    Reference_____

24. For a 2-inch fixture drain, the maximum distance from the trap weir to the vent fitting is _____ feet.

    a. 3   b. 5

    c. 6   d. 8

Reference_____

25. A vent shall not be installed within _____ pipe diameters of the trap weir.

    a. 2   b. 3

    c. 4   d. 6

Reference_____

Study Session
13

2018 IPC Sections 910 through 920
Vents II

OBJECTIVE: To develop an understanding of the code provisions for vents, circuit venting, combination drain and vent systems, island fixture venting and the uses of air admittance valves.

REFERENCE: Sections 910 through 920, 2018 *International Plumbing Code*

KEY POINTS:
- What is the difference between a common vent and an individual vent?
- What requirements apply when two fixture drains connect to the common vent at the same level? At different levels?
- What fixtures are permitted to be vented by a horizontal wet vent? A vertical wet vent?
- What are the connection requirements for the dry vent serving a wet vent system?
- How is a wet vented system sized? How is the connected dry vent sized?
- What criteria apply to a waste stack vent?
- A vent stack is required based on how many branch intervals?
- When is circuit venting permitted?
- Where do the vent connections occur in a circuit vented system?
- What is a combination waste and vent system? What fixtures may be vented?
- How is the piping sized for a combination waste and vent system?
- When can island fixture venting be used? Where are cleanouts required?
- How does a single stack vent system differ from other venting systems?
- What fixtures are permitted to connect to a single stack vent system? What limitations are placed on horizontal branches?
- Which types of vents are permitted to terminate to an air admittance valve?
- What is the minimum height above the fixture drain for the placement of the air admittance valve?

KEY POINTS:
(Cont'd)
- What provisions apply to the air admittance valve related to the location, access and ventilation of the space?
- Where are air admittance valves prohibited?

Topic: Individual Vent as Common Vent
Reference: IPC 911.1
Category: Vents
Subject: Common Vent

Code Text: *An individual vent is permitted to vent two traps or trapped fixtures as a common vent. The traps or trapped fixtures being common vented shall be located on the same floor level.*

Discussion and Commentary: For common venting, the vent is classified and sized as an individual vent. The fixture drains being common vented may connect to either a vertical or horizontal drainage pipe. Any two fixtures can be common vented. The fixtures being common vented must be located on the same floor level so as to control flow velocities by limiting the vertical drop. Unless adequate separation is provided where water closets are common vented, Section 706.3 requires directional drainage fittings to prevent the discharge action of one fixture from interfering with the other fixture or causing a blowback into another fixture.

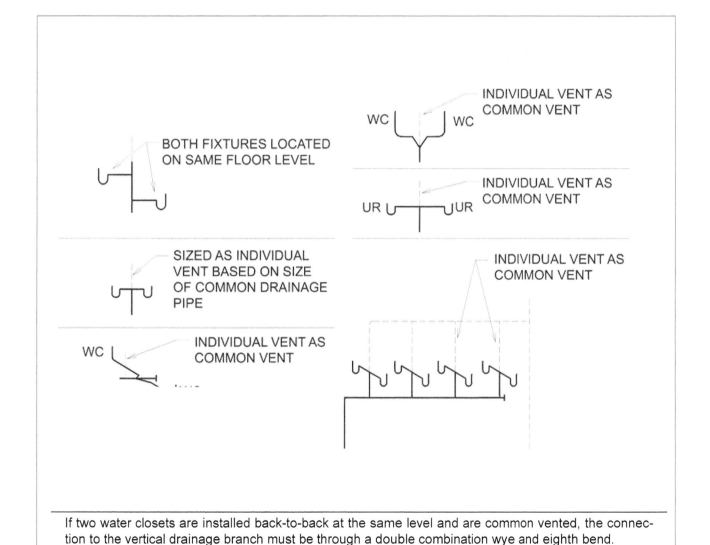

If two water closets are installed back-to-back at the same level and are common vented, the connection to the vertical drainage branch must be through a double combination wye and eighth bend.

Topic: Dry Vent Connection
Reference: IPC 912.2
Category: Vents
Subject: Wet Venting

Code Text: *The dry-vent connection for a horizontal wet-vent system shall be an individual vent or a common vent for any bathroom group fixture, except an emergency floor drain. Where the dry-vent connects to a water closet fixture drain, the drain shall connect horizontally to the horizontal wet-vent system. Not more than one wet-vented fixture drain shall discharge upstream of the dry-vented fixture drain connection. The dry-vent connection for a vertical wet-vent system shall be an individual vent or common vent for the most upstream fixture drain.*

Discussion and Commentary: The section of piping used as a wet vent is increased in size to function as both a drain and a vent. The increased size allows additional free area in the pipe to serve as a vent for a downstream fixture. Each fixture must connect separately to a horizontal wet vent. This means that fixture drains from two or more fixtures are not permitted to connect before discharging to the branch serving as a wet vent. The code permits a dry-vent connection to the horizontal drain of any fixture of a bathroom group including water closets but excluding emergency floor drains. Floor drains are not as likely to be used often to provide sufficient wash to the wet vent, and a stoppage in the vent is possible. Only one fixture is permitted upstream from the dry-vent connection.

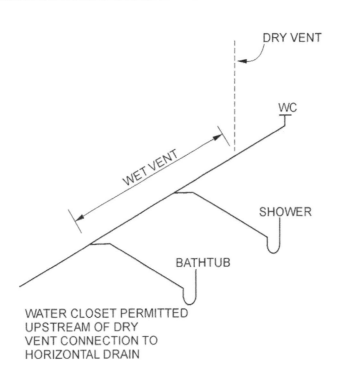

For horizontal wet venting, a water closet is permitted as the most upstream fixture. Only one fixture is permitted upstream of the dry vent connection, which in this case would connect to the water closet fixture drain. The dry vent must be sized in accordance with Section 912.3 based on the wet vent size established by Table 912.3.

Topic: Size
Reference: IPC 912.3
Category: Vents
Subject: Wet Venting

Code Text: *The dry vent serving the wet vent shall be sized based on the largest required diameter of pipe within the wet vent system served by the dry vent. The wet vent shall be of a minimum size as specified in Table 912.3, based on the fixture unit discharge to the wet vent.*

Discussion and Commentary: To ensure proper amount of air flow for the entire system, the size of the dry vent serving the wet vent is based on the largest pipe diameter within the wet vent system. This is the same criteria used for both systems. Table 912.3 establishes prescriptive wet vent pipe systems for different fixture unit loads from 1 dfu (a single lavatory or bidet) to 12 dfus (two bathroom groups).

TABLE 912.3
WET VENT SIZE

WET VENT PIPE SIZE (inches)	DRAINAGE FIXTURE UNIT LOAD (dfu)
$1\frac{1}{2}$	1
2	4
$2\frac{1}{2}$	6
3	12

For SI: 1 inch = 25.4 mm.

In a wet vented system, a single vent can provide airflow when fixtures are being discharged and relieve pressures that develop in the drain piping.

Study Session 13

Topic: Waste Stack Vent Permitted
Reference: IPC 913.1
Category: Vents
Subject: Waste Stack Vent

Code Text: *A waste stack shall be considered a vent for all of the fixtures discharging to the stack where installed in accordance with the requirements of this section.*

Discussion and Commentary: A waste stack vent uses the waste stack as the vent for fixtures other than urinals and water closets. The principles of use are based on some of the original research that was done in plumbing. The system has been identified by a variety of names, including vertical wet vent, Philadelphia single-stack and multifloor stack venting.

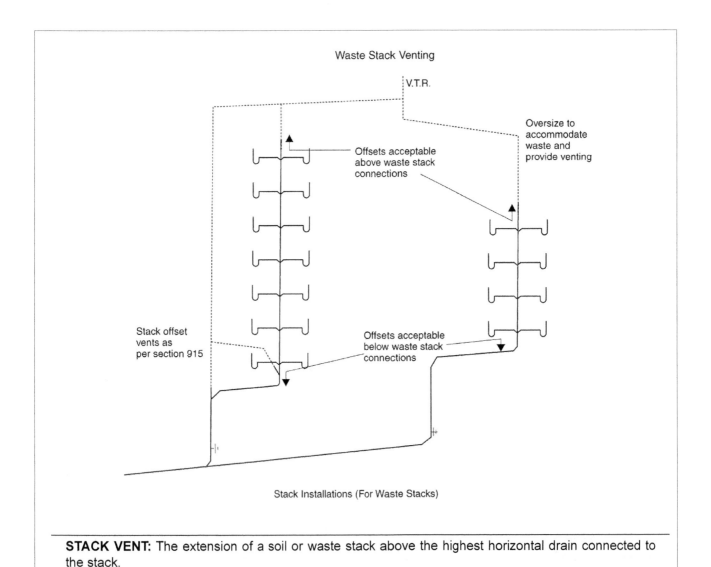

Stack Installations (For Waste Stacks)

STACK VENT: The extension of a soil or waste stack above the highest horizontal drain connected to the stack.

Topic: Stack Installation
Reference: IPC 913.2
Category: Vents
Subject: Waste Stack Vent

Code Text: *The waste stack shall be vertical, and both horizontal and vertical offsets shall be prohibited between the lowest fixture drain connection and the highest fixture drain connection. Every fixture drain shall connect separately to the waste stack. The stack shall not receive the discharge of water closets or urinals.*

Discussion and Commentary: Because the drainage stack serves as the vent, there are certain limitations on the design to prevent pressures in the system from exceeding plus or minus 1 inch of water column. Water closets and some urinals have a surging discharge that results in too great a pressure fluctuation in the system, so they are not allowed to connect to the stack system. The system may serve sinks, lavatories, bathtubs, bidets, showers, floor drains, drinking fountains and standpipes.

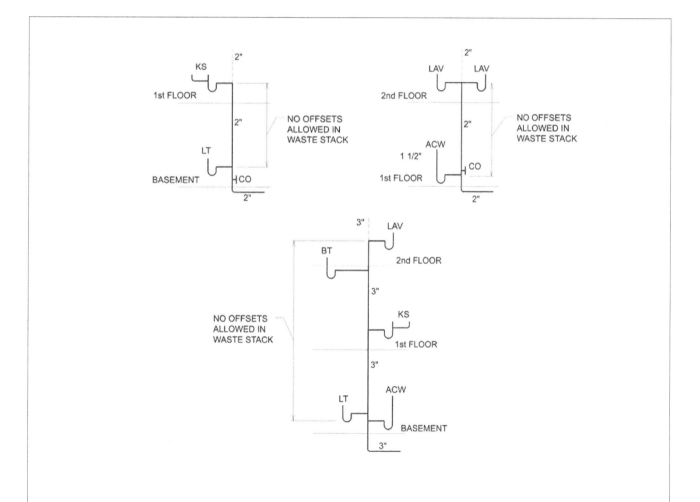

To preserve the desirable annular flow in the stack, offsets (of any degree) are prohibited. The stack must be vertical from the lowest fixture connection to above the highest fixture connection.

Topic: Stack Vent
Reference: IPC 913.3
Category: Vents
Subject: Waste Stack Vent

Code Text: *A stack vent shall be provided for the waste stack. The size of the stack vent shall be not less than the size of the waste stack. Offsets shall be permitted in the stack vent and shall be located not less than 6 inches (152 mm) above the flood level of the highest fixture, and shall be in accordance with Section 905.2. The stack vent shall be permitted to connect with other stack vents and vent stacks in accordance with Section 904.5.*

Discussion and Commentary: A full-size stack vent provides the vent opening to the outdoors, allowing the stack to remain at neutral pressures. Offsets are allowed in the stack vent because such offsets are dry and have no effect on the flow in the waste stack.

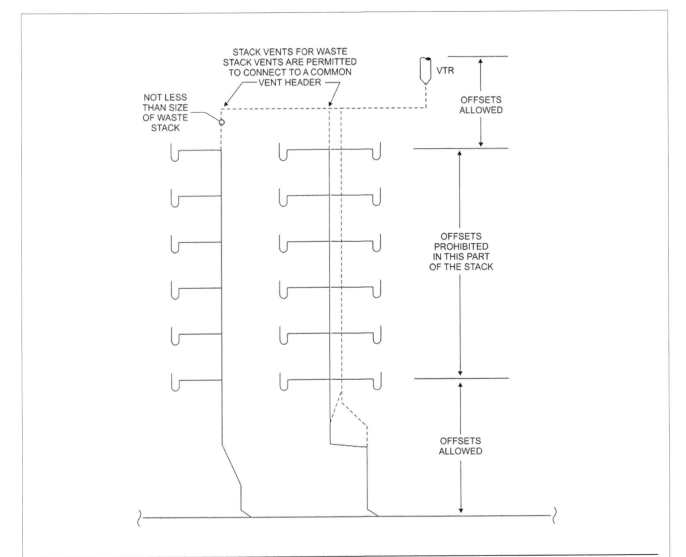

Stack dry vents must not run horizontally below the flood level rim of fixtures, because this may allow waste to enter the vent and impair its function.

Topic: Vent Connection
Reference: IPC 914.2
Category: Vents
Subject: Circuit Venting

Code Text: *The circuit vent connection shall be located between the two most upstream fixture drains. The vent shall connect to the horizontal branch and shall be installed in accordance with Section 905. The circuit vent pipe shall not receive the discharge of any soil or waste.*

Discussion and Commentary: The circuit vent must connect between the two most upstream fixture drains to allow proper circulation of air. The vent is located so that the most upstream fixture discharges past the vent connection, thereby washing that section of pipe and preventing the buildup of solids. For this reason, the most upstream fixture should not be a fixture that is seldom used (such as a floor drain).

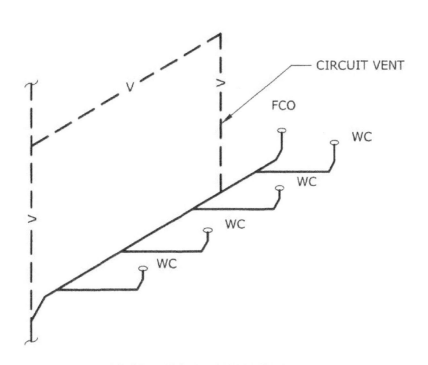

CIRCUIT VENT

Section 905 requires the vent to connect vertically to the drain and rise vertically to 6 inches above the flood level rim before offsetting horizontally.

Topic: Slope and Size of Horizontal Branch **Category:** Vents
Reference: IPC 914.3 **Subject:** Circuit Venting

Code Text: *The slope of the vent section of the horizontal branch drain shall be not greater than one unit vertical in 12 units horizontal (8-percent slope). The entire length of the vent section of the horizontal branch drain shall be sized for the total drainage discharge to the branch.*

Discussion and Commentary: The principle of a circuit vent is that the drainage branch is entirely horizontal. A maximum pitch of 1 to 12 is to keep the branch horizontal without any vertical offsets. The horizontal drainage branch must also be uniformly sized to establish consistent flow characteristics and the free movement of air. Because it is uniformly sized for its full length, the horizontal branch will be oversized for all but the most downstream portion. Table 710.1(2) is used to size the horizontal branch.

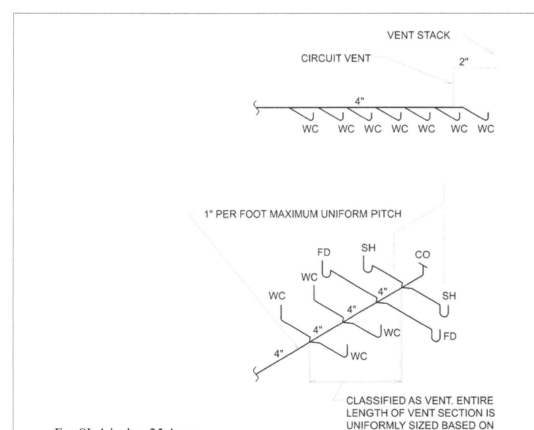

For SI: 1 inch = 25.4 mm

Circuit venting involves up to eight fixtures and a single vent. A dry vent connects between the two most upstream fixtures on the horizontal branch.

Topic: Relief Vent	Category: Vents
Reference: IPC 914.4	Subject: Circuit Venting

Code Text: *A relief vent shall be provided for circuit vented horizontal branches receiving the discharge of four or more water closets and connecting to a drainage stack that receives the discharge of soil or waste from upper horizontal branches.*

Discussion and Commentary: A relief vent is required under the following conditions: 1) If a circuit-vented horizontal branch connects to a drainage stack that is receiving drainage discharge from floors above, and 2) if more than three water closets connect to the circuit-vented horizontal branch. The relief vent will prevent any pressure differential in the drainage stack from affecting the horizontal branch by relieving the pressures.

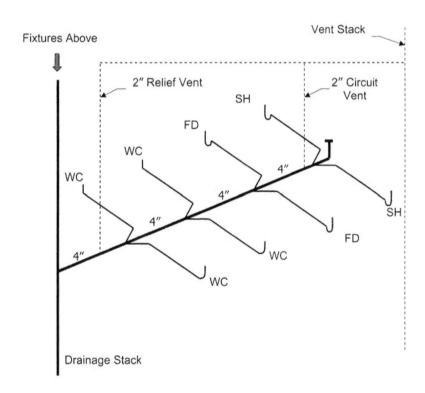

For SI: 1 inch = 25.4 mm

CIRCUIT VENT: A vent that connects to a horizontal drainage branch and vents two traps to a maximum of eight traps or trapped fixtures connected into a battery. **RELIEF VENT:** A vent whose primary function is to provide circulation of air between drainage and vent systems.

Topic: Limitation
Reference: IPC 916.1

Category: Vents
Subject: Island Fixture Venting

Code Text: *Island fixture venting shall not be permitted for fixtures other than sinks and lavatories. Residential kitchen sinks with a dishwasher waste connection, a food waste disposer, or both, in combination with the kitchen sink waste, shall be permitted to be vented in accordance with this section.*

Discussion and Commentary: Island fixture venting is a method of venting island sinks and lavatories. Other options such as a combination waste and vent regulated by Section 915 and air admittance valves in accordance with Section 918 are also available. Residential type sinks with dishwasher and/or food waste disposer connections are allowed to be served by an island vent even if not located in a residential occupancy.

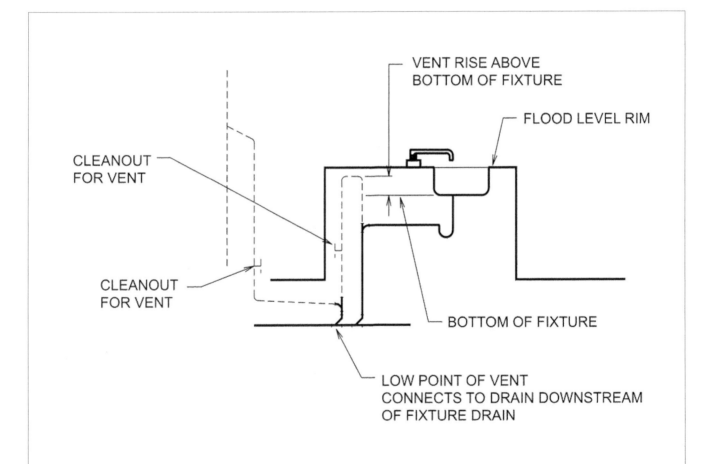

Island fixture venting is an option for plumbing fixtures located such that an individual vent cannot be installed without horizontal sections of piping below the flood level rim of the fixture served.

Topic: Where Permitted
Reference: IPC 917.1
Category: Vents
Subject: Single-Stack Vent System

Code Text: *A drainage stack shall serve as a single-stack vent system where sized and installed in accordance with Sections 917.2 through 917.9. The drainage stack and branch piping shall be the vents for the drainage system. The drainage stack shall have a stack vent.*

Discussion and Commentary: The drainage stack of a single-stack vent system serves as the vent for all connected fixtures. The pipe size of the stack is increased compared to conventional venting systems, and a number of limitations are placed on the fixtures and the developed length of piping between the fixture and the stack. Unlike a waste stack vent, a single-stack vent system permits water closets and urinals to discharge to the stack, and each fixture is not required to connect separately to the stack. The length of trap arms is limited to reduce suction on the traps, and oversized piping limits air pressure differentials.

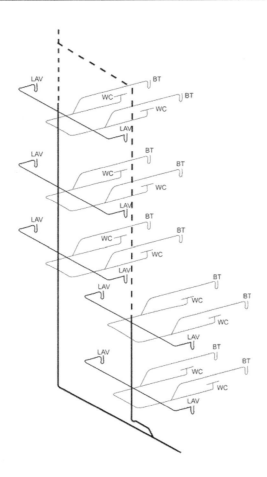

In a single-stack venting system, stacks greater than two branch intervals in height are prohibited from receiving the discharge from horizontal branches on the lower two floors.

Topic: Where Permitted
Reference: IPC 918.3
Category: Vents
Subject: Air Admittance Valves

Code Text: *Individual, branch and circuit vents shall be permitted to terminate with a connection to an individual or branch-type air admittance valve in accordance with Section 918.3.1. Stack vents and vent stacks shall be permitted to terminate to stack-type air admittance valves in accordance with Section 918.3.2.*

Discussion and Commentary: Air admittance valves are allowed to be used in a plumbing system, with certain limitations. Such valves can be used to relieve pressure in individual, branch and circuit vents as well as in stack vents and vent stacks as long as the correct type of air admittance valve is used. ASSE 1050 is the applicable standard for stack-type air admittance valves.

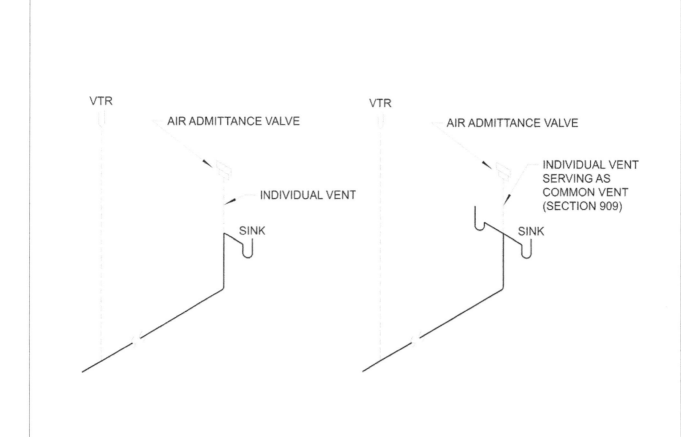

ASSE 1051 - Type A devices may only be used as individual vents for a single fixture drain. ASSE 1051 - Type B devices may serve as branch vents for one or more individual vents, including the dry vent connecting to a common vent, wet vent or circuit vent.

Topic: Stack
Reference: IPC 918.3.2

Category: Vents
Subject: Air Admittance Valves

Code Text: *Stack-type air admittance valves shall be prohibited from serving as the vent terminal for vent stacks or stack vents that serve drainage stacks having more than six branch intervals.*

Discussion and Commentary: This text places a restriction on air admittance valves to stacks that are six branch intervals or seven stories tall. Air admittance valves in stack applications function the same as they function in branch applications. The only difference between branch and stack venting is the location of the intervals.

STACK-TYPE AIR ADMITTANCE VALVE

FLOOR 7

6TH BRANCH INTERVAL

FLOOR 6

FLOOR 5

STACK-TYPE AIR ADMITTANCE VALVES LIMITED TO STACKS WITH NO MORE THAN 6 BRANCH INTERVALS

Stack-type air admittance valves must be located at least 6 inches above the flood level rim of the highest fixture being vented and at least 6 inches above insulation materials.

Study Session 13

Topic: Location
Reference: IPC 918.4
Category: Vents
Subject: Air Admittance Valves

Code Text: *Individual and branch-type air admittance valves shall be located a minimum of 4 inches (102 mm) above the horizontal branch drain or fixture drain being vented. Stack-type air admittance valves shall be located not less than 6 inches (152 mm) above the flood level rim of the highest fixture being vented. The air admittance valve shall be located within the maximum developed length permitted for the vent. The air admittance valve shall be installed not less than 6 inches (152 mm) above insulation materials.*

Discussion and Commentary: An air admittance valve has one moving part (a seal), which must be maintained a safe distance above the drain served. In the event of a drain stoppage, the seal may become inoperable or operate improperly if waste is permitted to rise into the air admittance valve assembly. An air admittance valve must be located a safe distance above insulation materials that may block air inlets or otherwise impair the operation of the device.

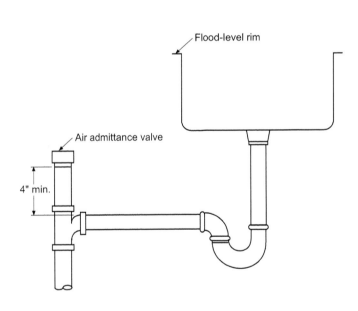

For SI: 1 inch = 25.4 mm

An individual or branch-type air admittance valve is not required to extend above the flood level rim of the fixture served, because in the event of a drain blockage, such device will trap air between it and the rising waste, thereby protecting the device from contamination.

Topic: Prohibited Installations
Reference: IPC 918.8
Category: Vents
Subject: Air Admittance Valves

Code Text: *Air admittance valves shall not be installed in nonneutralized special waste systems as described in Chapter 8 except where such valves are in compliance with ASSE 1049, are constructed of materials approved in accordance with Section 702.5 and are tested for chemical resistance in accordance with ASTM F1412. Air admittance valves shall not be located in spaces utilized as supply or return air plenums. Air admittance valves shall not be used to vent sumps or tanks except where the vent system for the sump or tank has been designed by an engineer. Air admittance valves shall not be installed on outdoor vent terminals for the sole purpose of reducing clearances to gravity air intakes or mechanical air intakes.*

Discussion and Commentary: Air admittance valves are designed and listed for a specific application, such as those approved for venting only a single fixture, those that serve as a branch vent for multiple fixtures on the same floor and those approved for stack vents. Versatile as they are, there are certain limitations that apply to air admittance valves. When used for venting chemical waste systems, air admittance valves must comply with the material provisions for chemical waste systems in Section 702.6, and the associated standards. As a precaution against adverse effects of negative and positive pressures on the operation of an air admittance valve, and possible contamination and circulation of environmental air with sewer gases leaking through a faulty air admission valve, the code prohibits location of these valves in supply or return air plenums.

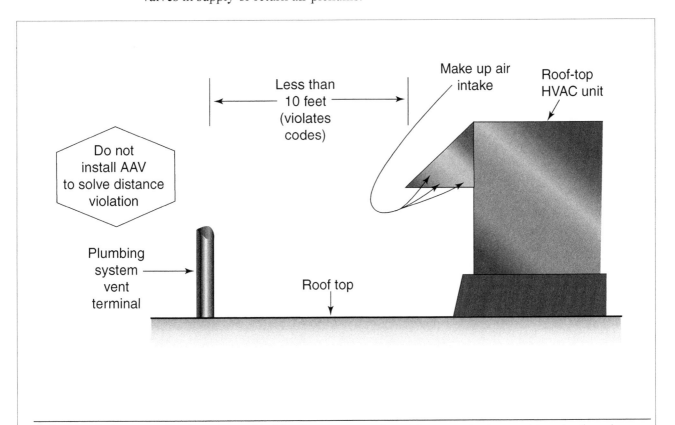

An air admittance valve is not permitted for the purpose of avoiding or reducing vent termination clearances to air intakes or openings into a building.

Study Session 13
IPC Sections 910 through 920

1. What is the minimum size required for a stack vent serving a 2½-inch waste stack?

    a. 1¼ inches
    b. 1½ inches
    c. 2 inches
    d. 2½ inches

    Reference _____

2. What is the minimum size required for a waste stack vent receiving the discharge of two drainage fixture units at each of three branch intervals?

    a. 1¼ inches
    b. 1½ inches
    c. 2 inches
    d. 2½ inches

    Reference _____

3. Provided the total discharge for the stack is not exceeded, what is the maximum number of drainage fixture units allowed to discharge to a 3-inch-diameter waste stack vent in any one branch interval?

    a. two
    b. four
    c. eight
    d. unlimited

    Reference _____

4. A common vent provides venting to _____ fixture(s).

    a. one
    b. two
    c. three
    d. four

    Reference _____

5. The vent or branch vent for multiple island fixture vents shall extend to a minimum of _____ inches above the highest island fixture being vented before connecting to the outside vent terminal.

   a. 3
   b. 4
   c. 6
   d. 12

   Reference _____

6. The maximum horizontal distance between a lavatory and the stack of a single stack vent system is _____ feet in developed length.

   a. 4
   b. 8
   c. 12
   d. 16

   Reference _____

7. A 3-inch stack of a single stack vent system is permitted to serve a maximum of _____ water closets.

   a. two
   b. three
   c. four
   d. six

   Reference _____

8. A relief vent is required when a circuit-vented branch receives the discharge of _____ and the branch connects to a drainage stack receiving drainage from above.

   a. 4 or more water closets
   b. 2 or more bathroom groups
   c. an automatic clothes washer
   d. more than 16 drainage fixture units

   Reference _____

9. A circuit vent is prohibited from receiving any drainage, but a relief vent is permitted to be a fixture drain when the relief vent receives a discharge of not more than _____ drainage fixture units (dfus).

   a. 2
   b. 4
   c. 6
   d. 8

   Reference _____

10. Which of the following fixtures is allowed to be vented by a combination waste and vent system?

    a. floor drain

    b. clinical sink

    c. urinal

    d. food waste disposer

    Reference _____

11. The slope of a horizontal combination waste and vent pipe shall not be greater than _____ inch per foot.

    a. 1/8
    b. 1/4
    c. 1/2
    d. 1

    Reference _____

12. In a combination waste and vent system, vertical piping is permitted for the connection between the _____.

    a. fixture outlet and the fixture trap

    b. stack and the building drain

    c. fixture drain and the horizontal combination waste and vent pipe

    d. building drain vent and the horizontal combination waste and vent pipe

    Reference _____

13. Where a 1 1/4-inch trap and fixture drain is connected to the vertical section of a combination waste and vent system, the maximum developed length between the trap weir and the vertical section is _____ feet.

    a. 2
    b. 3
    c. 5
    d. 6

    Reference _____

14. A minimum _____ -inch-diameter combination waste and vent pipe is required for receiving the discharge of 3 drainage fixture units.

    a. 1 1/2
    b. 2
    c. 3
    d. 4

    Reference _____

15. Island fixture venting is not permitted for a _____.
    a. sink
    b. clothes washer standpipe
    c. lavatory
    d. residential kitchen sink with a food waste disposer and dishwasher

    Reference _____

16. For a(n) _____ installation, cleanouts shall be provided to permit rodding of all vent piping located below the flood level rim of the fixtures.
    a. air admittance valve
    b. island fixture vent
    c. circuit vent
    d. combination waste and vent

    Reference _____

17. A(n) _____ is not permitted for venting the fixture drain from a water closet.
    a. air admittance valve
    b. circuit vent
    c. wet vent
    d. combination waste and vent

    Reference _____

18. Where two fixtures connect at different levels of a vertical drain pipe, the common vent pipe is sized based on _____.
    a. the larger of the two fixture drains
    b. the maximum discharge from the upper fixture drain
    c. the maximum discharge from the lower fixture drain
    d. the size of the fixture branch

    Reference _____

19. When a fixture is individually vented, the vent connects to _____.
    a. a drain receiving the discharge from more than one fixture drain
    b. the fixture branch receiving the discharge
    c. the fixture drain of the trapped fixture
    d. a minimum 1 1/2- inch drain

    Reference _____

20. Wet venting is permitted for any combination of fixtures _____.
    a. within two bathroom groups located on adjacent floors
    b. within two bathroom groups located on the same floor
    c. except water closets and urinals
    d. located on the same floor

    Reference_____

21. When a bathroom group is served by a horizontal wet vent, fixtures that are not within a bathroom group are required to connect _____.
    a. upstream from the horizontal wet vent
    b. downstream of the horizontal wet vent
    c. independently to the horizontal wet vent
    d. at an elevation above the water closet connection

    Reference_____

22. In a horizontal wet-vent system, how many wet-vented fixture drains are allowed to discharge upstream of the dry vent connection?
    a. none   b. one
    c. two   d. three

    Reference_____

23. An air admittance valve shall not serve as the vent stack terminal for drainage stacks having more than _____ branch intervals.
    a. six   b. five
    c. eight   d. ten

    Reference_____

24. In a waste stack vent system, the fixture drain of a _____ is permitted to connect separately to the waste stack.
    a. urinal   b. water closet
    c. bathroom group   d. standpipe

    Reference_____

25. An air admittance valve shall be installed a minimum of _____ inches above insulation materials.

    a. 8   b. 6

    c. 4   d. 2

Reference_____

Study Session 14

2018 IPC Chapter 10
Traps, Interceptor and Separators

OBJECTIVE: To develop an understanding of the overall code provisions that regulate the materials, design and installation of sanitary drainage. To develop an understanding of the specific provisions of the code that apply to joints and fittings in the sanitary drainage system.

REFERENCE: Chapter 10, 2018 *International Plumbing Code*

KEY POINTS:
- Where are traps required?
- What is the maximum vertical and horizontal distance from the fixture outlet to the trap weir?
- What requirements apply to combination fixtures on one trap?
- What limitations apply to grease interceptors serving as traps?
- Under what circumstances are floor drains without traps permitted to connect to a main trap?
- What are the key characteristics of traps?
- What types of traps are prohibited?
- Where are slip joints permitted in a trap assembly, and what type of joint seal is required?
- What are the minimum and the maximum depths of the liquid seal for a fixture trap?
- When would a deeper trap seal on fixture traps be allowed?
- When are house (building) traps permitted?
- When house traps are installed, what additional provisions apply?
- What type of protection is required for an underground acid-resisting trap?
- What specific provision applies to pipes and traps located in mental health centers?
- What is the purpose of interceptors and separators?
- How are the size, types, location, design and installation of interceptors and separators determined?
- What additional requirements apply to food waste disposers? Are they permitted to discharge to grease interceptors?

KEY POINTS:
(Cont'd)
- What type of occupancy does not require grease interceptors?
- What determines the retention capacity of grease interceptors?
- When is a water flow control device required, and what venting requirements apply?
- What are the location and access requirements for automatic grease removal devices?
- Where are oil separators required? Sand interceptors?
- What general venting, access and maintenance provisions apply to interceptors and separators?

Topic: Fixture Traps
Reference: IPC 1002.1

Category: Traps, Interceptors and Separators
Subject: Trap Requirements

Code Text: *Each plumbing fixture shall be separately trapped by a liquid-seal trap, except as otherwise permitted by this code. The vertical distance from the fixture outlet to the trap weir shall not exceed 24 inches (610 mm) and the horizontal distance shall not exceed 30 inches (762 mm) measured from the centerline of the fixture outlet to the centerline of the inlet of the trap. The height of a clothes washer standpipe above a trap shall conform to Section 802.4. A fixture shall not be double trapped.* See the exceptions for 1) fixtures with integral traps, 2) combination fixtures on one trap, 3) grease interceptors as traps and 4) multilevel parking structure floor drains with main trap.

Discussion and Commentary: The configuration of a trap interferes with the flow of drainage; however, the interference is minimal because of the construction of the trap and the relatively high inlet velocity of the waste flow. Double trapping of a fixture is prohibited because it will cause air to be trapped between two trap seals, and the *air-bound* drain will impede the flow. The maximum vertical distance of 24 inches from a fixture outlet to the trap weir is required to reduce odor and the growth of bacteria and to control the velocity of the drainage flow. A maximum horizontal distance of 30 inches must also be adhered to.

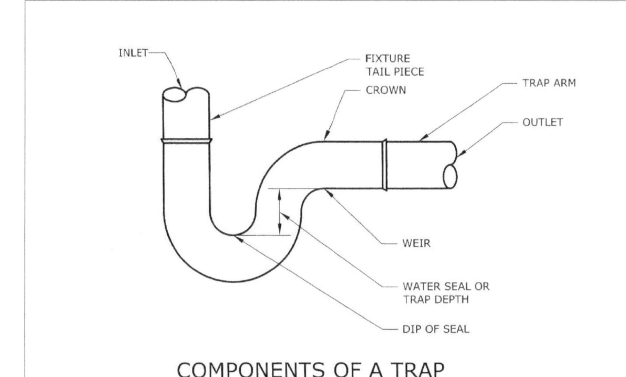

COMPONENTS OF A TRAP

The trap seal prevents sewer gases and aerosol-borne bacteria from entering the building space. Sewer gases often contain methane gas that in high concentrations can cause an explosion when exposed to an ignition source.

Topic: Design of Traps
Reference: IPC 1002.2

Category: Traps, Interceptors and Separators
Subject: Trap Requirements

Code Text: *Fixture traps shall be self-scouring. Fixture traps shall not have interior partitions, except where such traps are integral with the fixture or where such traps are constructed of an approved material that is resistant to corrosion and degradation. Slip joints shall be made with an approved elastomeric gasket and shall be installed only on the trap inlet, trap outlet and within the trap seal.*

Discussion and Commentary: A trap must have a pattern that allows unobstructed flow to the drain. Interior partitions are allowable where constructed of a material resistant to corrosion and degradation. For example, bottle traps have interior partitions and are sometimes used because their slim profile fits in limited spaces or provides a more appealing finished look to an exposed installation.

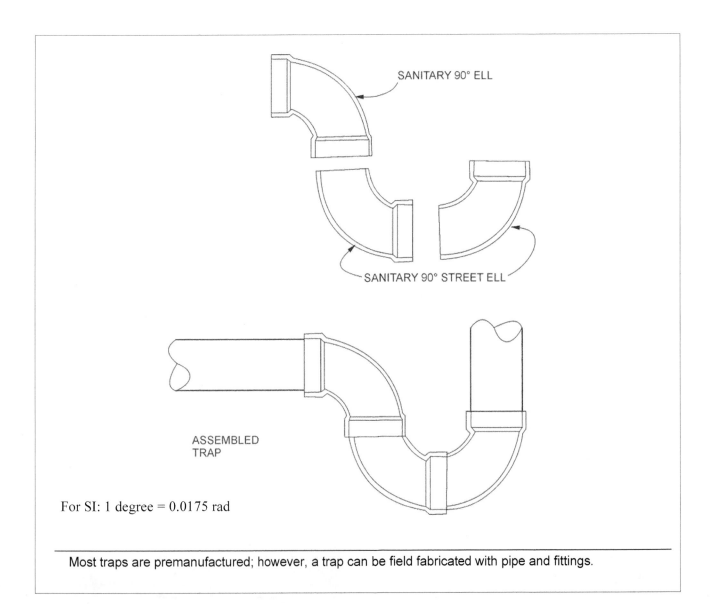

For SI: 1 degree = 0.0175 rad

Most traps are premanufactured; however, a trap can be field fabricated with pipe and fittings.

Topic: Prohibited Traps
Reference: IPC 1002.3

Category: Traps, Interceptors and Separators
Subject: Trap Requirements

Code Text: *The following types of traps are prohibited:*

1. *Traps that depend on moving parts to maintain the seal.*
2. *Bell traps.*
3. *Crown-vented traps.*
4. *Traps not integral with a fixture and that depend on interior partitions for the seal, except those traps constructed of an approved material that is resistant to corrosion and degradation.*
5. *"S" traps.*
6. *Drum traps.*
   Exception: Drum traps used as solids interceptors and drum traps serving chemical waste systems shall not be prohibited.

Discussion and Commentary: A trap is intended to be a simple U-shaped piping arrangement that offers minimal resistance to flow. Prohibited traps do not incorporate this simple design concept. In some cases, such as an "S" trap, the trap design is prohibited because it is subject to siphoning and losing its trap seal.

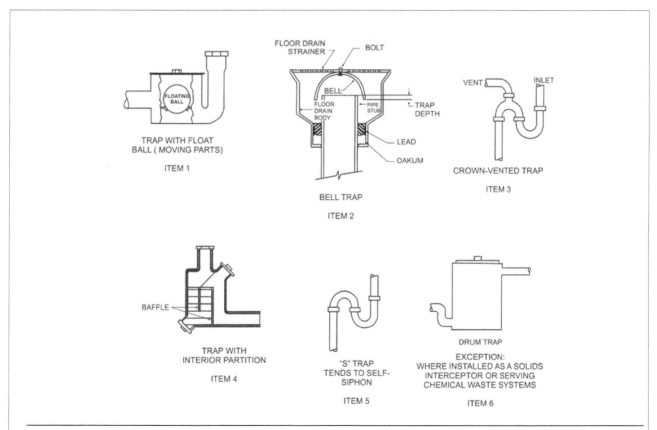

TRAP: A fitting or device that provides a liquid seal to prevent the emission of sewer gases without materially affecting the flow of sewage or wastewater through the trap.

Study Session 14

Topic: Size of Fixture Traps
Reference: IPC 1002.5
Category: Traps, Interceptors and Separators
Subject: Trap Requirements

Code Text: *Fixture trap size shall be sufficient to drain the fixture rapidly and not less than the size indicated in Table 709.1. A trap shall not be larger than the drainage pipe into which the trap discharges.*

Discussion and Commentary: The minimum fixture trap sizes are listed in Table 709.1. The minimum trap sizes for fixtures not listed in Table 709.1 must be the size of the fixture outlet, but in no case less than $1^1/_4$ inches. The code does not prescribe a maximum trap size; however, if a trap is oversized, it will not scour (cleanse) itself and will therefore be prone to clogging.

TABLE 709.1
DRAINAGE FIXTURE UNITS FOR FIXTURES AND GROUPS

FIXTURE TYPE	DRAINAGE FIXTURE UNIT VALUE AS LOAD FACTORS	MINIMUM SIZE OF TRAP (inches)
Automatic clothes washers, commercial[a,g]	3	2
Automatic clothes washers, residential[g]	2	2
Bathroom group as defined in Section 202 (1.6 gpf water closet)[f]	5	—
Bathroom group as defined in Section 202 (water closet flushing greater than 1.6 gpf)[f]	6	—
Bathtub[b] (with or without overhead shower or whirlpool attachments)	2	$1^1/_2$
Bidet	1	$1^1/_4$
Combination sink and tray	2	$1^1/_2$

(continued)

For SI: 1 inch = 25.4 mm

A trap that is larger than the drainage pipe into which it discharges is not allowed by the code. The reduced size in the direction of flow would be subject to frequent clogging because the outlet pipe would not allow a waste flow velocity adequate to scour and clean the trap.

Topic: Trap Setting and Protection
Reference: IPC 1002.7
Category: Traps, Interceptors and Separators
Subject: Trap Requirements

Code Text: *Traps shall be set level with respect to the trap seal and, where necessary, shall be protected from freezing.*

Discussion and Commentary: Traps must be set level to maintain the trap seal depth and reduce the possibility of self-siphoning. Losing the trap seal exposes building occupants to hazards associated with the contents of the sewer drainage system.

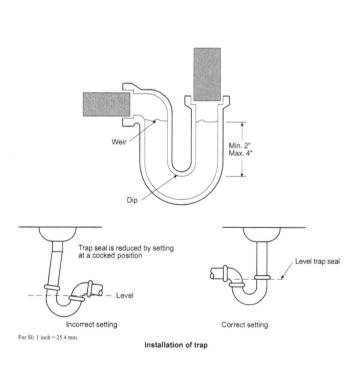

Installation of trap

TRAP SEAL: The vertical distance between the weir and the top of the dip of the trap.

Study Session 14

Topic: Approval	**Category:** Traps, Interceptors and Separators
Reference: IPC 1003.2	**Subject:** Interceptors and Separators

Code Text: *The size, type and location of each interceptor and of each separator shall be designed and installed in accordance with the manufacturer's instructions and the requirements of this section based on the anticipated conditions of use. Wastes that do not require treatment or separation shall not be discharged into any interceptor or separator.*

Discussion and Commentary: Each interceptor and separator must be designed for the specific installation because the installation depends on the materials being separated. When devices of this specialized nature are involved, no material other than that which requires treatment or separation should be allowed to discharge into the device, unless specifically recommended by the device manufacturer or the design engineer as performing a necessary function. This requires an analysis of the intended use and a determination of the peak load condition.

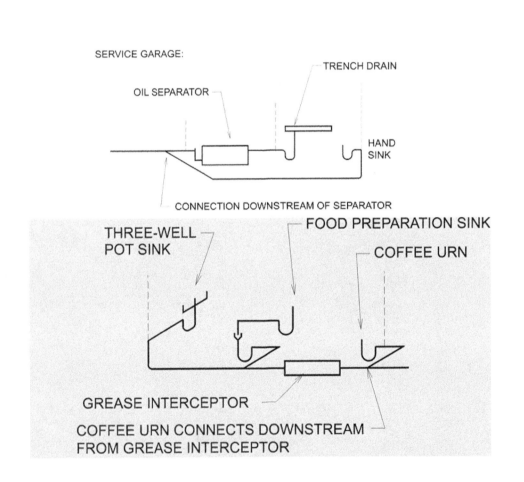

Many factors affect the design and installation, including the type of material being separated, proximity of equipment to the waste source, temperatures, flow rates and capacities.

Topic: Required Devices
Reference: IPC 1003.3.1

Category: Traps, Interceptors and Separators
Subject: Interceptors and Separators

Code Text: *A grease interceptor or automatic grease removal device shall be required to receive the drainage from fixtures and equipment with grease-laden waste located in food preparation areas, such as in restaurants, hotel kitchens, hospitals, school kitchens, bars, factory cafeterias and clubs. Fixtures and equipment shall include pot sinks, pre-rinse sinks; soup kettles or similar devices; wok stations; floor drains or sinks into which kettles are drained; automatic hood wash units and dishwashers without pre-rinse sinks. Grease interceptors and automatic grease removal devices shall receive waste only from fixtures and equipment that allow fats, oils or grease to be discharged.*

Discussion and Commentary: Interceptors are necessary to remove substances that are detrimental to the drainage system, sewage treatment plants or private sewage disposal systems. Many questions arise as to which fixtures in various occupancies such as restaurants should be connected to the interceptor. The code provides guidance by listing most of such fixtures in this section. Judgment is still required in questionable cases because the code allows only fixtures that allow the discharge of fats to be connected to the interceptor.

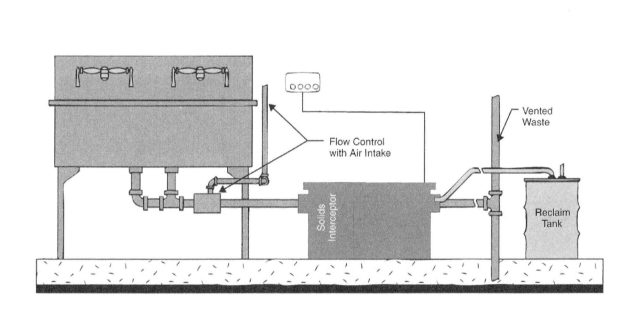

Occupancies that commonly require the removal of grease, fat or other solids such as sand include: motor vehicle repair shops, restaurants or cafeterias, hotels, hospitals, animal slaughtering facilities, fowl, fish or meat-packaging plants, and commercial laundries.

Topic: Food Waste Disposers
Reference: IPC 1003.3.2
Category: Traps, Interceptors and Separators
Subject: Interceptors and Separators

Code Text: *A food waste disposer shall not discharge to a grease interceptor.*

Discussion and Commentary: A food waste disposer's discharge is not permitted to pass through a grease interceptor. Food waste accumulating in a grease interceptor creates gases that interfere with the grease separation process and causes the interceptor to become less effective.

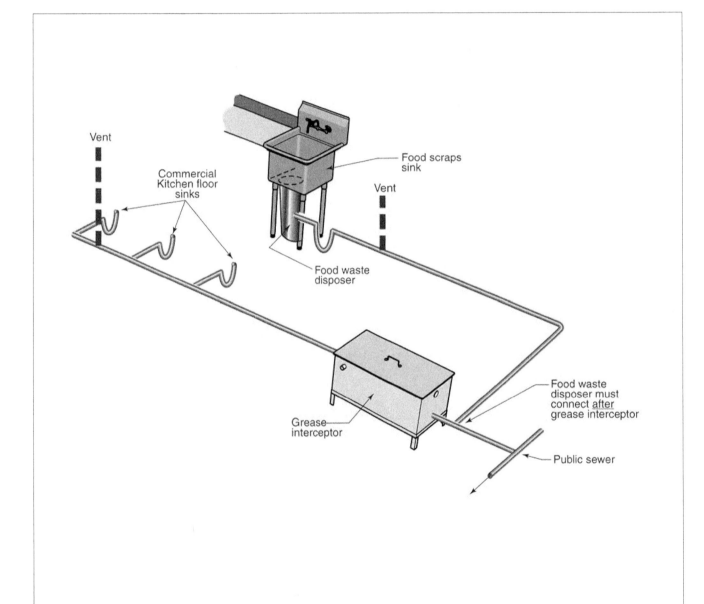

Drains serving food waste disposers must bypass grease interceptors and connect downstream of the interceptor.

Topic: Additives to Grease Interceptors	Category: Traps, Interceptors and Separators
Reference: IPC 1003.3.3	Subject: Interceptors and Separators

Code Text: *Dispensing systems that dispense interceptor performance additives to grease interceptors shall not be installed except where such systems dispense microbes for the enhancement of aerobic bioremediation of grease and other organic material, or for inhibiting growth of pathogenic organisms by anaerobic methods. Such microbial dispensing systems shall be installed only where the grease interceptor manufacturer's instructions allow such systems and the systems conform to ASME A112.14.6. Systems that discharge emulsifiers, chemicals or enzymes to grease interceptors shall be prohibited.*

Discussion and Commentary: Additives to grease interceptors are limited to microbes dispensed by systems that comply with ASME A112.14.6. The periodic maintenance (evacuation) of grease interceptors can be costly for operators. Reducing the frequency of cleaning by the addition of relatively inexpensive emulsifiers, chemicals or enzymes can be tempting. However, the results often are nonproductive or counterproductive to the operation of the interceptor. Microbes are the only effective additive for a grease interceptor.

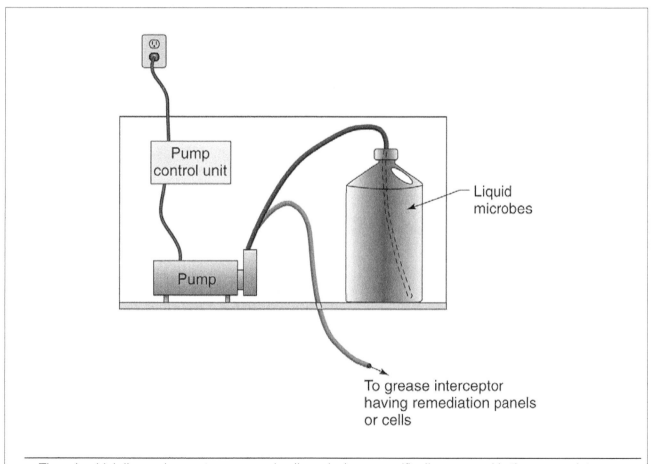

The microbial dispensing systems are only allowed where specifically approved in the grease interceptor manufacturer's instructions.

Study Session 14

Topic: Hydromechanical Grease Interceptors **Category:** Traps, Interceptors and Separators
Reference: IPC 1003.3.5 **Subject:** Interceptors and Separators

Code Text: *Hydromechanical grease interceptors; fats, oils, and greases disposal systems and automatic grease removal devices shall be sized in accordance with ASME A112.14.3, ASME 112.14.4, ASME A112.14.6, CSA B481.3 or PDI G101. Hydromechanical grease interceptors; fats, oils, and greases disposal systems and automatic grease removal devices shall be designed and tested in accordance with ASME A112.14.3, ASME 112.14.4, CSA B481.1, PDI G101 or PDI G102. Hydromechanical grease interceptors; fats, oils, and greases disposal systems and automatic grease removal devices shall be installed in accordance with the manufacturer's instructions. Where manufacturer's instructions are not provided, hydromechanical grease interceptors; fats, oils, and greases disposal systems and automatic grease removal devices shall be installed in compliance with ASME A112.14.3, ASME 112.14.4, ASME A112.14.6, CSA B481.3 or PDI G101.*

Discussion and Commentary: The referenced standards PDI G101 and ASME A112.14.3 describe a procedure for testing and rating a grease interceptor. The standards do not specify any construction requirements. After testing to the standard, a grease interceptor is certified for its flow rate and grease retention capacity. PDI G102 applies to testing and certification of alarm devices for interceptors. The alarm device on a hydromechanical grease interceptor monitors the level of fats, oils and grease (FOG) captured in the unit and provides both an audible alarm and a visual signal to indicate that the FOG needs to be removed. ASME A112.14.4 is the standard for automatic grease removal devices. Hydromechanical grease interceptors can be fitted with fats, oils and greases (FOG) disposal systems to extend the required cleaning intervals of the tank.

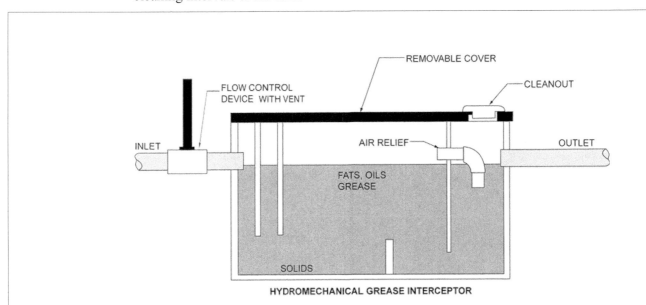

HYDROMECHANICAL GREASE INTERCEPTOR

A hydromechanical grease interceptor serves to intercept free-floating fats, oils and grease from waste water discharge. Continuous separation is accomplished by air entrainment, buoyancy and interior baffling.

Topic: Grease Interceptor Capacity
Reference: IPC 1003.3.5.1
Category: Traps, Interceptors and Separators
Subject: Interceptors and Separators

Code Text: *Grease interceptors shall have the grease retention capacity indicated in Table 1003.3.5.1 for the flow-through rates indicated.*

Discussion and Commentary: Grease interceptor retention capacity must be based on the flow-through rating of the grease interceptor and the discharge rate of the drainage pipe served. The waste flow capacity of a grease interceptor determines the quantity of grease that can be separated from the waste, which, in turn, dictates the required capacity of the grease interceptor to hold the collected grease.

TABLE 1003.3.5.1
CAPACITY OF GREASE INTERCEPTORS[a]

TOTAL FLOW-THROUGH RATING (gpm)	GREASE RETENTION CAPACITY (pounds)
4	8
6	12
7	14
9	18
10	20
12	24
14	28
15	30
18	36
20	40
25	50
35	70
50	100
75	150
100	200

For SI: 1 gallon per minute = 3.785 L/m, 1 pound = 0.454 kg.

a. For total flow-through ratings greater than 100 (gpm), double the flow-through rating to determine the grease retention capacity (pounds).

The maintenance frequency for a grease interceptor is directly proportional to the retention capacity of the device.

Topic: Rate of Flow Controls
Reference: IPC 1003.3.5.2
Category: Traps, Interceptors and Separators
Subject: Interceptors and Separators

Code Text: *Grease interceptors shall be equipped with devices to control the rate of water flow so that the water flow does not exceed the rated flow. The flow-control device shall be vented and terminate not less than 6 inches (152 mm) above the flood rim level or be installed in accordance with the manufacturer's instructions.*

Discussion and Commentary: To prevent an excessive flow rate through the grease interceptor, it must be either large enough to handle the flow, or a flow control device must be installed upstream of the grease interceptor and in accordance with the manufacturer's instructions. The flow control device acts as a restrictor to control the flow into the grease interceptor. Such devices are typically a fitting with a fixed orifice and an air intake or vent and are usually provided and sized by the manufacturer of the grease interceptor.

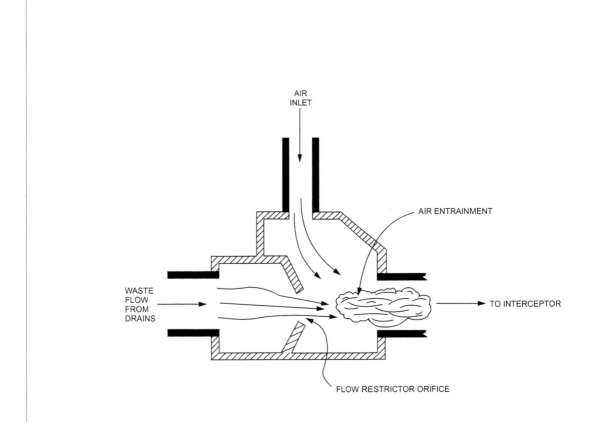

Flow control is achieved with a device installed upstream from the interceptor having an orifice that controls the rate of flow through the interceptor and an air intake (vent) downstream from the orifice that allows air to be drawn into the flow stream.

Topic: Automatic Grease Removal Devices **Category:** Traps, Interceptors and Separators
Reference: IPC 1003.3.6 **Subject:** Interceptors and Separators

Code Text: *Where automatic grease removal devices are installed, such devices shall be located downstream of each fixture or multiple fixtures in accordance with the manufacturer's instructions. The automatic grease removal device shall be sized to pretreat the measured or calculated flows for all connected fixtures or equipment. Ready access shall be provided for inspection and maintenance.*

Discussion and Commentary: This code text addresses automatic grease removal devices, their sizing and access requirements for inspection and maintenance. Automatic grease removal systems are an acceptable technology when installed properly. The ASME Standard A112.14.4 referenced in Section 1003.3.5 is related to automatic grease removal devices. Ready access must be provided to such devices.

GREASE REMOVAL DEVICE, AUTOMATIC (GRD). A plumbing appurtenance that is installed in the sanitary drainage system to intercept free-floating fats, oils and grease from wastewater discharge. Such a device operates on a time- or event-controlled basis and has the ability to remove freefloating fats, oils and grease automatically without intervention from the user except for maintenance.

Ready access means that a fixture, appliance or equipment can be directly reached without requiring the removal or movement of any panel, door or similar obstruction and without the use of a portable ladder, step stool or similar device.

Topic: Oil Separators Required
Reference: IPC 1003.4
Category: Traps, Interceptors and Separators
Subject: Interceptors and Separators

Code Text: *At repair garages where floor or trench drains are provided, car washing facilities, factories where oily and flammable liquid wastes are produced and hydraulic elevator pits, oil separators shall be installed into which oil-bearing, grease-bearing or flammable wastes shall be discharged before emptying into the building drainage system or other point of disposal.* See exception for hydraulic elevator pits where an approved alarm system is installed.

Discussion and Commentary: A separator is required in areas used for motor vehicle repairs and car-washing facilities with engine or undercarriage cleaning capability and at factories where oily and flammable liquid wastes are produced. In such facilities, floor drains are the primary receptors of wastes requiring treatment. It is not the intent of this section to require oil separators in a public or private garage. A garage used only as a parking facility is allowed to have floor drains connected to the drainage system without separators.

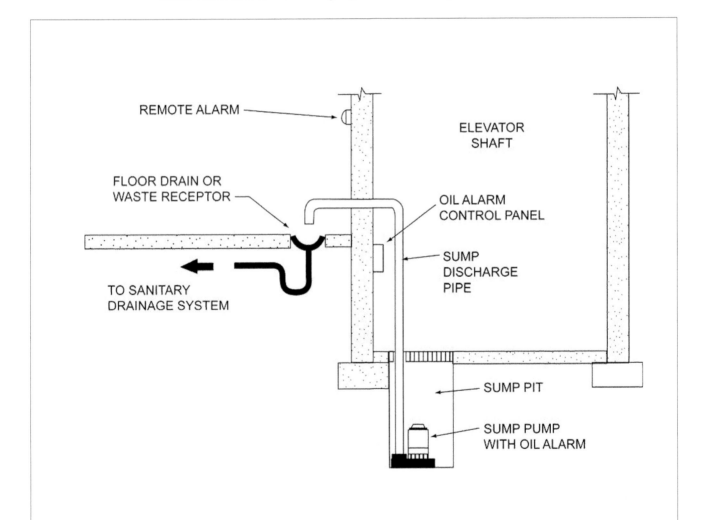

An approved alarm system that provides notification of an oil leak in a hydraulic elevator pit is considered equivalent to installing an oil separator. The alarm system shall not shut down pumps utilized to maintain emergency operation of the elevator by fire fighters. The pump discharge requires an indirect connection in accordance with Section 301.6.

Topic: Oil Separator Design
Reference: IPC 1003.4.2.1
Category: Traps, Interceptors and Separators
Subject: Interceptors and Separators

Code Text: *Oil separators shall have a depth of not less than 2 feet (610 mm) below the invert of the discharge drain. The outlet opening of the separator shall have not less than an 18-inch (457 mm) water seal.*

Discussion and Commentary: The sizing specified in this section relates to an open-tank-type separator. The minimum depth is necessary to provide retention capacity for sludge and solids and to obtain efficient retention of oil or other volatile liquid wastes by minimizing turbulent flow through the separator. The outlet must be designed to provide at least 18 inches of liquid seal to provide for the storage of oil to at least that depth.

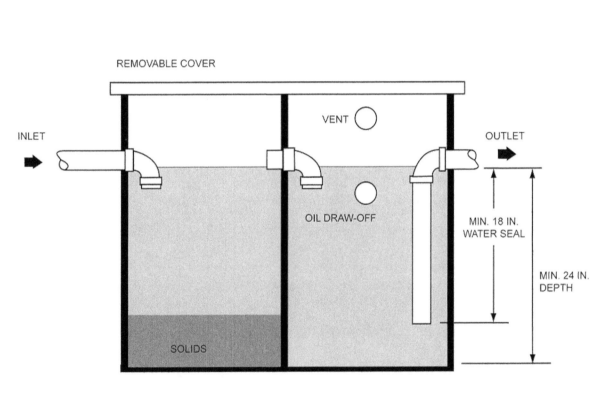

OIL SEPARATOR

For SI: 1 inch = 25.4 mm

A separator or interceptor is a device designed and installed to separate and retain for removal, by automatic or manual means, deleterious, hazardous or undesirable matter from normal wastes, while permitting normal wastes to discharge into the drainage system by gravity.

Topic: Garages and Service Stations **Category:** Traps, Interceptors and Separators
Reference: IPC 1003.4.2.2 **Subject:** Interceptors and Separators

Code Text: *Where automobiles are serviced, greased, repaired or washed or where gasoline is dispensed, oil separators shall have a capacity of not less than 6 cubic feet ($0.168m^3$) for the first 100 square feet ($9.3\ m^2$) of area to be drained, plus 1 cubic foot ($0.28\ m^3$) for each additional 100 square feet ($9.3\ m^2$) of area to be drained into the separator. Parking garages in which servicing, repairing or washing is not conducted, and in which gasoline is not dispensed, shall not require a separator. Areas of commercial garages utilized only for storage of automobiles are not required to be drained through a separator.*

Discussion and Commentary: In addition to the general design requirements for oil separators in Section 1003.4.2.1, this section specifically applies to motor vehicle garages or service stations where lubrication, oil changing, fuel dispensing, repair work, or hand or mechanical washing takes place. The intent of this section is to require oil separators in locations where flammable or combustible liquids would otherwise be discharged into the drainage system, typically in occupancies provided with floor or trench drains.

The requirement for an oil separator does not, in itself, create the requirement for floor or trench drains. Where a drainage system is provided in these occupancies, provisions must be made to prevent flammable and combustible liquids from entering the drainage system, sewers and waste treatment facilities.

Topic: Clothes Washer Discharge Interceptor   **Category:** Traps, Interceptors and Separators
Reference: IPC 1003.6   **Subject:** Interceptors and Separators

Code Text: *Clothes washers shall discharge through an interceptor that is provided with a wire basket or similar device, removable for cleaning, that prevents passage into the drainage system of solids $1/2$ inch (12.7 mm) or larger in size, string, rags, buttons or other materials detrimental to the public sewage system.* See the exceptions for clothes washers in dwelling units and a single clothes washer designed for dwelling units.

Discussion and Commentary: Commercial laundries and similar establishments must be equipped with an interceptor that is capable of preventing string, lint and other solids from entering the sewage system. The filter, screen or basket must allow for cleaning and removing intercepted solids.

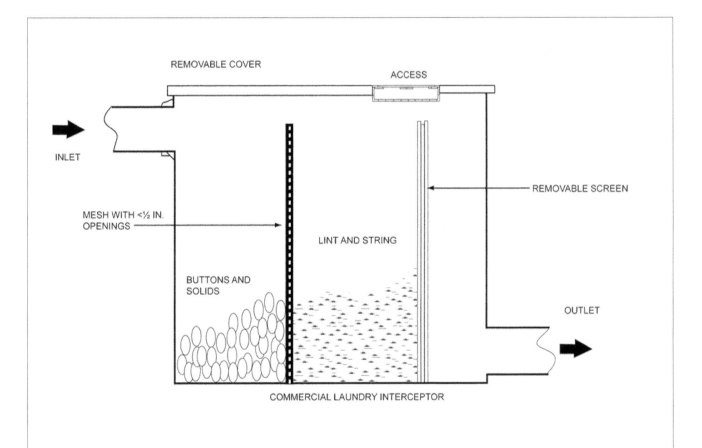

There are various acceptable designs for clothes washer interceptors in commercial laundry and similiar facilities. Lint screens or baskets are not required in the standpipe or drainage system serving a washing machine in an individual dwelling unit or for a single clothes washer installed in other occupancies but designed for use in dwelling units. For example, a small restaurant or a hand car wash might have a single "residential type" clothes washer for washing towels. There is no need to have interceptors for these minor applications.

Topic: Venting
Reference: IPC 1003.9
Category: Traps, Interceptors and Separators
Subject: Interceptors and Separators

Code Text: *Interceptors and separators shall be designed so as not to become air bound. Interceptors and separators shall be vented in accordance with one of the methods in Chapter 9.*

Discussion and Commentary: Most interceptors and separators require venting of the containment tank. Typically, a vent is required to allow the escape or admittance of air to compensate for the variable fluid level in the tank. Oil and gasoline separators require independent vents to help control and dissipate vapor buildup that may occur in the holding tank.

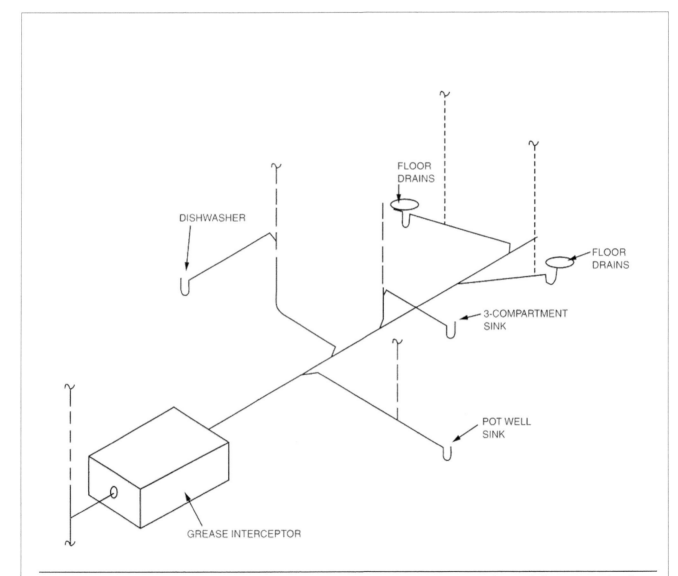

Interceptors and separators with integral traps must be vented to prevent the tank from emptying its contents by siphon action.

Study Session 14
IPC Chapter 10

1. A three-compartment pots-and-pans sink is permitted to be installed on one trap, provided _____.

    a. the vertical distance from the fixture outlet to the trap weir does not exceed 30 inches

    b. the waste outlets are not more than 30 inches apart

    c. one compartment is not more than 8 inches deeper than another compartment

    d. the horizontal distance from any one outlet to the trap inlet is not more than 24 inches

    Reference _____

2. A _____ trap is approved on a dental cuspidor, where it is designed to capture solids such as dental gold, silver or porcelain.

    a. bell
    b. strap
    c. drum trap
    d. crown-vented

    Reference _____

3. Exposed traps are prohibited in _____.

    a. trauma centers
    b. accessible public restrooms
    c. food service establishments
    d. mental health facilities

    Reference _____

4. All of the following are requirements for trap design and installation, except_____.

    a. the trap must be level

    b. elastomeric slip joints are allowed only on the trap inlet

    c. the trap seal must have a two- to four-inch liquid depth

    d. trap seal protection is required for emergency floor drains

Reference _____

5. Which trap design is prohibited in all applications?

    (a.) a trap designed with a floating ball-check

    b. interceptor type drum trap

    c. a trap integral to the fixture

    d. a deep seal trap

Reference 1002.3

6. When required to discharge to a combined building sewer system, floor drains in a _____ are not required to be individually trapped.

    a. food preparation facility   (b.) multilevel parking garage

    c. warehouse   d. factory

Reference _____

7. Trap seals subject to evaporation shall be protected by a trap seal primer or a _____.

    a. deep seal trap

    b. backwater valve

    c. flush valve

    (d.) barrier-type device

Reference _____

8. A grease interceptor serving as a trap, in accordance with the manufacturer's instructions, can be located a maximum of _____.

   a. 30 inches in developed length from the fixture outlet to the inlet of the interceptor

   (b.) 60 inches in developed length from the fixture outlet to the inlet of the interceptor

   c. 30 inches horizontally from the centerline of the fixture outlet to the inlet of the interceptor

   d. 24 inches vertically from the fixture outlet to the inlet of the interceptor

   Reference_____

9. Where the trap seal is dependent on an interior partition, only approved traps constructed of corrosion resistant material or _____ are permitted.

   a. traps integral to the fixture
   b. readily accessible traps
   c. traps with primer valves
   d. self-scouring traps with slip joint connections

   Reference __1002.2__

10. Where the manufacturer's design permits, a grease interceptor is allowed to serve as a fixture trap for how many fixtures?

    a. one   b. two
    c. three   d. four

    Reference _____

11. Substances that are detrimental to the sewer system are prevented from being discharged into the drainage system by _____.

    a. filters   (b.) strainers
    c. traps or backwater valve   d. interceptors or separators

    Reference _____

Study Session 14

12. Which of the following fixtures in a food preparation facility is not allowed to discharge to a grease interceptor?

     a. dishwashers without prerinse sinks
     b. food waste disposer
     c. pot and pan sinks
     d. automatic hood wash units

     Reference _____

13. Systems that dispense performance additives to grease interceptors are only permitted when they dispense _____.

     a. emulsifiers   b. microbes
     c. chemicals   d. enzymes

     Reference _____

14. A grease interceptor is not required for the kitchen of a _____.

     a. factory   b. hospital
     c. school   d. dwelling unit

     Reference _____

15. An auto repair garage has an oil separator receiving drainage from a repair bay that has an area of 100 feet x 27 feet. What is the minimum capacity in cubic feet required for the oil separator to serve the garage work area?

     a. 6   b. 27
     c. 32   d. 40

     Reference _____

16. The water seal for a sand interceptor shall be not less than _____ inches.

     a. 6   b. 8
     c. 12   d. 18

     Reference _____

17. The minimum height of the vent termination for a flow control device on a grease interceptor is _____ inches above the flood rim of the connected fixture or as required by the manufacturer.

   a. 12
   b. 18
   (c.) 6
   d. 24

   Reference _____

18. Automatic grease removal devices are required to be sized according to the calculated _____.

   a. flows during peak usage
   (b.) flows of all connected fixtures
   c. average flows of the fixtures
   d. flow rate from the highest volume fixture

   Reference _____

19. Design requirements, including provisions for venting, intend to prevent interceptors and separators from _____.

   a. contamination
   b. wastewater discharge
   c. backflow
   (d.) becoming air bound

   Reference _____

20. The vertical distance from the fixture outlet to the trap weir shall not exceed _____ inches

   a. 18
   (b.) 24
   c. 30
   d. 36

   Reference _____

21. Each fixture trap shall have a liquid seal of not less than _____ inches.

   a. $1^{1}/_{2}$
   b. $2^{1}/_{2}$
   (c.) 2
   d. 4

   Reference _____

Study Session 14

22. Where an acid-resisting trap is installed underground, such trap shall be embedded in concrete extending _____ inches beyond the bottom and sides of the trap.

   a. 2
   b. 3
   c. 4
   d. 6 ✓

   Reference_____

23. The capacity of a grease interceptor with a total flow-through rating of 10 gpm is _____ pounds.

   a. 14
   b. 18
   c. 20 ✓
   d. 24

   Reference_____

24. Oil separators shall have a depth of not less than _____ inches below the invert of the discharging drain.

   a. 24 ✓
   b. 36
   c. 30
   d. 42

   Reference_____

25. The outlet opening of an oil separator shall have a water seal of not less than _____ inches.

   a. 6
   b. 12
   c. 18 ✓
   d. 24

   Reference_____

Study Session

15

2018 IPC Chapters 11 through 14
Storm Drainage, Special Piping and Storage Systems, Nonpotable Water Systems and Subsurface Landscape Irrigation Systems

OBJECTIVE: To develop an understanding of the code provisions applicable to the removal of water associated with storm and rainfall and of the precautions against the structural failure of a flat roof. To develop an understanding of the code provisions that apply to systems for nonflammable medical gas and nonmedical oxygen systems. To gain an understanding of requirements related to the collection, storage, treatment and distribution of nonpotable water including subsurface landscape irrigation systems.

REFERENCE: Chapters 11 through 14, 2018 *International Plumbing Code*

KEY POINTS:
- Where is a storm drainage system required? Where are the approved discharge locations?
- When is storm water permitted to drain into a sanitary sewer?
- When are cleanouts and backwater valves required for storm drainage systems?
- What pipe materials are permitted for inside storm drain conductors? Building storm sewer pipe? Subsoil storm drain pipe?
- Where is a main trap required in a storm drainage system?
- When a combined sewer is utilized, where is the storm drain connected and with what type of fitting?
- Are floor drains permitted to be connected to a storm drain?
- What controls roof drain design and installation?
- What rainfall criteria are used for the sizing of a storm drainage system?
- What is the basis for sizing vertical storm drainage conductors and leaders? Horizontal piping? Semicircular gutters?
- How are vertical walls taken into consideration when sizing roof drains?
- What condition triggers the need for a secondary drainage system? Where must it discharge?
- What requirements apply to siphonic and controlled flow roof drain systems?

KEY POINTS:
(Cont'd)

- What location is approved for the discharge of building subdrains?
- What requirements apply to sump pumps, sump pits and pump discharge piping?
- What minimum water quality requirements apply to nonpotable water systems? When is filtration required? Disinfection?
- Where is signage required for nonpotable water use? What must appear on the sign?
- What provisions apply to nonpotable water storage tanks?
- When are operation and maintenance manuals required for nonpotable water systems?
- What are the trenching and separation requirements for buried nonpotable water piping?
- What provisions apply to on-site nonpotable water reuse systems?
- What fixtures are permitted to drain to an on-site nonpotable water reuse system? What other sources may be used if approved by the code official? What sources are prohibited?
- What are the permitted uses for gray water?
- What requirements apply to nonpotable rainwater collection and distribution systems?
- What provisions apply to nonpotable reclaimed water systems?
- What type of nonpotable water system is approved for connection to a subsurface landscape irrigation system?
- What site tests are required for subsurface landscape irrigation systems?
- What design and installation requirements related to absorption and seepage apply to subsurface landscape irrigation systems?
- What material, size and location requirements apply to distribution piping for subsurface landscape irrigation system?

Topic: Change in Size	Category: Storm Drainage
Reference: IPC 1101.5	Subject: General Provisions

Code Text: *The size of a drainage pipe shall not be reduced in the direction of flow.*

Discussion and Commentary: One of the fundamental requirements of any form of drainage system is that the piping is not permitted to be reduced in size in the direction of drainage flow. This is also the case with storm drainage systems. A size reduction creates an obstruction to the flow of discharge, possibly resulting in a backup, an interruption of service in the drainage system or a stoppage occurring in the piping.

Storm drainage system is a drainage system that carries rainwater, surface water, subsurface water and similar liquid wastes.

Topic: Roof Design
Reference: IPC 1101.7
Category: Storm Drainage
Subject: General Provisions

Code Text: *Roofs shall be designed for the maximum possible depth of water that will pond thereon as determined by the relative levels of roof deck and overflow weirs, scuppers, edges or serviceable drains in combination with the deflected structural elements. In determining the maximum possible depth of water, all primary roof drainage means shall be assumed to be blocked. The maximum possible depth of water on the roof shall include the height of the water required above the inlet of the secondary roof drainage means to achieve the required flow rate of the secondary drainage means to accommodate the design rainfall rate as required by Section 1106.*

Discussion and Commentary: The roof structure must be capable of supporting the maximum ponding of water that will occur when the primary roof drainage means are blocked. In Section 1108, the code requires the installation of a secondary (emergency) roof drainage system to limit the amount of rainwater that could be retained on top of the roof. This also limits the potential increased load to be structurally supported by the roof.

	FLOW RATE (gpm)									
	Depth of water above drain inlet (hydraulic head) (inches)									
DRAINAGE SYSTEM	1	2	2.5	3	3.5	4	4.5	5	7	8
4-inch-diameter drain	80	170	180							
6-inch-diameter drain	100	190	270	380	540					
8-inch-diameter drain	125	230	340	560	850	1,100	1,170			
6-inch-wide, open-top scupper	18	50	*	90	*	140	*	194	321	393
24-inch-wide, open-top scupper	72	200	*	360	*	560	*	776	1,284	1,572
6-inch-wide, 4-inch-high, closed-top scupper	18	50	*	90	*	140	*	177	231	253
24-inch-wide, 4-inch-high, closed-top scupper	72	200	*	360	*	560	*	708	924	1,012
6-inch-wide, 6-inch-high, closed-top scupper	18	50	*	90	*	140	*	194	303	343
24-inch-wide, 6-inch-high, closed-top scupper	72	200	*	360	*	560	*	776	1,212	1,372

For SI: 1 inch = 25.4 mm, 1 gallon per minute = 3.785 L/m.
Source: Factory Mutual Engineering Corp. Loss Prevention Data 1-54.

FLOW RATE, IN GALLONS PER MINUTE, OF VARIOUS ROOF DRAINS AT VARIOUS WATER DEPTHS AT DRAIN INLETS (INCHES)

There have been documented cases of roof structural collapse that are due to roof drain blockage causing excessive rainwater ponding.

Topic: Subsoil Drain Pipe
Reference: IPC 1102.5
Category: Storm Drainage
Subject: Materials

Code Text: *Subsoil drains shall be open-jointed, horizontally split or perforated pipe conforming to one of the standards listed in Table 1102.5.*

Discussion and Commentary: The referenced table specifies acceptable piping materials for subsoil drainage systems. Each material must comply with its own specific standard as shown in the table. All of the criteria and limitations of the standards are applicable unless otherwise specified in the code.

TABLE 1102.5
SUBSOIL DRAIN PIPE

MATERIAL	STANDARD
Cast-iron pipe	ASTM A74; ASTM A888; CISPI 301
Polyethylene (PE) plastic pipe	ASTM F405; ASTM F667; CSA B182.1; CSA B182.6; CSA B182.8
Polyvinyl chloride (PVC) Plastic pipe (type sewer pipe, SDR35, PS25, PS50 or PS100)	ASTM D2729; ASTM D3034, ASTM F891; CSA B182.2; CSA B182.4
Stainless steel drainage systems, Type 316L	ASME A112.3.1
Vitrified clay pipe	ASTM C4; ASTM C700

SUBSOIL DRAIN: A drain that collects subsurface water or seepage water and conveys such water to a place of disposal.

Topic: Fittings
Reference: IPC 1102.7
Category: Storm Drainage
Subject: Materials

Code Text: *Pipe fittings shall be approved for installation with the piping material installed, and shall conform to the respective pipe standards or one of the standards listed in Table 1102.7. The fittings shall not have ledges, shoulders or reductions capable of retarding or obstructing flow in the piping. Threaded drainage pipe fittings shall be of the recessed drainage type.*

Discussion and Commentary: Each fitting is designed to be installed in a particular system with a given material or combination of materials. Drainage pattern fittings must be installed in drainage systems. Vent fittings are limited to the venting system. There are also fittings available that could be used in any type of plumbing system. Fittings must be the same material as, or compatible with, the pipe. This prevents any chemical or corrosive action between dissimilar materials.

TABLE 1102.7
PIPE FITTINGS

MATERIAL	STANDARD
Acrylonitrile butadiene styrene (ABS) plastic	ASTM D2661; ASTM D3311; CSA B181.1
Cast-iron	ASME B16.4; ASME B16.12; ASTM A888; CISPI 301; ASTM A74
Coextruded composite ABS and drain DR-PS in PS35, PS50, PS100, PS140, PS200	ASTM D2751
Coextruded composite ABS DWV Schedule 40 IPS pipe (solid or cellular core)	ASTM D2661; ASTM D3311; ASTM F628
Coextruded composite PVC DWV Schedule 40 IPS-DR, PS140, PS200 (solid or cellular core)	ASTM D2665; ASTM D3311; ASTM F891
Coextruded composite PVC sewer and drain DR-PS in PS35, PS50, PS100, PS140, PS200	ASTM D3034
Copper or copper alloy	ASME B16.15; ASME B16.18; ASME B16.22; ASME B16.23; ASME B16.26; ASME B16.29
Gray iron and ductile iron	AWWA C110/A21.10
Malleable iron	ASME B16.3
Plastic, general	ASTM F409
Polyethylene (PE) plastic pipe	ASTM F2306/F2306M
Polyvinyl chloride (PVC) plastic	ASTM D2665; ASTM D3311; ASTM F1866
Steel	ASME B16.9; ASME B16.11; ASME B16.28
Stainless steel drainage systems, Type 316L	ASME A112.3.1

Many pipe standards also include provisions regulating fittings. There are, however, a number of standards that strictly regulate pipe fittings.

Topic: Floor Drains	**Category:** Storm Drainage
Reference: IPC 1104.2	**Subject:** Conductors and Connections

Code Text: *Floor drains shall not be connected to a storm drain.*

Discussion and Commentary: To prevent contamination of storm water discharge with chemicals, waste or sewage, the code prohibits the connection of floor drains to a storm drain. A floor drain connected to a storm drainage system invites the discharge of sanitary waste into the storm system, which, considering that storm drainage is discharged to the environment without treatment, would create an environmental hazard.

DRAINAGE SYSTEM. Piping within a public or private premise that conveys sewage, rainwater or other liquid wastes to a point of disposal. A drainage system does not include the mains of a public sewer system or a private or public sewage treatment or disposal plant.

Storm. A drainage system that carries rainwater, surface water, subsurface water and similar liquid wastes.

Areaway drains serving subsurface spaces outside of the building, such as window wells or basement or cellar entrance wells, are not considered to be floor drains when applying this section.

Topic: General Requirements
Reference: IPC 1105.1
Category: Storm Drainage
Subject: Roof Drains

Code Text: *Roof drains shall be installed in accordance with the manufacturer's instructions. The inside opening for the roof drain shall not be obstructed by the roofing membrane material.*

Discussion and Commentary Section 1102.6 requires roof drains to comply with ASME A112.6.4, Roof, Deck, and Balcony Drains, or ASME A112.3.1, which applies to stainless steel drainage systems and components. The manufacturer's instructions govern the installation of roof drains to comply with the referenced standards. Emphasis is placed on maintaining the full opening of the roof drain as designed. This is in response to documented cases of roof membranes overlapping the drain outlet opening and impeding the flow of storm drainage.

ROOF DRAIN: A drain installed to receive water collecting on the surface of a roof and to discharge such water into a leader or a conductor.

Topic: Size of Storm Drain Piping
Reference: IPC 1106.2
Category: Storm Drainage
Subject: Size of Conductors, Leaders and Drains

Code Text: *Vertical and horizontal storm drain piping shall be sized based on the flow rate through the roof drain. The flow rate in storm drain piping shall not exceed that specified in Table 1106.2.*

Discussion and Commentary: Testing of many different sizes and configurations of roof drains from a variety of manufacturers indicated that the roof drain assembly is the limiting factor in the design of storm drain systems. Therefore, storm drainage piping must be sized based on the published roof drain flow rate and anticipated ponding at the roof drain. The design process is to 1) choose a specific roof drain based on manufacturer's published flow rate data, 2) verify that the head-of-water required for that flow rate does not exceed the structural capacity of the roof and 3) choose pipe sizes that can accommodate the design flow rate. The location and elevation of secondary roof drains and scuppers must be closely coordinated with the design of the head-of-water of the primary roof drain. The designer's choice of a secondary roof drain must also take into account the head-of-water above the drain to achieve the design flow with respect to the structural capabilities of the roof.

TABLE 1106.2
STORM DRAIN PIPE SIZING

PIPE SIZE (inches)	CAPACITY (gpm)				
	VERTICAL DRAIN	SLOPE OF HORIZONTAL DRAIN			
		$1/16$ inch per foot	$1/8$ inch per foot	$1/4$ inch per foot	$1/2$ inch per foot
2	34	15	22	31	44
3	87	39	55	79	111
4	180	81	115	163	231
5	311	117	165	234	331
6	538	243	344	487	689
8	1,117	505	714	1,010	1,429
10	2,050	927	1,311	1,855	2,623
12	3,272	1,480	2,093	2,960	4,187
15	5,543	2,508	3,546	5,016	7,093

For SI: 1 inch = 25.4 mm, 1 foot = 304.8 mm, 1 gallon per minute = 3.785 L/m.

Table 1106.2 covers the sizing of vertical and horizontal storm drain piping.

Topic: Vertical Leader Sizing
Reference: IPC 1106.3
Category: Storm Drainage
Subject: Size of Conductors, Leaders and Drains

Code Text: *Vertical leaders shall be sized based on the flow rate from horizontal gutters or the maximum flow rate through roof drains. The flow rate through vertical leaders shall not exceed that specified in Table 1106.3.*

Discussion and Commentary: Unlike the flow in horizontal pipe, full flow in a vertical pipe is not possible under gravity-flow conditions. The sizing of leaders is based on the maximum probable capacity of a vertical pipe, which is approximately 29 percent of the pipe's cross-sectional area.

TABLE 1106.3
VERTICAL LEADER SIZING

SIZE OF LEADER (inches)	CAPACITY (gpm)
2	30
2 × 2	30
1½ × 2½	30
2½	54
2½ × 2½	54
3	92
2 × 4	92
2½ × 3	92
4	192
3 × 4¼	192
3½ × 4	192
5	360
4 × 5	360
4½ × 4½	360
6	563
5 × 6	563
5½ × 5½	563
8	1208
6 × 8	1208

For SI: 1 inch = 25.4 mm, 1 gallon per minute = 3.785 L/m.

Table 1106.3 covers the sizing of vertical leaders that typically receive the discharge from gutters. The maximum flow rate for the appropriately sized leader is based on the gutter flow rate capacity.

Topic: Vertical Walls
Reference: IPC 1106.4
Category: Storm Drainage
Subject: Size of Conductors, Leaders and Drains

Code Text: *In sizing roof drains and storm drainage piping, one-half of the area of any vertical wall that diverts rainwater to the roof shall be added to the projected roof area for inclusion in calculating the required size of vertical conductors, leaders and horizontal storm drainage piping.*

Discussion and Commentary: This section includes the requirement for the mandatory inclusion of half of the area of vertical walls, including parapet walls, that are adjacent to and above a roof area, into the calculation for projected horizontal roof area when sizing storm drainage components. This requirement acknowledges that such vertical walls can catch and divert rainwater onto the roof. As such, this additional water must be accounted for in the sizing of the components that will catch and discharge this water.

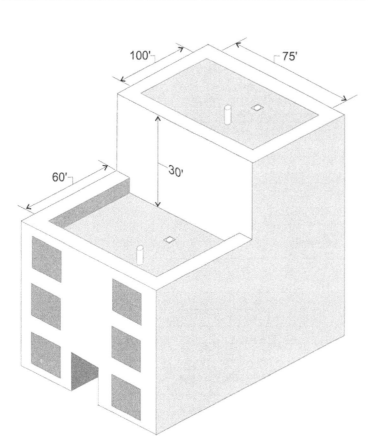

LOWER ROOF
PROJECTED ROOF AREA
60 × 75 = 4,500 sq.ft.

VERTICAL WALL AREA
$$\frac{30 \times 75}{2} = \frac{2,250}{2} \text{ sq.ft.}$$
$$= 1,125 \text{ sq.ft.}$$

PROJECTED ROOF AREA USED
TO SIZE LOWER ROOF DRAINS
4,500 + 1,125 = 5,625 sq.ft.

For SI: 1 foot = 304.8 mm, 1 square foot = 0.093 m²

The additional volume of water from building vertical walls must also be accounted for in the design of a controlled flow system.

Topic: Size of Roof Gutters
Reference: IPC 1106.6
Category: Storm Drainage
Subject: Size of Conductors, Leaders and Drains

Code Text: *Horizontal gutters shall be sized based on the flow rate from the roof surface. The flow rate in horizontal gutters shall not exceed that specified in Table 1106.6.*

Discussion and Commentary: The flow in gallons per minute of 1-inch-per-hour rainfall on 1 square foot of horizontal surface (or projected horizontal surface) is 0.0104 gallons per minute. Thus, the flow rate in gallons per minute can be directly and easily compared to the capacities of the leaders and gutters in the tables.

TABLE 1106.6
HORIZONTAL GUTTER SIZING

GUTTER DIMENSIONS[a] (inches)	SLOPE (inch per foot)	CAPACITY (gpm)
$1^{1}/_{2} \times 2^{1}/_{2}$	$1/_{4}$	26
$1^{1}/_{2} \times 2^{1}/_{2}$	$1/_{2}$	40
4	$1/_{8}$	39
$2^{1}/_{4} \times 3$	$1/_{4}$	55
$2^{1}/_{4} \times 3$	$1/_{2}$	87
5	$1/_{8}$	74
$4 \times 2^{1}/_{2}$	$1/_{4}$	106
$3 \times 3^{1}/_{2}$	$1/_{2}$	156
6	$1/_{8}$	110
3×5	$1/_{4}$	157
3×5	$1/_{2}$	225
8	$1/_{16}$	172
8	$1/_{8}$	247
$4^{1}/_{2} \times 6$	$1/_{4}$	348
$4^{1}/_{2} \times 6$	$1/_{2}$	494
10	$1/_{16}$	331
10	$1/_{8}$	472
5×8	$1/_{4}$	651
4×10	$1/_{2}$	1055

For SI: 1 inch = 25.4 mm, 1 foot = 304.8 mm, 1 gallon per minute = 3.785 L/m, 1 inch per foot = 83.3 mm/m.

a. Dimensions are width by depth for rectangular shapes. Single dimensions are diameters of a semicircle.

The size and number of conductors or leader connections to a roof gutter system must be adequate to prevent overflow of the gutters.

Topic: Sizing
Reference: IPC 1108.3
Category: Storm Drainage
Subject: Secondary (Emergency) Roof Drains

Code Text: *Secondary (emergency) roof drain systems shall be sized in accordance with Section 1106 based on the rainfall rate for which the primary system is sized. Scuppers shall be sized to prevent the depth of ponding water from exceeding that for which the roof was designed as determined by Section 1101.7. Scuppers shall have an opening dimension of not less than 4 inches (102 mm) in height and have an opening width equal to the circumstances of the roof drain required for the area served. The flow through the primary system shall not be considered when sizing the secondary roof drain system.*

Discussion and Commentary: The sizing tables contained in Chapter 11 are based on handling the anticipated rainfall rate (in inches per hour) for a particular horizontal projected roof area. This area is to include at least 50 percent of the area of adjacent vertical walls that can convey rainwater onto the roof. The actual process of sizing the components of a secondary drainage system is identical to sizing the primary system. The same tables and rainfall rates are used. Instead of installing a secondary system of roof drains and pipes, many designers install scuppers to allow rainwater to overflow the roof.

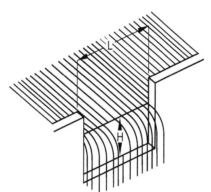

	CAPACITY OF SCUPPER (gallons per minute)									
Head (H) (inches)	Length (L) of scupper (inches)									
	4	6	8	10	12	18	24	30	36	48
1	10.7	17.4	23.4	29.3	35.4	53.4	71.5	89.5	107.5	143.7
2	30.5	47.5	64.4	81.4	98.5	149.4	200.3	251.1	302.1	404.0
3	52.9	84.1	115.2	146.3	177.8	271.4	364.9	458.5	552.0	739.0
4	76.7	124.6	172.6	220.5	269.0	413.3	557.5	701.8	846.0	1135.0
6	123.3	211.4	299.5	387.5	476.5	741.1	1005.8	1270.4	1535.0	2067.5

For SI: 1 inch = 25.4 mm, 1 foot = 304.8 mm, 1 gallon per minute = 3.785 L/m.
Based on the Francis formula:
$Q = 3.33 (L - 0.2H) H^{1.5}$
where:
Q = Flow rate (cubic feet per second).
L = Length of scupper opening (feet).
H = Head on scupper [feet (measured 6 feet back from opening)].

Although the code states that the minimum scupper dimension is 4 inches, it is necessary to increase the length dimension to keep the ponding depth at or below the level for which the roof was designed.

Topic: Minimum Number of Drains
Category: Storm Drainage
Reference: IPC 1110.4
Subject: Controlled Flow Systems

Code Text: *Not less than two roof drains shall be installed in roof areas 10,000 square feet (929 m²) or less and not less than four roof drains shall be installed in roofs over 10,000 square feet (929 m²) in area.*

Discussion and Commentary: For controlled flow systems, a system redundancy safety precaution is built into the design by the requirement for a minimum of two drains for roof areas of 10,000 square feet or less. The objective is that if one drain becomes clogged, the other would allow water to drain. For larger buildings in excess of 10,000 square feet of roof area, a minimum of four roof drains is required.

CONTROLLED FLOW DRAINAGE
AREA: 8,000 SQ.FT.
MINIMUM 2 ROOF DRAINS

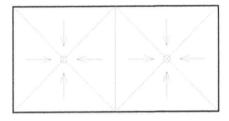

CONTROLLED FLOW DRAINAGE
AREA: 45,000 SQ.FT.
MINIMUM 4 ROOF DRAINS

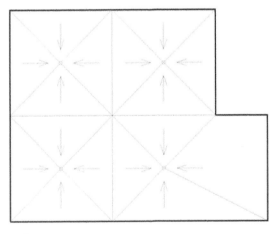

For SI: 1 square foot = 0.093 m²

Although no specific requirements exist in this section about how to design the controlled flow system, the potential for partial clogging of part of the system must be evaluated so that the contained water will drain off the roof without any structural or other problems.

Topic: Subsoil Drains
Reference: IPC 1111.1
Category: Storm Drainage
Subject: Subsoil Drains

Code Text: *Subsoil drains shall be open-jointed, horizontally split or perforated pipe conforming to one of the standards listed in Table 1102.5. Such drains shall not be less than 4 inches (102 mm) in diameter. Where the building is subject to backwater, the subsoil drain shall be protected by an accessibly located backwater valve. Subsoil drains shall discharge to a trapped area drain, sump, dry well or approved location above ground. The subsoil sump shall not be required to have either a gas-tight cover or a vent. The sump and pumping system shall comply with Section 1113.1.*

Discussion and Commentary: Table 1102.5 summarizes the applicable standards for subsoil drain pipes. The pipes listed in the table include Cast Iron, Concrete, Copper, PE, PVC, Stainless Steel and Vitrified Clay, mostly regulated with the applicable ASTM or CSA Standards. The minimum allowable size for a subsoil drain pipe is 4 inches.

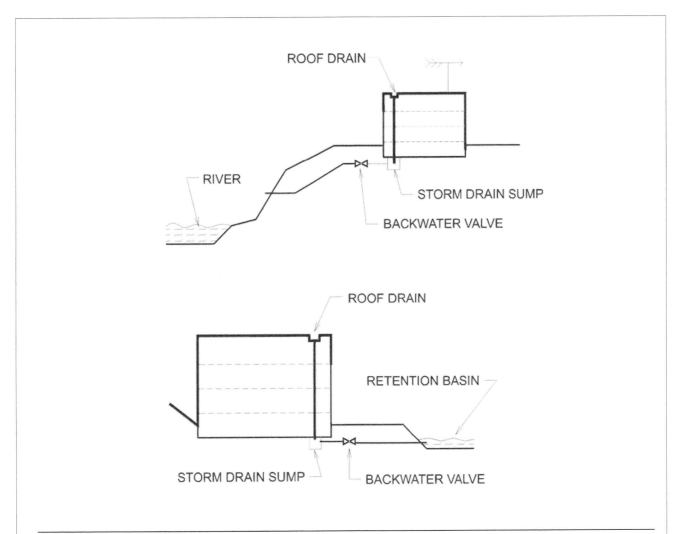

As with other below-grade piping, subsoil drain piping is required to have an accessible backwater valve if the area being drained is subject to backwater conditions.

Topic: Nonflammable Medical Gases **Category:** Special Piping and Storage Systems
Reference: IPC 1202.1 **Subject:** Medical Gases

Code Text: *Nonflammable medical gas systems, inhalation anesthetic systems and vacuum piping systems shall be designed and installed in accordance with NFPA 99.* See the exceptions for portable systems, cylinder storage and vacuum exhaust terminations.

Discussion and Commentary: NFPA 99 applies to all nonflammable medical gas, inhalation anesthetic and permanently installed vacuum piping systems, with the exception of portable systems and the storage of gas cylinders. The mechanical exhaust of vacuum piping systems is also exempted from the NFPA 99 requirements and must comply with the requirements of the *International Mechanical Code* (IMC).

Gases such as oxygen, nitrous oxide, compressed air, carbon dioxide, helium, nitrogen and various mixtures of these gases are typically used in nonflammable medical-gas piping systems.

Topic: Signage Required
Reference: IPC 1301.3
Category: Nonpotable Water Systems
Subject: General Provisions

Code Text: *Nonpotable water outlets such as hose connections, open ended pipes and faucets shall be identified at the point of use for each outlet with signage that reads as follows: "Nonpotable water is utilized for [application name]. CAUTION: NONPOTABLE WATER – DO NOT DRINK." The words shall be legibly and indelibly printed on a tag or sign constructed of corrosion-resistant waterproof material or shall be indelibly printed on the fixture. The letters of the words shall be not less than 0.5 inch (12.7 mm) in height and in colors in contrast to the background on which they are applied. In addition to the required wordage, the pictograph shown in Figure 1301.3 shall appear on the signage required by this section.*

Discussion and Commentary: Provisions for collecting, storing and using various types of nonpotable water recognize the growing need for water conservation and the increase in development of water conservation programs in many regions of the United States. The code addresses rainwater, reclaimed water and on-site nonpotable water reuse systems. On-site nonpotable water reuse systems include but are not limited to gray water systems. Nonpotable water is not safe for drinking, bathing or cooking purposes, and the code requires clear warning signs at nonpotable water outlets such as hose connections and yard hydrants.

In addition to a written warning in ½-inch high letters, nonpotable water outlets also require a pictograph indicating the water is not safe for drinking.

Topic: Sources
Reference: IPC 1302.2
Category: Nonpotable Water Systems
Subject: On-Site Nonpotable Water Reuse Systems

Code Text: *On-site nonpotable water reuse systems shall collect waste discharge from only the following sources: bathtubs, showers, lavatories, clothes washers and laundry trays. Where approved and as appropriate for the intended application, water from other nonpotable sources shall be collected for reuse by on-site nonpotable water reuse systems.*

Discussion and Commentary: Alternative on-site nonpotable water includes gray water collected from approved plumbing fixtures. Unless specifically prohibited, nonpotable water collected for use from other sources must be approved by the code official. Rainwater collection and distribution systems are covered separately in Section 1303.

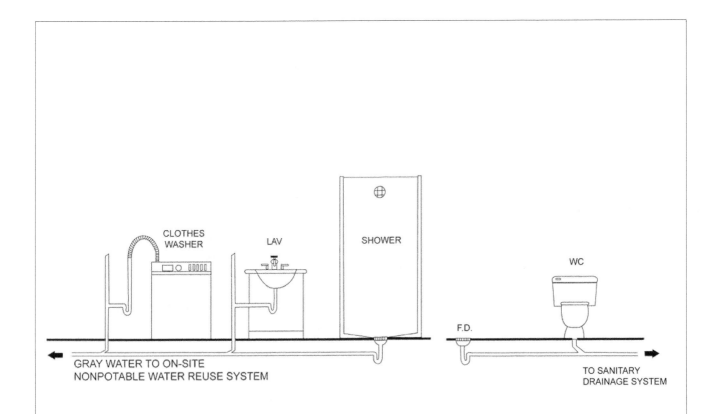

Gray water is waste water discharged from lavatories, bathtubs, showers, clothes washers and laundry trays. Waste from toilets, urinals, kitchen sinks, dishwashers, wet-hood scrubbers, reverse osmosis systems and water softeners are not permitted for use in an on-site nonpotable water reuse system.

Topic: Disinfection and Treatment **Category:** Nonpotable Water Systems
Reference: IPC 1302.6 **Subject:** On-Site Nonpotable Water Reuse Systems

Code Text: *Where the intended application for nonpotable water collected on site for reuse requires disinfection or other treatment or both, it shall be disinfected as needed to ensure that the required water quality is delivered at the point of use. Nonpotable water collected on site containing untreated gray water shall be retained in collection reservoirs for a maximum of 24 hours. Gray water used for flushing water closets and urinals shall be disinfected and treated by an on-site water reuse treatment system complying with NSF 350.*

Discussion and Commentary: Not all alternative on-site nonpotable water reuse systems require disinfection, but each must be evaluated as to the appropriate application including any disinfection or treatment. Gray water, defined as the waste from lavatories, bathtubs, showers, washing machines and laundry tubs, does require disinfection when used for flushing water closets and urinals. Where chlorine is used for disinfection, Section 1301.2.1 limits the residual levels to not more than 4 ppm of chloramines or free chlorine when tested in accordance with ASTM D1253.

TABLE 1302.7.1
LOCATION OF NONPOTABLE WATER REUSE STORAGE TANKS

ELEMENT	MINIMUM HORIZONTAL DISTANCE FROM STORAGE TANK (feet)
Critical root zone (CRZ) of protected trees	2
Lot line adjoining private lots	5
Seepage pits	5
Septic tanks	5
Water wells	50
Streams and lakes	50
Water service	5
Public water main	10

For SI: 1 foot = 304.8 mm.

On-site nonpotable water reuse, including gray water, for subsurface landscape irrigation systems does not require disinfection. The maximum retention time for untreated gray water is 24 hours.

Topic: First-Flush Diverters
Reference: IPC 1303.4
Category: Nonpotable Water Systems
Subject: Nonpotable Rainwater Collection Systems

Code Text: *First-flush diverters shall operate automatically and shall not rely on manually operated valves or devices. Diverted rainwater shall not be drained to the roof surface, and shall be discharged in a manner consistent with the storm water runoff requirements of the jurisdiction. First-flush diverters shall be provided with access for maintenance and service.*

Discussion and Commentary: Nonpotable rainwater systems collect rainwater from approved roof surfaces only. A first-flush diverter allows a predetermined amount of rainwater at the beginning of each rainfall to bypass the storage system and discharge as storm water runoff. This prevents an excessive amount of roof debris and contaminants from entering the storage tank. A typical installation diverts the initial runoff into a length of vertical pipe that is capped at the bottom with a cleanout plug. When the pipe is filled, additional rainfall flows directly into the rainwater storage tank. The diverter pipe has a small-diameter outlet at the bottom that slowly releases the water to empty the pipe for the next rainfall.

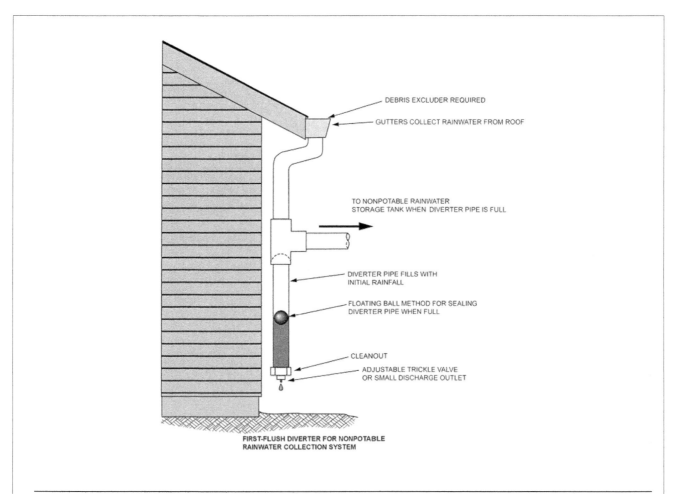

FIRST-FLUSH DIVERTER FOR NONPOTABLE RAINWATER COLLECTION SYSTEM

A debris excluder and first-flush diverter must be installed to limit the amount of debris and contaminants reaching the rainwater collection tank. Debris excluders must be self-cleaning. First-flush diverters require automatic operation without manual valves or devices.

Topic: Distribution Piping
Reference: IPC 1403.2

Category: Subsurface Landscape Irrigation Systems
Subject: Installation

Code Text: *Distribution piping shall be not less than 3 inches (76 mm) in diameter. Materials shall comply with Table 1403.2. The top of the distribution pipe shall be not less than 8 inches (203 mm) below the original surface. The slope of the distribution pipes shall be not less than 2 inches (51 mm) and not greater than 4 inches (102 mm) per 100 feet (30 480 mm).*

Discussion and Commentary: Chapter 14 covers the design and installation of subsurface landscape irrigation systems connected to nonpotable water from on-site water reuse systems such as a gray water system. The irrigation system distribution piping must be PVC or PE plastic pipe typically used in seepage beds with a minimum diameter of 3 inches to provide adequate air flow and prevent blockages. The minimum 8-inch burial depth intends to deliver the irrigation water to just below the topsoil layer. The minimum slope is 2 inches in 100 feet, and the maximum slope is 4 inches in 100 feet to ensure a slow flow across the entire length of pipe and maximum absorption into the soil.

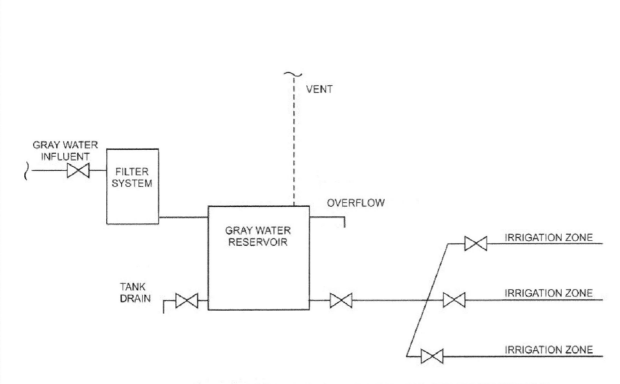

GRAY WATER OR OTHER ON-SITE NONPOTABLE WATER REUSE SYSTEMS FOR SUBSURFACE LANDSCAPE IRRIGATION

On-site nonpotable water reuse systems require a bypass valve installed on the collection piping upstream of each storage tank to allow for servicing. In addition, backwater valves are required on tank overflow pipes and drain pipes. Tank overflow and drain pipe discharge is governed by local ordinances of the jurisdiction.

Quiz

Study Session 15
IPC Chapters 11 through 14

1. For other than one- and two-family dwellings, rainwater from roofs shall drain to a(n) _____.

    a. sanitary sewer   b. storm sewer

    c. street   d. approved location

    Reference _____

2. Which of the following is a prohibited connection in a storm drainage system?

    a. trap   b. floor drain

    c. quarter bend   d. backwater valve

    Reference _____

3. The maximum retention time for untreated gray water in a collection reservoir is _____ hours.

    a. 24   b. 48

    c. 36   d. 72

    Reference _____

4. The absorption field of a subsurface landscape irrigation system using nonpotable water shall maintain a minimum horizontal distance of _____ feet to the water service line.

    a. 2   b. 5

    c. 10   d. 25

    Reference _____

5. A _____ valve shall be installed on the collection piping upstream of the storage tank of an on-site nonpotable water reuse system.

    a. backwater   b. shutoff
    c. check   d. bypass

    Reference _____

6. On-site nonpotable water reuse systems shall not receive the discharge from a _____.

    a. shower   b. kitchen sink
    c. clothes washer   d. laundry tray

    Reference _____

7. For a nonpotable rainwater collection system, a _____ is required to prevent contaminated rainwater from entering the storage tank at the beginning of each rain event.

    a. bypass valve
    b. gutter guard
    c. first-flush diverter
    d. leader filter

    Reference _____

8. What is required between the connection of a storm water conductor and a combined building sewer?

    a. vent   b. trap
    c. strainer   d. backwater valve

    Reference _____

9. Where is the cleanout required on a trapped vertical conductor that discharges to a horizontal combined sewer?

    a. on the sewer side of the trap
    b. on the building side of the trap
    c. less than 10 pipe diameters downstream of the conductor
    d. a minimum of 10 pipe diameters downstream from the conductor

    Reference _____

10. For all installations, the following are required for nonpotable water storage tanks except _____.

    a. an overflow pipe

    b. a rated capacity label

    c. makeup water

    d. a vent

    Reference _____

11. A secondary roof drainage system is permitted to discharge _____.

    a. below ground into a subsoil drainage system

    b. above grade to the ground around the building

    c. into a building sump discharging to a combined sewer

    d. to vertical primary roof drain conductors

    Reference _____

12. For a building of 11,500 square feet of projected roof area, what is the minimum required number of roof drains in a controlled flow roof drain system?

    a. one   b. two

    c. three   d. four

    Reference _____

13. A 3$\frac{1}{2}$-inch by 4-inch rectangular vertical leader for storm drainage is approved for draining a maximum flow rate of _____ gallons per minute (gpm).

    a. 92   b. 192

    c. 360   d. 563

    Reference _____

14. A secondary roof drainage system is designed to be _____ the size of the primary system.

    a. one-half   b. one and one-half times

    c. two times   d. equal to

    Reference _____

15. All of the following materials are approved for subsoil storm drainage pipe, except _____.

    a. ABS plastic pipe, ASTM D2661
    b. PVC plastic pipe, ASTM D2729
    c. vitrified clay pipe, ASTM C4
    d. cast-iron pipe, ASTM A74

    Reference _____

16. Which of the following is not a requirement of a building subsoil sump pit?

    a. gas-tight cover   b. solid floor
    c. accessible   d. 24-inch minimum depth

    Reference _____

17. The maintenance and operation of nonflammable medical gas systems is regulated by which of the following codes?

    a. *International Plumbing Code*® (IPC®)
    b. *International Mechanical Code*® (IMC®)
    c. *International Fuel Gas Code*® (IFGC®)
    d. *International Fire Code*® (IFC®)

    Reference _____

18. Distribution piping for a subsurface landscape irrigation system using nonpotable water shall be not less than _____ inches in diameter.

    a. 1½   b. 2
    c. 3   d. 4

    Reference _____

19. Where a vertical wall measuring 60 feet long by 10 feet high diverts rainwater to the adjacent roof area, _____ square feet must be added to the projected roof area for sizing the storm drainage system.

    a. 60   b. 150
    c. 300   d. 600

    Reference _____

20. A 4-inch horizontal storm drain pipe with a ⅛-inch-per-foot slope has a flow rate capacity of _____ gallons per minute (gpm).

    a. 55
    b. 81
    c. 115
    d. 163

    Reference_____

21. Gray water used for flushing water closets and urinals requires _____.

    a. a warning label at the fixture
    b. filtering through a 600-micron filter
    c. a blue dye
    d. disinfection

    Reference_____

22. For nonpotable rainwater collection and distribution systems, storage tank outlets must be located at least _____ inches above the bottom of the tank.

    a. 4
    b. 8
    c. 2
    d. 6

    Reference_____

23. A 4-inch semicircular roof gutter with a ⅛-inch-per-foot slope has a flow rate capacity of _____ gallons per minute (gpm).

    a. 106
    b. 87
    c. 55
    d. 39

    Reference_____

24. A subsoil drain discharging to a sump shall be open-jointed, split or perforated pipe not less than _____ inches in diameter.

    a. 1½
    b. 2
    c. 3
    d. 4

    Reference_____

25. Below-grade storage tanks with a capacity of 800 gallons or greater and used for non-potable water systems require a manhole at least _____ inches in diameter.

   a. 24
   b. 18
   c. 30
   d. 20

   Reference_____

Answer Keys

Study Session 1
2018 *International Plumbing Code*

1.	c	Sec. 101.2, Exception
2.	c	Sec. 102.2
3.	d	Sec. 101.3
4.	b	Sec. 102.1
5.	c	Sec. 102.2
6.	a	Sec. 102.8.1
7.	b	Sec. 105.2
8.	b	Sec. 105.2.1
9.	c	Sec. 105.3.2
10.	d	Sec. 104.7
11.	a	Sec. 103.2
12.	a	Sec. 102.8
13.	c	Sec. 106.3.1
14.	b	Sec. 106.3
15.	a	Sec. 107.2
16.	d	Sec. 106.2
17.	d	Sec. 106.5.3
18.	b	Sec. 109.1
19.	d	Sec. 106.5.5
20.	b	Sec. 105.3.3
21.	b	Sec. 106.5.1
22.	a	Sec. 106.5.6
23.	b	Sec. 109.1
24.	a	Sec. 106.3.1
25.	d	Sec. 107.6

Study Session 2
2018 *International Plumbing Code*

1.	b	Sec. 301.3, Exception
2.	c	Sec. 301.7
3.	d	Sec. 301.6, Exception
4.	c	Sec. 303.4
5.	c	Sec. 304
6.	b	Sec. 305.4
7.	c	Sec. 305.4
8.	d	Sec. 306.2
9.	b	Sec. 305.6
10.	b	Sec. 307.5
11.	c	Sec. 307.6
12.	c	Sec. 305.6
13.	c	Sec. 305.3
14.	d	Sec. 306.2.3
15.	b	Sec. 306.3
16.	b	Sec. 306.3
17.	a	Sec. 307.4
18.	d	Sec. 305.1
19.	a	Sec. 305.1
20.	b	Sec. 305.6
21.	a	Sec. 306.2.2
22.	d	Sec. 305.4.1
23.	c	Sec. 306.2.1
24.	a	Sec. 306.4
25.	d	Sec. 305.5

Study Session 3
2018 *International Plumbing Code*

1. b Table 308.5
2. b Sec. 308.6
3. d Table 308.5
4. d Table 308.5, Footnote a
5. c Table 308.5, Footnote b
6. a Sec. 315.1
7. b Sec. 309.2, Item 3
8. a Sec. 312.1.1, Item 1
9. b Sec. 312.2
10. d Sec. 312.1
11. d Sec. 312.5
12. a Secs. 314.1 and 314.2.1
13. d Sec. 314.2.3.1
14. b Sec. 308.9
15. d Sec. 311.1
16. a Secs. 312.2 through 312.8
17. d Sec. 312.5
18. c Sec. 308.7.1
19. c Table 308.5
20. a Sec. 312.6
21. c Sec. 312.9
22. c Sec. 314.2.2
23. b Sec. 314.2.2, Table 314.2.2
24. c Sec. 314.2.3, Item 1
25. d Sec. 314.2.3, Items 1 and 2

Study Session 4
2018 *International Plumbing Code*

1. b   Sec. 410.2
2. b   Table 403.1
3. c   Table 403.1
4. c   Table 403.1
5. d   Sec. 405.3.2
6. d   Sec. 406.2
7. d   Sec. 406.2
8. c   Sec. 405.9
9. a   Sec. 405.3.1
10. b   Sec. 406.2
11. b   Sec. 410.4
12. d   Sec. 405.3.5
13. c   Sec. 410.5
14. c   Sec. 405.3.5, Exception 1
15. a   Sec. 405.4.3
16. b   Sec. 407.2
17. c   Sec. 405.3.1
18. d   Sec. 403.3.3, Exception
19. b   Sec. 405.1
20. a   Sec. 403.2, Exception 3
21. d   Sec. 403.3.3
22. c   Sec. 403.3.4
23. c   Sec. 405.3.1
24. b   Sec. 408.3
25. b   Sec. 411.2

Study Session 5
2018 International Plumbing Code

1.	d	Secs. 425.2 and 425.3
2.	a	Sec. 424.2
3.	c	Sec. 412.7
4.	b	Secs. 419.5 and 202
5.	a	Sec. 421.4.2
6.	b	Sec. 421.4, Exception
7.	b	Sec. 426.5
8.	d	Sec. 412.3
9.	c	Sec. 412.3
10.	c	Sec. 417.1
11.	c	Sec. 424.2
12.	b	Sec. 413.3
13.	b	Sec. 413.4
14.	d	Sec. 416.3
15.	a	Sec. 421.5.2
16.	c	Sec. 415.2
17.	b	Sec. 415.3.2
18.	a	Sec. 411.3
19.	b	Sec. 415.1.1
20.	b	Sec. 415.3.1
21.	c	Sec. 412.10
22.	b	Sec. 419.3
23.	a	Sec. 421.3
24.	d	Sec. 426.5
25.	c	Sec. 412.5

Study Session 6
2018 *International Plumbing Code*

1. d Secs. 501.3, 503.1 and 504.1
2. c Sec. 504.2
3. d Sec. 504.5
4. c Sec. 502.5
5. d Sec. 504.5
6. c Sec. 504.7
7. a Sec. 504.7.1
8. d Sec. 504.6, Item 10
9. c Sec. 504.6, Items 8, 11, 12
10. a Sec. 504.5
11. d Sec. 504.6, Item 7
12. c Sec. 505.1
13. c Sec. 504.7
14. b Sec. 501.6
15. b Sec. 503.1
16. b Sec. 501.5
17. c Sec. 501.2
18. c Sec. 501.7
19. a Sec. 502.3
20. d Sec. 504.3
21. a Sec. 504.7.1
22. d Sec. 504.7.2
23. c Sec. 504.4.1
24. b Sec. 502.3
25. b Sec. 502.3

Study Session 7
2018 *International Plumbing Code*

1. b   Sec. 602.3.1
2. c   Sec. 604.8
3. b   Sec. 604.8
4. c   Sec. 604.9
5. b   Sec. 604.24.1
6. d   Sec. 605.2.1
7. a   Sec. 604.8
8. d   Table 605.4
9. a   Sec. 605.4
10. b   Sec. 605.7
11. b   Sec. 605.23.1
12. d   Secs. 605.14.3 and 605.21.4
13. c   Sec. 604.6
14. c   Sec. 605.3
15. b   Table 604.5, Footnote a
16. b   Secs. 605.12.3 and 605.13.6
17. b   Table 604.4
18. b   Sec. 604.4, Exception 1
19. a   Sec. 602.3.5.1
20. a   Sec. 603.1
21. c   Sec. 603.2
22. d   Sec. 603.2
23. c   Sec. 605.15.2, Exception
24. a   Sec. 605.21.3
25. c   Table 604.5

Study Session 8
2018 *International Plumbing Code*

1. d   Sec. 606.2
2. d   Sec. 606.4
3. c   Sec. 607.1.2
4. b   Table 606.5.4
5. c   Sec. 606.1, #8
6. b   Table 608.1
7. d   Sec. 608.9.2
8. d   Sec. 607.3
9. a   Sec. 608.17.4
10. d   Sec. 608.17.5
11. c   Sec. 608.9.2
12. c   Sec. 608.16.1
13. a   Table 608.9.2.2
14. d   Table 608.18.1
15. b   Sec. 610.1, Item 2
16. c   Sec. 608.3.1
17. c   Sec. 606.5.9
18. b   Sec. 608.14.4
19. c   Sec. 608.9.1
20. b   Sec. 608.8, Exception
21. c   Sec. 608.16.4.1
22. c   Sec. 607.2
23. b   Sec. 608.16.4.2
24. b   Table 608.16.1
25. a   Sec. 606.5.1

Study Session 9
2018 *International Plumbing Code*

1.	d	Sec. 701.3
2.	c	Sec. 702.5
3.	d	Sec. 705.16.4
4.	b	Tables 702.1 and 702.2
5.	c	Sec. 702.6
6.	d	Sec. 705.12.1
7.	a	Sec. 705.10.2
8.	b	Sec. 705.16.2
9.	c	Sec. 705.16.7
10.	d	Secs. 705.7, 705.12.1, 705.13.1, 705.14.1
11.	c	Sec. 706.3
12.	b	Table 706.3
13.	d	Sec. 706.4
14.	c	Table 704.1
15.	a	Sec. 704.3
16.	a	Sec. 703.3
17.	a	Sec. 704.2
18.	d	Table 704.1
19.	a	Sec. 705.2.2
20.	c	Sec. 705.10.1
21.	b	Sec. 705.16.4
22.	a	Sec. 705.18
23.	c	Sec. 706.2
24.	b	Table 706.3
25.	d	Table 706.3

Study Session 10
2018 *International Plumbing Code*

1. a   Sec. 709.4.1
2. b   Table 710.1(1)
3. c   Sec. 708.1.5, Exception 1
4. d   Sec. 709.2 and Table 709.2
5. c   Sec. 709.3
6. a   Table 709.1 and Sec. 202
7. a   Table 710.1(1), Footnote a
8. b   Sec. 202
9. d   Sec. 712.1
10. a   Secs. 712.2 and 712.3.2
11. b   Sec. 712.3.4
12. c   Sec. 712.3.2
13. d   Sec. 712.3.5
14. c   Sec. 712.4.2, Exception 1
15. b   Table 712.4.2
16. c   Sec. 708.1.6
17. c   Sec. 712.2
18. c   Sec. 713.3.2 and Table 704.1
19. b   Sec. 712.3.2
20. a   Sec. 714.1, Exception
21. b   Sec. 716.2
22. d   Sec. 708.1.1
23. a   Sec. 708.1.4
24. c   Sec. 708.1.3
25. b   Sec. 708.1.9

Study Session 11
2018 International Plumbing Code

1. a   Sec. 802.1.1
2. c   Sec. 802.1.6
3. c   Sec. 802.1.2
4. c   Sec. 802.3
5. b   Sec. 802.4.1
6. b   Sec. 802.4
7. c   Sec. 803.1
8. b   Sec. 802.4
9. a   Sec. 803.2
10. d   Sec. 802.4.3
11. a   Sec. 802.1.6
12. b   Sec. 802.4
13. d   Sec. 802.1.4
14. c   Sec. 802.3
15. d   Sec. 802.4.3
16. b   Sec. 802.4.3.1
17. a   Sec. 802.4
18. d   Sec. 802.4.2
19. b   Sec. 802.3.1
20. b   Sec. 801.2
21. a   Sec. 802.1
22. b   Sec. 802.1.2
23. b   Sec. 802.3.2
24. d   Sec. 803.1
25. a   Sec. 802.1.1

Study Session 12
2018 *International Plumbing Code*

1. b   Sec. 901.2
2. a   Sec. 901.2
3. c   Sec. 901.3
4. b   Sec. 902.3
5. a   Sec. 904.1
6. c   Sec. 904.4
7. b   Sec. 903.2
8. c   Sec. 903.2 and Appendix D
9. c   Sec. 903.1
10. b   Sec. 903.5
11. d   Sec. 903.6
12. d   Sec. 903.7
13. d   Sec. 905.4
14. c   Sec. 909.1 and Table 909.1
15. d   Sec. 909.2
16. d   Sec. 909.1, Exception
17. a   Sec. 906.1
18. d   Sec. 906.2
19. b   Sec. 908.2
20. d   Sec. 907.1
21. d   Sec. 906.2
22. c   Table 906.5.1
23. d   Sec. 908.1
24. d   Table 909.1
25. a   Sec. 909.3

Study Session 13
2018 *International Plumbing Code*

1.	d	Sec. 913.3
2.	d	Table 913.4
3.	d	Table 913.4
4.	b	Secs. 911.1 and 202
5.	c	Sec. 916.2
6.	c	Sec. 917.4.2
7.	a	Sec. 917.2
8.	a	Sec. 914.4
9.	b	Sec. 914.4.2
10.	a	Sec. 915.1
11.	c	Sec. 915.2.1
12.	c	Sec. 915.2
13.	c	Sec. 915.2.5 and Table 909.1
14.	b	Table 915.2.2
15.	b	Sec. 916.1
16.	b	Sec. 916.3
17.	d	Sec. 915.1
18.	b	Sec. 911.3 and Table 911.3
19.	c	Sec. 910.1
20.	b	Secs. 912.1 and 912.1.1
21.	b	Sec. 912.1
22.	b	Sec. 912.2.1
23.	a	Sec. 918.3.2
24.	d	Sec. 913.2
25.	b	Sec. 918.4

Answer Keys

Study Session 14
2018 *International Plumbing Code*

1. b   Sec. 1002.1, Exception 2
2. c   Sec. 1002.3, Item 6 Exception
3. d   Sec. 1002.10
4. b   Secs. 1002.2, 1002.4, 1002.4.1 and 1002.7
5. a   Sec. 1002.3, Item 1
6. b   Sec. 1002.1, Exception 4
7. d   Sec. 1002.4.1.4
8. b   Sec. 1002.1, Exception 3
9. a   Sec. 1002.2
10. a   Sec. 1002.1, Exception 3
11. d   Sec. 1003.1
12. b   Secs. 1003.3.1 and 1003.3.2
13. c   Sec. 1003.3.3
14. d   Sec. 1003.3.4
15. c   Sec. 1003.4.2.2
16. a   Sec. 1003.5
17. c   Sec. 1003.3.5.2
18. b   Sec. 1003.3.6
19. d   Sec. 1003.9
20. b   Sec. 1002.1
21. c   Sec. 1002.4
22. d   Sec. 1002.9
23. c   Table 1003.3.5.1
24. a   Sec. 1003.4.2.1
25. c   Sec. 1003.4.2.1

Study Session 15
2018 *International Plumbing Code*

1.	d	Sec. 1101.2
2.	b	Sec. 1104.2
3.	a	Sec. 1302.6
4.	b	Sec. 1402.3 and Table 1402.3
5.	d	Sec. 1302.8.1
6.	b	Sec. 1302.2.1
7.	c	Sec. 1303.4
8.	b	Sec. 1103.1
9.	b	Sec. 1103.4
10.	c	Secs. 1301.9.4, 1301.9.5, 1301.9.7 and 1301.9.9
11.	b	Sec. 1108.2
12.	d	Sec. 1110.4
13.	b	Table 1106.3
14.	d	Sec. 1108.3
15.	a	Table 1102.5
16.	a	Secs. 1111.1 and 1113.1.2
17.	d	Sec. 1201.1
18.	c	Sec. 1403.2
19.	c	Sec. 1106.4
20.	c	Table 1106.2
21.	d	Secs. 1301.2.2 and 1302.6.1
22.	a	Sec. 1303.10.3
23.	d	Table 1106.6
24.	d	Sec. 1111.1
25.	a	Sec. 1301.9.6

Specify and Approve with
CONFIDENCE

When facing new or unfamiliar materials, how do you know if they comply with building codes and standards?

- ICC-ES® Evaluation Reports are the most widely accepted and trusted technical reports for code compliance. When you specify products or materials with an ICC-ES report, you avoid delays on projects and improve your bottom line.

- ICC-ES® Reports save time and resources, and permit quick and easy access to compliance information relevant to a product to determine its code or standard compliance and installation requirements.

- ICC-ES® provides a one-stop shop for the evaluation, listing and now testing of innovative building products through our newly formed cooperation with Innovation Research Labs, a highly respected ISO 17025 accredited testing lab with over 50 years of experience.

- ICC-ES® is a subsidiary of ICC®, the publisher of the codes used throughout the U.S. and many global markets, so you can be confident in their code expertise.

WWW.ICC-ES.ORG | 800-423-6587 x3877

SOLAR RATING & CERTIFICATION CORPORATION
A member of the ICC Family of Companies

Solar Rating & Certification Corporation (ICC-SRCC)

ICC-SRCC, a program of the ICC Evaluation Service, is an accredited certification body with programs for the certification and performance rating of solar heating and cooling products and small wind turbines. ICC-SRCC certifications and ratings are specified by many jurisdictions and programs that promote the use of solar heating and cooling technologies.

ICC-SRCC's certifications and listings assist code enforcement professionals, allowing them to quickly confirm the code compliance of solar heating and cooling products and small wind turbines. Consumers benefit from objective, third-party performance data that allows them to compare products and find the best options for their project.

ICC-SRCC CERTIFIES:
- Solar thermal collectors
- Domestic solar water heating systems
- Solar air heating systems
- Solar pump stations
- Solar pool heating systems
- Small wind turbines

ICC-SRCC BENEFITS INCLUDE:
- Evaluations of compliance to ICC-SRCC Standards 100, 300 and 400 that are referenced in many codes throughout North America
- Objective performance ratings and energy savings estimates for solar water heaters
- Proof of compliance with many federal, state and local rebate programs
- Web-based directory of certifications and ratings

Need more information?
Contact the Solar Rating & Certification Corporation today!
www.solar-rating.org | 1-888-422-7233, x7735
Connect with us on Twitter and LinkedIn

ASSESSMENT center

The ICC Assessment Center (formerly known as ICC Certification & Testing) provides nationally recognized credentials that demonstrate a confirmed commitment to protect public health, safety, and welfare. Raise the professionalism of your department and further your career by pursuing an ICC Certification.

ICC Certifications offer:

- Nationwide recognition
- Increased earning potential
- Career advancement
- Superior knowledge
- Validation of your expertise
- Personal and professional satisfaction

Exams are developed and maintained to the highest standards, which includes continuous peer review by national committees of experienced, practicing professionals. ICC is continually evolving exam offerings, testing options, and technology to ensure that all building and fire safety officials have access to the tools and resources needed to advance in today's fast-paced and rapidly-changing world.

Enhancing Exam Options

Effective July 2018, the Assessment Center enhanced and streamlined exam options and now offers only computer based testing (CBT) at a test site and PRONTO. We no longer offer paper/pencil exams.

Proctored Remote Online Testing Option (PRONTO)

Taking your next ICC certification exam is more convenient, more comfortable and more efficient than ever before with PRONTO.

PRONTO provides a convenient testing experience that is accessible 24 hours a day, 7 days a week, 365 days a year. Required hardware/software is minimal – you will need a webcam and microphone, as well as a reasonably recent operating system.

Whether testing in your office or in the comfort of your home, your ICC exam will continue to maintain its credibility while offering more convenience, allowing you to focus on achieving your professional goals. The Assessment Center continues to add exams to the PRONTO exam catalog regularly.

18-15617

Checkout all the ICC Assessment Center has to offer at iccsafe.org/certification

People Helping People Build a Safer World®

Valuable Guides to Changes in the 2018 I-Codes®

FULL COLOR! HUNDREDS OF PHOTOS AND ILLUSTRATIONS!

SIGNIFICANT CHANGES TO THE 2018 INTERNATIONAL CODES®

Practical resources that offer a comprehensive analysis of the critical changes made between the 2015 and 2018 editions of the codes. Authored by ICC code experts, these useful tools are "must-have" guides to the many important changes in the 2018 International Codes.

Key changes are identified then followed by in-depth, expert discussion of how the change affects real world application. A full-color photo, table or illustration is included for each change to further clarify application.

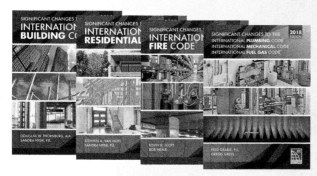

SIGNIFICANT CHANGES TO THE IBC, 2018 EDITION
#7024S18

SIGNIFICANT CHANGES TO THE IRC, 2018 EDITION
#7101S18

SIGNIFICANT CHANGES TO THE IFC, 2018 EDITION
#7404S18

SIGNIFICANT CHANGES TO THE IPC/IMC/IFGC, 2018 EDITION
#7202S18

ORDER YOUR HELPFUL GUIDES TODAY!
1-800-786-4452 | www.iccsafe.org/books

HIRE ICC TO TEACH

Want your group to learn the Significant Changes to the I-Codes from an ICC expert instructor? Schedule a seminar today!

email: **ICCTraining@iccsafe.org** | phone: **1-888-422-7233 ext. 33818**